RECORDED POETRY AND POETIC RECEPTION
FROM EDNA MILLAY TO THE CIRCLE OF
ROBERT LOWELL

RECORDED POETRY AND POETIC RECEPTION FROM EDNA MILLAY TO THE CIRCLE OF ROBERT LOWELL

Derek Furr

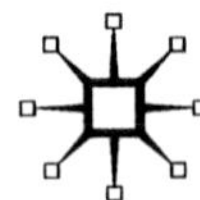

RECORDED POETRY AND POETIC RECEPTION FROM EDNA MILLAY TO THE CIRCLE OF ROBERT LOWELL
Copyright © Derek Furr, 2010.

Materials written by James Weldon Johnson are published here by permission of Dr. Sondra Kathryn Wilson, Executor for the Estate of Grace and James Weldon Johnson.

Photo of Edna St. Vincent Millay is used with the permission of the Edna St. Vincent Millay Society.

First published in 2010 by
PALGRAVE MACMILLAN®
in the United States—a division of St. Martin's Press LLC,
175 Fifth Avenue, New York, NY 10010.

Where this book is distributed in the UK, Europe and the rest of the world, this is by Palgrave Macmillan, a division of Macmillan Publishers Limited, registered in England, company number 785998, of Houndmills, Basingstoke, Hampshire RG21 6XS.

Palgrave Macmillan is the global academic imprint of the above companies and has companies and representatives throughout the world.

Palgrave® and Macmillan® are registered trademarks in the United States, the United Kingdom, Europe and other countries.

ISBN: 978–0–230–10377–1

Library of Congress Cataloging-in-Publication Data is available from the Library of Congress.

A catalogue record of the book is available from the British Library.

Design by Newgen Imaging Systems (P) Ltd., Chennai, India.

First edition: July 2010

10 9 8 7 6 5 4 3 2 1

Printed in the United States of America.

CONTENTS

ACKNOWLEDGMENTS

I owe the idea for this study to my friend and former colleague Raphael Allison. In the autumn of my first year on the faculty of the Master of Arts in Teaching Program at Bard College, Raphael knocked on my office door and asked whether I liked listening to poetry recordings. He had heard of an archive at Harvard and had a friend with whom we could stay in Cambridge, so if I was game, he said, maybe we could each make a list of recordings that interested us and go together to check out the archive. It would be, in a sense, a scholarly road trip. Later that month, as we drove through the Berkshire mountains and across Massachusetts to the Woodberry Poetry Room, we played a random assortment of cassette recordings of poets and began the conversations about poetry, sound, textuality, and reception that inspired us both to research and write about the audio archive of modernist poetry. That I have managed to complete this book and see it to publication is, first and foremost, a tribute to Raphael, who has been a constant source of encouragement and thoughtful criticism.

There are many others who have offered guidance, talked with me about the ideas in this book, and read and commented on drafts. Lesley Wheeler has been chief among them. Lesley was writing about Millay for her book on poetic voices when she attended a panel that Raphael and I had put together for the Modernist Studies Association conference. Our conversations about Millay and sound were the first of several on the topics in this book, and Lesley has been a gracious critic and guide at every stage of this book's development. When the book was still in its formative stages, I received important advice and encouragement from Deirdre D'Albertis, Jessica Feldman, and Ann Lauterbach, as well as from fellow scholars at the annual meeting of the Modernist Studies Association and the Lifting Belly conference on women's poetry. Jaime Alves, Myra Armstead, Julia Emig, and Wendy Urban-Mead provided helpful readings of chapters and, moreover, cheered me forward with the work despite the demanding schedule of the MAT program. The reviewers of my manuscript for Palgrave Macmillan offered invaluable suggestions about the overall shape of the argument in its final stages, and I am especially grateful to Brigitte Shull for recognizing the project's potential and Lee Norton for shepherding it through to publication. Students in my summer 2009 section of LI 526, Poetic Voices, also deserve special recognition; their listening sometimes challenged, sometimes confirmed, my own, and it helped shape the course described in the appendix. For their photo of microgrooves on a long-playing record, I thank Brian McIntyre and Chris Supranowitz of the Institute of Optics, University of Rochester. For technical assistance with waveform photos, I thank Paul Collins.

Library archives and, importantly, non-circulating holdings of recordings have been indispensable to this research. Among the many librarians and archivists who have helped in some way with this project, I owe a special debt of gratitude to Dean Rogers, Katerine Beutner, Don Share, Jeff Katz, Jane Hryshko, and the staff of the Interlibrary Loan Department at Bard College, where I have the distinction of being the first faculty member to request an LP through ILL. For access to recordings and other archival materials cited in this book, I am grateful to the following: The George Edward Woodberry Poetry Room Collection, Houghton Library, Harvard University; The Rodgers and Hammerstein Archives of Recorded Sound, New York Public Library for the Performing Arts; The Recorded Sound Reference Center, Library of Congress; The Edna St. Vincent Millay Papers and The Elizabeth Bishop Papers, Vassar College Special Collections; The George J. Mitchell Department of Special Collections and Archives, Bowdoin College; The James Weldon Johnson Papers, Beinecke Rare Book and Manuscript Library, Yale University; The Susan Howe Papers, Mandeville Special Collections Library, University of California at San Diego; The Anne Sexton Papers, Harry Ransom Humanities Research Center, The University of Texas at Austin; The Carter A. Towbin Poetry Room, Bard College.

A portion of chapter two appeared in an earlier form in my article "Remembering Bishop, Bishop Remembering," *Twentieth-Century Literature,* Spring 2007; a portion of chapter three appeared in an earlier form in my article "Listening to Millay," *Journal of Modern Literature,* Winter 2006.

Finally, for their willingness to listen to poetry on the road to hockey matches, and their particular adoration of Wanda Coleman's "I Live For My Car," I thank my sons, Samuel and Jacob. And for her perceptive criticism and practical advice, infinite patience and abiding love, I thank Caroline Ramaley—"haply, I think on thee, and then my state / Like to the lark at break of day arising / From sullen earth, sings hymns at heaven's gates."

INTRODUCTION

LISTENING TO RECORDED POETRY

In the September 16, 2008, podcast of "Poetry Off the Shelf," Curtis Fox of the Poetry Foundation announced the release of the *Essential American Poets* project, conceived as a way of introducing readers to "essential" U.S. poets. Drawing on recordings from the Library of Congress and the Poetry Archive of the United Kingdom, as well as its own holdings, the Foundation has begun to create an online archive that includes audio and text—an archive that, given the dynamic nature of the web, will grow over time. So far, determining which poets are essential has been the work of Donald Hall and Andrew Motion, and Fox interviewed Hall for the podcast.

The interview was taken up primarily by Fox's and Hall's reflections on recordings of Theodore Roethke reading "My Papa's Waltz" and Gwendolyn Brooks reading "We Real Cool." But their conversation began with claims about the importance of listening to poetry. Fox asked, "What do you get from listening to a poem, as opposed to just reading it on the page?" Hall's reply is worth quoting in full:

> I think you get a great deal. The sound of poetry is where I enter poetry. I…when I was twelve years old, when I first fell in love with it, was sound. And I also think, it's important to hear it in the poet's own voice. Now, some poets are very good readers, some are rather poor [here Fox agrees, laughing]. I would always want to hear them, at some point or other, in their own voices. It is a sort of help, like, uh, helping somebody cross a street or something, to hear the voice, the quality of the voice, the tone of it, the flesh of it…(Hall, "Interview")

Hall and Fox went on to the example of Ezra Pound as one whose voice surprised them and changed their idea of his poetry. Fox cued Pound's reading of the ironic "Cantico del Sole," after which Hall exclaimed that despite the poor sound quality, "the voice is there, the man is there."

Almost seventy-five years earlier, in the winter of 1932–33, listeners across the United States gathered around their radios on Sunday evenings to listen to Edna St. Vincent Millay read her work on NBC. So taken were they by Millay's readings that many wrote letters of appreciation, nearly fifteen hundred altogether. These letters specifically address the qualities of Millay's voice and the value of listening, and they confess to a kind of intimacy with the poet that listening promotes. "It's simply intoxicating," one of her listeners remarked in a December 1932 letter to Millay, "Don't, don't ever change, and become stiff or formal or eloquent...You sound so real, so natural, so—so very much alive..." (quoted in Milford 367). Over the airwaves and, later, on record, Millay's voice was "there," the woman was there.

I begin with these anecdotes—which will prove representative—because they give rise to a question that has been fundamental to this study. Post-structuralist skepticism of presence notwithstanding, and even if discs, lengths of tape, and computer chips do not actually hold the "flesh" of a human voice, why has the poet's reading—her voicing of her own work—been important to her audience, so much so in fact that for over a century, we have recorded it? One set of answers to this loaded question is implied by Millay's listener and improvised by Donald Hall: the poet's voice is unique, her performance—whether artful, natural, or poorly executed—embodies the work and helps us understand it and connect to it, which is analogous to understanding and connecting to the poet herself. While commonly held, these answers are deceptively simple, masking the complexity of what we hear when we press "play" and listen. For poetry performance, recording technology, and listener response shaped the modern poet's voice.

Audio recording of poets reading their work was an essential twentieth-century practice, inside and outside of the academy, not only among innovative "sound" poets and postmodern artists, whose experiments have been the subject of recent critical analysis, but also among the full range of poets clustered under the broad rubrics "modern" and "modernism." These widely dispersed recordings of poetry and commentary constitute a vast but rarely studied archive of poetic voices, an archive that deserves close listening and that is the primary source for this work. Through an analysis of recorded poetic events such as public readings, studio sessions, memorial services, and concerts, this study describes how and why poetry was recorded in the United States from the 1930s through the "confessional" poetries of the 1960s and early 1970s, and seeks to delineate ways of listening to the audio poem. It seeks to provide a model for framing the study of archival audio materials by considering the kind of recording and the voice of the poet's performance. Close listening and reception study play an essential role throughout, providing critical insight into the relationship among reading style, historical context, and the vicissitudes of taste. Taking up the aural traces of reading events, this book demonstrates that the recorded poem often troubles the shape and sounds of the poem as we've received it in print. Voice timbre and pitch, ambient sounds in the live recording, the juxtaposition of poetries not commonly anthologized together, the audio poem resonates in ways unique to the medium and causes us to attend equally to poetic craft, material form, and contextual constraints.

In this introductory chapter, I will first consider who's listening to the audio archive and where my study fits in the critical discourse on sound and modern poetry. I will then define "audio archive" and the kinds of recordings that factor into this study. Finally, I will turn to what criticism and theory have taught us about how and why to listen. I will describe the model for listening that I propose and outline the major "scenes" of modern poetry on record that this study considers.

Who's Listening Now?

Pitched as a response to readers' shared desire to hear great poetry, the Poetry Foundation's project to recover and distribute twentieth-century poetry audio illustrates the symbiotic relationship between technology and interest. As recordings are made easily accessible, public and scholarly interest increases, which in turn drives efforts to recover and disseminate recordings. Recent history bears this out. In this section, I will briefly recount this history, with an emphasis on what recordings have been made available and who in the scholarly community is listening to them.

In 1987, the *New York Times* reported a surge in the market for audiobooks, aided in part by the advent of inexpensive, high quality cassettes. It noted that Harper and Row had recently acquired Caedmon—one of the first commercial spoken word recording companies—that Random House had opened an audio division, and that many small companies were also entering the fray (Mitgang). While defining only a fractional segment of this market, poetry audio has been a stable part of it all along. The early 1990s saw the release of two successful compilations of poets reading their work. Random House's *Voice of the Poet* series and Sourcebooks' *Poetry Speaks* included previously unreleased live recordings, as well as reissues of studio recordings produced by Caedmon, the Library of Congress, Harvard Vocarium, and others; these earlier poetry recording ventures will be the subject of chapter one. At the time of this writing, *Poetry Speaks* has entered its second, expanded edition, and many of the *Voice of the Poet* recordings are being reissued on compact disc. Appealing both to entertainment and to educational interests, these compilations are largely "greatest hits" of mainstream twentieth-century poetry on record: from Walt Whitman and Robert Browning reading into the Edison phonograph, to Robert Frost quietly intoning "Stopping By Woods on a Snowy Evening" and Sylvia Plath sternly reprimanding "Daddy."

Alongside such large-scale, popular compilations are the smaller, more specialized ventures of universities and the Academy of American Poets, whose recordings are available by catalog and website sales. These recordings are almost entirely live, involve several readings by one or two poets, and rarely include events prior to 1960. From the Academy, for example, one can order a complete recording of Czeslaw Milosz reading at the Guggenheim in 1974, and of Allen Ginsberg and Kamau Brathwaite reading together at the New School in October 1994. The Academy of American Poets' small, specialized recordings are to Random House's large-scale reissues as the Library of Congress recordings were to Caedmon in the early decades of poetry audio. That is to say, one is academic to the other's popular, while together they represent the broad mainstream of modern poetry.[1]

Compact disc compilations are quickly giving way to a more dynamic medium, the Internet audio archive. Many of these archives duplicate each other's holdings and draw on the same sources as *Poetry Speaks* and *Voice of the Poet*. But the best among them have begun to make important poetry recordings of the past and present freely accessible. At the time of this writing, the deepest online archives, besides that of the Poetry Foundation, are PennSound, Ubuweb, the UK Poetry Archive, and the website of the Academy of American Poets. All of these online resources offer an array of live and studio recordings of poetry readings, taped interviews with poets, and roundtable discussions of poetry. Ubuweb and PennSound, which holds a place of honor as one of the first such sites, generally emphasize the twentieth-century avant-garde. On Ubuweb, the focus is experimental sound and performance poetries. At PennSound, there is a rich representation from poets in the objectivist, New York School, and Language poetry traditions. PennSound takes advantage of multiple aspects of digital technology by offering live webcasts from classrooms and poetry readings and hosting a regular podcast, PoemTalk, in which a circle of poets and critics "offer a close, but not too close, reading" of a poem held in PennSound's audio archive.[2] The Academy of American Poets and the UK Poetry Archive provide short biographies of poets, frequently with audio of twentieth-century poets reading their work. The range of twentieth-century poetries on these two sites is wider than on PennSound or Ubuweb—we get work by Robert Frost as well as Lyn Hejinian—but the representation is less adventurous. For David Antin or Jaap Blonk, see Ubuweb and PennSound. For Edna Millay, see the Academy's site. For John Ashbery, go to any of these sites.

The differences among these collections, however, are balanced by their fundamental similarity: a shared assumption that the poet's reading is important and instructive. In the introduction to his path-breaking collection *Close Listening*, Charles Bernstein argues that the poet's reading deserves greater status in our study and preservation of literary history. He writes, "When the audiotape archive of a poet's performance is acknowledged as a significant, rather than incidental, part of her or his work, a number of important textual and critical issues emerge" (7). While it is doubtful that Bernstein would agree with Hall's claim that in a recording of Pound we have "the man," he suggests that such recordings do have a significant place in the textual history of poet's work. That place is readily apparent in the work of poets such as David Antin or Jaap Blonk; Antin's talk poems and Blonk's vocal pyrotechnics are actualized in performance by the artists.[3] The rationale for listening to recordings of poets whose primary modes of practice and dissemination are print text is less apparent. In this study, I will follow from Bernstein's claim and seek to address the "textual and critical issues" that emerge from close listening to poets such as Elizabeth Bishop, Louise Bogan, and Robert Lowell.

Besides the shared assumption that the poet's reading is significant, these compilations and websites tend to consider the particular setting of the poet's reading to be minimally important. Very little, if any, information is given about the time, place, and rationale of the recording, even on the Academy and PennSound sites, where efforts to situate the events have clearly been made. While it's possible that very little information is extant about many of these recordings, the effect is to isolate the poet's voice—to detach it from the recording techniques and social contexts that framed it. Finally, across all of these compilations and sites, edited studio recordings and unedited live recordings and everything in between are presented equally. Are all these kinds of readings of equal value? As we will see in the chapters ahead, they offer vastly different forms of information and listening experiences.

As the audio archive becomes increasingly accessible, who is listening to it in an effort to answer the wide range of practical and theoretical questions that it raises? Contemporary critical interest in the audio archive per se should be dated to Bernstein's *Close Listening*, but almost two decades after its publication in 1998, it is helpful to situate that collection in a larger group of contemporary studies in poetic sound and voice. I want to turn now to a review of those studies and suggest how *Recorded Poetry and Poetic Reception* may contribute.

My study of poetry audio takes up both poetic sound and voice. The critical literature on those two topics is vast and interconnected, but it has been cogently summarized by Lesley Wheeler, whose *Voicing American Poetry* (2008) offers a history of poetry reading in the twentieth-century United States. In "Sounding Poetic Voice," Wheeler notes that "while poetic voice is a metaphor, it also exceeds metaphor—this phrase evokes a physical process, a medium for art, and a means for social change" (18). In the poetry workshop, "voice" conjures a numinous essence, something that defines a writer's uniqueness. This neo-Romantic inner voice is projected outward in the activist voice of feminist poetics, in which acquiring voice and boldly speaking the self are evidence of political progress. Wheeler points out that such metaphoric meanings of voice originate in the physical voice. That the print text inscribes bodily voice and that the poetic line and breath are analogous were essential claims of poet Charles Olson, and the physiological characteristics of voice production have been the concern of studies in reading and language acquisition (23–27).

Despite this range of uses, "poetic voice" tends always to imply the presence of a speaker embodied in the artifact, whether print or audio. Wheeler writes that "it is difficult to discuss sound in poetry without invoking someone's body, and the attendant implications of presence and identity are troubling for readers schooled in post-structuralist critique" (21). The recorded voice, Hall claimed, holds the poet himself; as we shall see, most twentieth-century listeners felt this way and, consequently, described listening to a poet as a physically intimate experience. The very title *The Voice of the Poet* suggests not only that the poetry and the poet's physical voice are one, but also that the recording embodies the voice.

Such assumptions were the subject of Derrida's deconstruction of voice-as-presence in *Speech and Phenomena*. The power of the voice, as Derrida describes it, originates in an illusion of unmediated presence. Having no "worldly form," the voice appears to issue from a true self, one that hears its own voice before speaking and is then heard by others. The voice or the spoken word, Derrida argues, appears to *be* the subject: "My words are 'alive' because they seem not to leave me: not to fall outside me, outside my breath, at a visible distance; not to cease to belong to me, to be at my disposition 'without further props'" ("From Speech" 19). However, when words are imagined or spoken, there is movement through time, suggesting to Derrida that voice and "self-presence" are traces, on the same field of play as printed words or perceived objects.

Among contemporary critics of literature and sound, the most provocative heir to Derrida has been Garrett Stewart. Stewart's concept of "phonemic reading" draws attention to the phonic slippage between and within words:

> Literary language induces its own aural (if silent) feedback, not so much to thicken itself into "literariness" as continually to "reanalyze" the medium called "language" on which it is staked. In phonemic reading as practiced here, then, what is read is language itself, its deepest transformative logic, not just its given textual manifestations. (*Reading Voices* 102)

"Reading" in his study is most often *silent* reading, and Stewart is more concerned with the potential meaning latent in "linguistic accident than with aesthetic craft" (25). On the topic of recorded literature per se, Stewart is generally silent. Although "transegmental drift" is most obviously encountered in the speech stream of oral language, its presence in written language suggests to him that "the evocalization of transegmental alternatives is not sonic at all but phonemic" (127). Be that as it may, when one listens to a recorded poem without benefit of the script, transegmental drift is one of several provocative accidents that can open up the poem. I will explore these in greater detail in my deformations of a recording by Wallace Stevens at the end of this introduction and, later, of readings by Allen Tate and Dylan Thomas, as part of an analysis of Caedmon and Library of Congress recordings from mid-century.

The recorded voice is necessarily situated in time—the time of the recording and of the listening. In *Distant Reading* (2005), Peter Middleton concludes that "staging, authorship, sound, and intersubjectivity are constitutive elements of a poetry reading that are revealed as elements of reading itself..." (59). The event of the reading is, that is to say, analogous to reading as an event. The same can be said of close listening. When we listen to a recording, we hear the poet's assumptions about what a poet and poem sound like, and we hear her audience, not only as ambient noise on the recording, but also as instrumental in the development of her vocal quality and reading style. W. B. Yeats, for instance, read in an incantatory mode that tends to elicit laughter from students in my classroom. But his had been the dominant mode of reading poetry for decades and would continue to have proponents well into the mid-twentieth century. Yeats prefaced his recording of "The Lake Isle of Innisfree" with an apologia. "I'm going to read my poem with great emphasis upon the rhythm," he declares, and while "that may seem strange if you are not used to it," he insists that it gave him "a devil of a lot of trouble to get into verse the poems I'll read, and that's why I will not read them as if they were prose" ("Lake"). In close listening, it is critical to distinguish between reading and listening "then" versus "now"—a distinction that will prove basic to the model of listening I propose later in this introduction. Poetry, in Yeats' estimation, may be distinguished from prose by its rhythms, which demand to be emphasized in performance; the recordings of Edna Millay, Edith Sitwell, Dylan Thomas, and Allen Ginsberg, among others, suggest a similar set of assumptions. Put simply, how we listen to Yeats may well differ from how he was once heard, and foregrounding the distinction can often be critical to an analysis of the recorded poem.

Literary critics have responded to post-structuralist concerns about presence by examining the materiality of poetic voice and placing voice in specific historical contexts. John Picker's study *Victorian Soundscapes* (2003) is a case in point. In a chapter on early recording technology, Picker analyzes the late Victorian reception of Edison's phonograph, especially of recordings of poets reading from their work. He notes that, on the one hand, Edison's representatives and the poets that they recorded considered the recordings a form of embalming: as they understood it, their voices were literally etched onto cylinders, giving the voices a kind of corporeality as well as longevity. On the other hand, the disembodied character of the recorded voice, when played back, evoked awe and wonderment, as if the voice had a ghostly life of its own.

As in Picker's work, the relationship among voice, recording, and social history is critical to many of the studies in Adalaide Morris' *Sound States: Innovative Poetics and Acoustical Technologies* (1997). From that important volume, two essays on literature and audiotape are especially relevant to my study. In "Voices Out of Bodies, Bodies Out of Voices," N. Kathryn Hayles demonstrates that audiotape allows both preservation of a voice and alteration of it (77). Hayles is interested in what this implies about the nature of authorial subjectivity. Focusing on Beckett's *Krapp's Last Tape* and Burroughs' *The Ticket that Exploded*, she maintains that "audiotape functioned not only as a theme, a metaphor, or a vehicle for expression but as a mode of relation that produced a certain kind of postmodern subjectivity" (75).

Michael Davidson arrives at similar conclusions about the relationship between audio technology and postmodern subjectivity. Invoking the useful phrase "technologies of presence" in an essay by that name, Davidson traces a brief history of how tape recording shaped contemporary poetics. He argues that tape recording became a basic tool of the "surveillance culture" of the post–World War II era, thereby making the voice something to be overheard in a context that predetermined its meanings and, at worst, criminalized it. Poets such as Olson, Robert Creeley, and Allen Ginsberg responded by wresting control of the recorder "as an accomplice in the recovery of more authentic speech" ("Technologies"

103). After these initial "authentic speech" uses of recording came the work of Paul Blackburn, David Antin, and later Laurie Anderson and Steve Benson. This line of poets traces a gradual movement away from treating the recorder as a means of archiving the authentic and toward treating voice as a construct.

That movement has been made by many contemporary artists whose experiments in sound, or sound and technology, deconstruct presence and redefine the boundaries of the poetical. The innovative works in language and noise of artists such as John Cage, Jackson Mac Low, Anderson, and Blonk, as well as the ethnopoetics of writers such as Kamau Brathwaite have defined the principal soundscape for most criticism of poetry recording specifically, and of poetry, voice, and sound generally, since the 1990s. This is evident not only in Middleton's work and in the Bernstein and Morris collections, but also in Kahn and Whitehead's *Wireless Imagination* (1992), the influential work of Al Filreis, Marjorie Perloff, Jed Rasula, and Steve MacCaffery, and in the majority of the papers presented as part of the focus on sound and poetry at the 2006 MLA convention in Philadelphia. The soundscape here is rich and diverse; Cage's recordings of his mesostics dissolve lyric subjectivity, while Brathwaite's vocalizations of *Born to Slow Horses* reconstitute it elsewhere, differently. But by and large, critics of sound and modern poetry have preferred what Bernstein calls "anti-expressivist poetics," verse outside of "official verse culture," and poetries that are aligned against authorial presence or the notion of a "poet's voice" (*Close Listening* 12, 16).

I would argue that, ironically, this preference has closed our ears to a portion of the audio archive and, therefore, to the full range of meanings of modern poetry in performance. Insisting on the importance of "aurality" as opposed to "orality" as a framing concept for close listening, Bernstein claims that "the poetry reading enacts the poem not the poet; it materializes the text not the author; it performs the work not the one who composed it. In short, the significant fact of the poetry reading is less the presence of the poet than the presence of the poem" (13). My research in the audio archive suggests something quite different from this: among other things, that the "presence of the poet" is always at issue, at least for listeners and usually for the reader herself; that poetry readings (and, in different ways, recordings) materialize both text and author in ways that complicate twentieth-century literary critical insistences upon separating the two; that many important poetry performances in the modern era have been very much about "the one who composed" the work as well as the work itself.

The difference, of course, comes in part from what one chooses to listen to. In this study, I attempt to extend our understanding of the audio archive by close listening to recordings of modern poets, in the studio and at readings, for whom the text was primary and for whom readings and recordings were principally a means of disseminating their work. While "avant-garde" is a floating signifier, and "modernist" a vexed category, in respect to twentieth-century poetry and sound those terms have come to suggest, conveniently, a difference between mainstream or establishment practices and experimental, antiestablishment modes. As Bernstein justly asserts, for most modernist poets, audio recording was either secondary to the writing or was principally a means to generate writing. For the avant-garde, by contrast, experiments in poetic language often involved performance and recording. What I will show, however, is that precisely because modernist poets—such as Lowell and Eliot, Bishop, Johnson, or Sexton—were tethered to the text, they faced the differences that reading aloud and recording made in the poetry and for the representation of a self. It will become clear that despite the primacy of print, modernism was for many an experience in listening, and on tape and record, we are left with a wealth of modern voiced poems and commentaries that repay the kind of close listening critics have rightly given to the late-twentieth-century avant-garde.

Modernist recordings have played a role in a few critical studies besides those mentioned earlier. In her contribution to *The Unraveling Archive: Essays on Sylvia Plath* (2007), Kate Moses surveys and differentiates among Plath's recordings. Don Share, librarian of the Woodberry Poetry room, has written and presented on the history of the Harvard Vocarium, whose recordings factor in several of the following chapters. Taking a lead from Kamau Brathwaite and Derek Walcott, Charles Pollard acknowledges the importance of Eliot's recordings in the shaping of Caribbean modernism in a chapter of his *New World Modernisms* (2004), and Eliot's "The Waste Land" recordings were the subject of the earliest among these studies: Richard Swigg's "Sounding *The Waste Land:* T.S. Eliot's 1933 Recording." But sustained studies of the audio archive of modernism, broadly construed, and of the variety of questions it raises and problems it presents remain to be written. *Recorded Poetry and Poetic Reception* is an attempt at a beginning. It complements Wheeler's groundbreaking study by focusing in detail on the recorded poetic voice, describing some of the major scenes and kinds of modernist poetry recording and providing critical analysis of these recordings alongside their more familiar print versions. Like Bernstein's work, it advocates close listening, but it listens closely to modernist poets whom the most important critics of poetry and sound have tended to ignore.

What Are We Listening To?

I will turn now to some preliminary considerations of the archive itself. In this section of the introduction, I will describe the nature of the archive and its recordings, and outline the principal reasons why modern poetry was recorded.

As a name for the body of twentieth-century poetry recordings, "archive" can be misleading, insofar as it implies careful preservation, specific location, and organization—as in the highly ordered structure of the William Blake online archive, or the specific coordinates of a university library's cataloged and climate-controlled special collections. For the audio archive does not (yet) have the meticulous, if hidden, hierarchical arrangement of online and library archives—a form of order that has been a source of tension between proponents and critics of digitization, and that has given pause to critics of the cultural studies move to historicize.[4] The audio archive is, however, a body of scarce historical materials that demand study, description, preservation, and duplication, all of the kind we associate with and provide for the early editions, manuscripts, journals, and ephemera of many writers. Recognizing that important archival materials have yet to find their way into (or out of) official archives, *PMLA* and *Modernism/Modernity* have begun devoting space to the publication of "little known documents" (*PMLA*) and matters "out of the archive" (*Modernism/Modernity*).

The audio poetry archive consists of commercial and noncommercial recordings. The former—a range of studio and live recordings, most now out of print—have been largely ignored by scholarship. Reproduced in small quantities and marketed, for the most part, to specialized audiences, these recordings—unlike their print counterparts—have been somewhat haphazardly collected by community and university libraries; most major libraries own, for instance, editions of all of Edna Millay's books, but few have her recordings. Noncommercial recordings—often single recordings that, except in a few cases, have not been reproduced and marketed—are dispersed across a range of libraries, colleges, and other institutions where poetry has been read and recorded. Efforts to describe and catalog noncommercial recordings, whether locally produced or acquired as part of a poet's "papers," vary dramatically. Harvard's Woodberry Poetry Room and the Recorded Sound Reference Center at the Library of Congress represent the minority in their careful, descriptive bibliography and integration into a searchable catalog. Based on my experiences in researching this book, I venture to say that significant recordings in the audio archive remain tucked away in closets and drawers, on tape that will eventually be unplayable, either because the materials have deteriorated or because players will be nearly impossible to find. Be that as it may, even commercial recordings on more stable media rarely show up in bibliographies of modern poets' works, and many by such small labels as Musicraft or Yale's Carillon are nearly as difficult to get as their locally produced, noncommercial counterparts. All of this neglect seems to suggest that the work of Bernstein, Morris, and others notwithstanding, poetry recordings are considered ephemera, with only marginal value to scholarship. But why are James Weldon Johnson's recordings of *God's Trombones*, a great modernist experiment in what he called "Aframerican" voice, not essential listening for students and scholars of modern poetry, and why are recordings by Edna Millay and Anne Sexton—for whom to read aloud and be heard were critical—marginal to study of their lives and work? All of the modernist poets, including such establishment writers as Stevens, Moore, Lowell, and Bishop, recorded their work. Recordings of poets reading their work often find their way into classrooms, but generally as a kind of curiosity, a sideline to serious print material. One of the goals of this study is to bring these recordings "out of the archive" as examples of how aural and print media together may inform an understanding of modern poetry—in both scholarship and the classroom.[5]

So far, I have categorized the recordings in the audio archive as commercial and noncommercial, but defining what we're listening to leads me to consider when poetry is recorded, and why. As I argued earlier, avant-garde experiments with recording technology and the poetics of sound are one part of the archive that has elicited theory and criticism. But the largest section of the archive is made up of recorded poetry readings—a scene I will describe as "on the stage" throughout this study. The ubiquitous practice of recording poetry readings seems to be principally documentary, the irony being that the documents generally go unheard. The practice assumes that a poet's reading is important, not something to be lost, that it has at least some potential value for posterity. As audible inscriptions of an event, live recordings of poetry readings include a poet's commentary on her work, sometimes involve audience feedback, and always capture ambient sounds that tend to place the reading in time and space. Together, this host of data points asks us to consider what is worth attending to in close listening, a question I will attempt to answer in the chapters ahead.

Two subsets of "on the stage" readings are the recorded radio broadcast and what I will simply call the "occasional" recording. Again, the purpose of these recordings seems to have been documentary, and the two often overlap. Because radio traded on illusions of presence, listening to recordings of, for example, Edna Millay's NBC broadcasts or Dylan Thomas' musings on the BBC invites attempts to reconstruct the scene of listening; drawing on letters and commentary from listeners, I will often place listening "then" and "now" in tension with one another. As "occasional," I include recordings of poetry forums, inaugurations, elocution contests, memorial services, and other occasions in which readings of poetry play an important, if not a central, role. These recordings place a host of voices and kinds of discourse into dialogue, and they raise questions about the public role of poetry in the twentieth century.

Unlike live recordings, studio recordings were generally made with an eye to preservation and commerce, though most were never intended for mass consumption, and they share the documentary impulse of the recorded poetry reading. Sound quality has been carefully controlled, and the commercial versions of these recordings come with liner notes, record jackets, and other components of what Jerome McGann called the "bibliographic code," discussed later here and in each of the chapters ahead. As I will show, what we listen to in the audio archive is often much more than the poet's voice. The packaging and the line-up of voices shape our experience, as do the technologies of sound editing and engineering.

With so much to attend to, a method for listening proves critical. In the final section of this introduction, I will review the theory and practice of listening that inform this study. I will describe the method I propose and preview the design and goals of the chapters ahead.

How To Listen and Why

Close (silent) reading and close listening are analogous practices, and throughout this study, I will move back and forth between them in my responses to audio poems. Even in the usually silent practice of close analysis of a literary text, words are sounded internally, or even subvocalized, in the process of decoding and comprehension, as research in reading has made clear.[6] There is always sound in reading, whether or not we are aware of it. But listening to poetry read aloud brings out possible resonances that tend to lie dormant in the quiet, solitary act of reading. For despite the practical similarities between reading and listening to a poem, the experience of listening differs in significant ways from that of reading.

Most crucially, listening to someone read has a social dimension that involves the casting of a text in a particular voice. In his meditation on the phenomenology of listening, Jean Luc Nancy proposes that when we listen, sound is at once outside and inside us, simultaneously connecting and distinguishing us from the source of the sound. To listen is to be open and opened, he argues: "In this open and above all opening presence, in acoustic spreading and expansion, listening takes place at the same time as the sonorous event, an arrangement that is clearly distinct from that of vision," because "visual presence is already there, available, before I see it, whereas sonorous presence arrives..." (14). For Nancy, listening is therefore always an event, situated in time and space, contingent on sounds being produced in the moment of the listening. Reading, too, is an "event," as reception theorists such as Hans Robert Jauss and Jerome McGann have argued. When we read, we enter into a history of readings from a particular moment and place. However unawares, we take part in a discourse that attends the text we hold. But the critical difference between my reading a poet and my listening to her is the sound of another—in the case of the recordings in this study, the sound of the poet's reading voice. We experience that voice as different from ours, and it is that voice, not our own, which carries the text. Having been heard, the voice of the poet often echoes within us when we read her work.

As sound, and as sound in a particular voice, the recorded poem conveys meaning beyond that of the words being spoken. In a series of acoustic readings of feminist theory, Ruth Salvaggio has argued that the instability of language, its tendency to suggest meanings in addition to, at odds with, or at a slant with the intentions of rhetoric, is most apparent in sound. In this respect, Salvaggio's "sounding language" is analogous to Garrett Stewart's "phonemic reading," but Salvaggio stresses the physical effects of sound on the reader: "Sound stimulates other sensatory modes of expression and response. Heard messages are tactile, reverberating in ear, mouth, mind. Words become kinetic, moving on and beyond the page. Thought resembles less the stable and staid intellect, more the rhythms of a breathing body" (66). In the voiced text, the implied sounds of print are further expanded to include such vocal effects as timbre, accent, and breath. These sounds may enhance the text, frame our understanding of it, or signify beyond its surface meanings.

At the same time, they suggest a "breathing body"—in the audio poems of the archive, the specific body of the poet whose reading was the occasion of the original recording. This has important implications for how we listen to poetry on record. In *Poetry and the Fate of the Senses* (2002), Susan Stewart writes that "sounds in poems are never heard outside an expectation of meaning" because poetry readers tend to assume that sound and sense are integrated (79). Though Stewart writes about the intersection of listening and reading, her claim may be applied uniquely to how we listen to the poet read. For we bring to such a scene of listening an expectation that the poet's reading will be meaningful—that the poem in the voice of its author will speak to us in a way that another's reading would not. Writing about the problematic concept of "voice" in poetry, Stewart again makes an observation that may be meaningfully applied to the performed poem:

> What do we mean when we speak of "voice" in poetry? To indulge in such creative writing workshop clichés as that of "the poet finding his or her own voice" is to substitute a reifying and mystifying version of subjectivity for what is in fact most profound and engaging about poetic voice— that is, the plays of transformation it evokes beyond the irreducibility of its own grain, its own potential for silence...In listening, I am listening to the material history of your connection to all the dead and the living who have been impressed upon you. The voice, with the eyes, holds within itself the life of the self—it cannot be another's. (110)

A poet's voice is, to borrow a phrase from Elizabeth Bishop, "flowing and flown"—that is to say, connected to a history of writing and voicings and yet unique in its conformation, which is dynamic and irreducible (*Complete* 66). Stewart's ideas here echo Julia Kristeva's now-familiar concept "intertextuality," the voice in Stewart's formulation having the same qualities as the literary text in Kristeva's. I want to add, however, that while the recorded poems considered in this study are, as I suggested earlier, tethered to a text, they are nonetheless constitutionally different from their printed versions. In the audio poem, the field of signification is wider than in print, as when the *sound* of one poet's voice echoes another—as Sexton calls up Millay—or a way of reading aloud joins together fundamentally different poets—Allen Tate and Louise Bogan, for example. At the same time as the connections are being generated, however, the unique timbre of a voice turns our attention to a specific point of reference, the poet who reads and the text she holds. In an essay on the possibilities of reclaiming a "self" in poetry after deconstruction, Peter Middleton wonders, "Why can't the self in the poem be large enough to contain impersonality and personality, along with multitudes, bodies, and communities?" (106). Heard in the poet's voice, the poem projects just such a self.

Listening to the recorded poem requires not only close attention to the stream of sounds, but also to the print text and performer. When we begin with the recording, as I often do in this study, the print text becomes, like a score, a script with many possible soundings. Whether or not the poet's sounding should be authoritative is a question of great import, and I will consider it in detail in the chapters ahead. None of this is to say that, to paraphrase Pater, the printed poem aspires to the condition of music, or that reading aloud should be an effort to recover the utterance at the point of composition, though Dylan Thomas will argue as much, as we shall see. Rather, I mean to suggest that text, audio, and context describe a circle that constitutes the scene of listening to poetry from the audio archive. Even as we lean toward the center of the circle to hear the poet's voice, echo, static, and resonance will cause us to turn our heads or glance at the page. Throughout this study, therefore, the "voices" of audio and print media are considered together—recordings alongside letters, manuscript variants, and other artifacts. For it is not my contention that audio should be given a privileged position, rather that it should be considered an integral part of a poet's output and of the documentary materials of the literary historical record.

Given these many factors, how should we proceed to listen to and study the recordings in the modernist audio archive? At the risk of seeming prescriptive, but in the interest of clarity and utility, I want to propose a set of questions to guide scholarly work with these materials; the questions derive from my experiences in the archive and are an integral part of the description and analysis in the chapters that follow. The order of the questions will vary, though I would argue that whether one seeks to study a single recorded poem or an entire event, all apply.

What are the sound and sense of the recorded poem? As I suggest later in this introduction, answering this question depends in part on our situating the reading historically and accounting for its material condition. But I invoke "sound and sense," not as an endorsement of the somewhat dated poetry textbook that took this as its name, but because the phrase implies that there is meaning in a poem's sounds, broadly construed here to include the poet's vocalization as well as the sonorous linguistic, syntactic, and metrical workings of the text. For close listening, as I practice it in this study, is a variety of formalism. Like close reading, it involves careful attention to the language and formal procedures of a poem, and throughout *Recorded Poetry and Poetic Reception*, I will argue that the recorded modernist poem should be studied among the textual variants of a poet's oeuvre. But because the recorded poem, as sound, is not fully analogous to the poem in print, close listening also involves interventions into the recorded poem that take advantage of its difference from the print variant. As Charles Bernstein writes, "Close listenings may contradict 'readings' of poems that are based exclusively on the printed text and that ignore the poet's own performances, the 'total' sound of the work, and the relation of sound to semantics" (*Close Listening* 4). In a recording of a poetry reading, there are many places of entry and points of departure. The poem unfolds as we listen, and words and sounds besides those in the poem itself enter into the experience; in the chapters ahead, we will have occasion to examine the role they play in the meaning of the recording. More importantly, whether on the stage or in the studio, the poet's reading often generates a form that contrasts with the printed version we hold in our hands. In the tension between sound and print, things fall apart in ways that open up the forms and ideas of often familiar modernist poems.

For this reason, close listening includes de-forming the audio and print texts. I take the concept of "deformance" from Jerome McGann and Lisa Samuels. Following Emily Dickinson's suggestive comments about reading a poem backward, McGann and Samuels reverse the lineation of Wallace Stevens' "The Search for Sound Free from Motion" to make the case that performative critical models can "release or expose the poem's possibilities of meaning" (28). That is the goal of de-forming the audio poem as I practice it here, through rendering audio into print, by overlaying various soundtracks of poetry recordings, or through other technological interventions into the stream of sounds. Briefly, by way of a preliminary example, consider what happens if we transcribe Wallace Stevens' slow, methodical reading of "The Idea of Order at Key West."[7] Pensive, even dolorous, Stevens' reading is notable for its frequent pauses; Stevens isolates short phrases, drawing out and emphasizing syllables, such that the first stanza of "Idea" might be written as follows:

> She sang
> Beyond the genius of the sea.
> The water never formed
> To mind
> Or voice
> Like a body wholly body,
> Fluttering its empty sleeves.
> And yet,
> Its mimic motion made constant cry,
> Caused constantly
> A cry that was not ours,
> Although we understood,
> Inhuman,
> Of the veritable ocean.

Short lines, some isolating single words, and long, heavy pauses give the impression of a poet who is working out an idea or cautiously articulating an argument that he has not yet fully formed. Stevens seems to be searching; the pause after "to mind" implies that "or voice" occurs to him as he thinks the poem, and it establishes the productive tension between thought and speech, between sense and sound, around which the poem develops.

Alongside this transcription and the audio, the familiar text of Stevens' opening stanza stands in marked contrast: seven blank verse lines, beginning with a single, end-stopped sentence that seems to announce a thesis, and concluding with a rhyme, "ocean" with "motion" of line four. Without Stevens' printed poem as a guide, one level of meaning is occluded by close listening alone, for Stevens works out an "idea of order" within the structure of a received form we cannot hear. Along with Stevens' injunction to Ramon Fernandez in the final stanzas, the fact of the poem's form is essential to the claim it makes about the relationship between experience and aesthetic ordering: that the words and sounds of experience seem to betray implicit structures before the artist's "rage for order" (130). At the same time, Stevens' reading re-actualizes a coming-into-order, the processes of thought that have been disciplined by the metrical demands of a traditional form. His extended pause at "And yet" points to the way that the stanza, like his thinking, pivots in the midst of the fourth line. In the transcription, the two complete thoughts occupy two sets of seven short lines that, semantically, convey the same essential ideas as the seven-line stanza. What remains, however, is the increased ordering of the blank verse stanza: a visual ordering, centered on the semi-colon in line four, balanced on each side by lines three and five with their caesurae, framed by end-stopped pairs in lines one and two, six and seven.

As I mean to suggest with this brief analysis of a Stevens recording, the goal of close listening in the audio archive is not to reaffirm axioms about the absolute integrity of the text—a perspective, admittedly, held by several of the poets whom this study will treat. On the contrary, listening necessarily violates the text's putative integrity, for the poem nearly always sounds different from its print representation. Close listening is about working with the differences in the interest of further understanding the poem's craft and possibilities.

What is the state of the recording? In essence, this is a question of descriptive bibliography, of how the material characteristics of the text—in this case, the recorded poem and ancillary materials—subtly shape our responses. Contingent on space and the sophistication of audio equipment, quality of sound is only the most obvious of these characteristics. What we hear as the poet's voice on a recording often bears the traces of technological interventions; since the advent of magnetic tape, ambient and incidental noise have been edited out or strategically left in, and the poetic voice has altered in ways that I will consider in detail in chapter one. Besides the sound per se, there is the nature of the material that conveys it—broadly speaking, disc, tape, or digital file—and how that affects the presentation of the audio poem. Commercially produced long-playing records were often accompanied by cover art and extensive liner notes; cassettes and compact discs followed suit, and these frame our listening. All three formats provided limited recording space, thereby influencing choice and arrangement of readings. Online digitization of these and noncommercial recordings has made poets' recordings more accessible and easier to locate, and this welcome opening up of the archive makes it all the more critical that scholars take stock of the relationship between the audio poem and its presentation. For example, while online archives make early recordings easy to search, scan, and even transform electronically, they rarely include images or text from the original albums, an important historical source of information and meaning. The recorded poem online may or may not be the same as its earlier tape or disc version, just as the reading may differ from the print.

Consider two reissued forms of Gertrude Stein's 1935 studio recordings.[8] *Five American Women Poets*, a cassette/compact disc compilation produced by the Random House *Voice of the Poet* series, positions Stein as a female modernist alongside H.D., Edna St. Vincent Millay, Louise Bogan, and Muriel Rukeyser. Granted a certain degree of uniformity in the selection—all the writers are educated, white women whose careers began before 1940—the variety of voices and styles is remarkable, and that appears to be the simple, implicit point: that modernist poetry by women cannot be reduced to a single mode or agenda. The grouping encourages comparison and essentially creates dialogue among the poets. No doubt there were constraints on the design of this commercial compilation that had little to do with the editor's perspective on modern poetry by women; aside from the very limited number of recordings of Stein and H.D., for example, there may have been the desire to give voice to poets for whom a single-author recording could not be justified. Note that Elizabeth Bishop, Sylvia Plath, and Adrienne Rich have their own discs in the *Voice of the Poet* series. Be that as it may, Stein holds the place of matriarch on *Five American Women Poets*. Hers is the first voice, contrasting with the high-toned seriousness of H.D., who follows her, and with Millay's playful histrionics; Bogan seems to echo H.D., and with Rukeyser's "Islands," the humor in Stein's delivery finds resonance. With this brief review, I mean to suggest that the specific arrangements of a recording shape reception, as do the technical qualities of sound; while some cassette and disc players allow the listener to skip or search for tracks, the default mode of tape and disc is linear, just as the liner notes for either enfold the recording and suggest ways of listening. Later in the study, we will examine these effects in detail, and listen to several of these women more closely.

In contrast with the Stein of *Five Women Poets*, consider the same recordings as they are presented by PennSound. Assuming that we navigate to Stein via the site's author index, we will find her positioned in a long, alphabetical catalogue of poets, primarily from the post–1960 avant-garde. Stein's nearest neighbors, at the time of this writing, are Brian Kim Stefans and Lamont Steptoe, but that need have little bearing on our listening. For we may easily listen to any of the poets from the list in any order, and the same holds true for listening to Stein's actual recordings, which have been saved as separate sound files. We may stream or download these, the latter feature allowing us to create our own lists. While tape recording did allow listeners to transfer tracks from different sources to a single tape, the ease of digital mixing makes audio anthologizing infinitely various. Although the Stein recordings "Matisse," "A Valentine for Sherwood Anderson," "If I Told Him: A Completed Portrait of Picasso," and "A Portrait of Christian Berard" on PennSound are the same as those on *Five American Women Poets*, the context of the readings and state of the recordings themselves differ dramatically from one site to the other, and a goal of scholarship in the audio archive should be to account for different presentations of the recordings that affect reception. Because the vast majority of recordings in the archive remain on tape and record, artifacts in those formats will be the focus of my study. To the topic of digitization and the re-archiving of modernist poetry on record, I will return in the epilogue.

What is the scene of the reading? Many of the characteristics of a poetry recording derive from, or are at least fundamentally influenced by, the specific time, place, and circumstances of the reading. The tone of the poet's delivery, for instance, differs dramatically between studio readings and live performances, the latter generally being more informal and conversational than the former. Choice of texts in the studio generally tends to the well-known or the would-be canonical, whereas on the stage, poets will offer up works in progress and comment on their process, sometimes in the middle of the poem. As Lesley Wheeler shows, styles of reading changed dramatically over the course of the century, such that the sound of the recorded poem may be traced in part to a particular moment in the history of poetry performance and recording. It follows that reception study is essential to work in the audio archive, first because the event of the recording itself is an instance of reception, and second because our current reactions to a poet's recorded performance betray historical difference. In short, the "scene" of the reading—its place, time, and intended audience—frames and influences its purpose, and is basic to the shape of the recorded poetic voice.

The four core chapters of this study span the long era of modernism as it is represented in audiotape and disc, from the late 1930s to the early 1970s, but they are organized topically, rather than chronologically. Earlier, I wrote that the audio archive could be divided between two general scenes—the studio reading and the live recording "on the stage." Framed by those broad categories, chapters one and two form a pair, the first dealing with poets and producers in the studio, the second treating an especially rich variant of the live recording, in which poets and critics read and discuss another's work. Whether live or from the studio, the audio recording of a poet reading her work points us toward complex issues of authenticity, persona, and authority. Chapters three and four, therefore, focus on the differences between reading in one's own voice and reading in character, the two prevalent subject positions taken by poets in the audio archive. Essential to these chapters is an analysis of how modernist poets shaped their public voice and sounded their materials in response to listeners. The archive offers many examples of recordings in the studio and on stage, in first person and in the voice of another. My approach to this array of possibilities has been to work in detail with a specific set of recordings that I consider representative and to show how close listening, with attention to the state of the materials and their reception, extends our understanding both of the poets in question and of the issues posed by the audio archive of modernism. I have, moreover, chosen to focus on poets whose work in sound and recording has generally not been studied, even though they actively read and recorded their work. So while the seminal work of Olson, Creeley, and writers from the Beat and Black Arts movements, for example, fall within the time frame of *Recorded Poetry and Poetic Reception*, I have been interested in the difference made by close listening to such print-based writers as Robert Lowell and Elizabeth Bishop, or to performers such as James Weldon Johnson and Anne Sexton, whose contributions to the audio archive of modernism deserve fuller evaluation than they have so far received from literary criticism.

Chapter one, "Making Poetry Records, Remaking Poetic Voices: Caedmon and the Library of Congress," examines the relationship among recording technology, voice, and what we hear when we listen to poetry on record. I tell the story of two critically important, and fundamentally different, mid-century recording ventures—the work of Caedmon Records and of the Library of Congress' *Twentieth Century Poetry in English* project. Focusing on recordings of Dylan Thomas, whose voice launched Caedmon, of Robert Lowell, who jump-started the Library of Congress project, and of a range of modernist poets who got behind the microphone at Lowell's request, I consider how such factors as sound quality, tape editing, and packaging affect what we hear. With Lowell in charge, the Library of Congress venture was a deliberate exercise in canon-formation; with Thomas as its primary voice, Caedmon's purpose was to capitalize on the poetic voice as entertainment. The Library of

Congress and Caedmon examples resonate with nearly all "in the studio" archival recordings.

The scenes of chapter two, "Poets and Critics Live at the Forum: The Occasional Recording and Elizabeth Bishop," are gatherings of poets and critics to commemorate or appraise the work of a colleague. Such events are important markers in the reception history of a writer, and they constitute an important subset of recordings in the archive: the occasional poetry recording. As a case study, I analyze three recordings from the life and work of Elizabeth Bishop. The first is an example of poets "at the forum," and in a reading and conversation with Susan Howe and Charles Ruas, we hear Bishop resisting the call to perform. The concerns for reception implicit in that recording resonate with the second example from the chapter, a commemorative reading that Bishop gave in honor of Robert Lowell. I compare her readings and remarks at the commemoration to drafts of her elegy for Lowell, "North Haven," and argue that together they take us deeper into Bishop's concerns about a poet's critical afterlife. That afterlife is the subject of the third example of the occasional poetry recording, a memorial service for Bishop, which, I argue, anticipates the themes of Bishop's posthumous canonization as a major modernist voice. The three recordings demonstrate the potential of such ephemera as instances of reception and collections of apparently disparate poetry and voices, and I suggest ways that my analysis of the Bishop memorial can be a model for studying similar artifacts from the archive.

In the third and fourth chapters, the focus shifts from kinds of recordings to the persona of the poet on record—in first person, or in another's voice. Reading on stage—on radio, in an auditorium, in a small lecture hall—has been the primary mode of personal connection between the modernist poet and her audience, as Lesley Wheeler shows. That connection has been particularly crucial for modern expressive poetry in its various forms. In chapter three, "Authenticity and Audience: Millay, Sexton, and Vocal Connections," I investigate how the "I" of the poem of personal expression and experience is shaped by negotiations between poet and listeners. The live readings, recordings, and popular reception of Edna St. Vincent Millay and Anne Sexton are especially rich material in this regard, for these poets were instrumental in the development of an aesthetic that emphasized presence and the intimacy of vocal expression—an aesthetic of the "beautiful throat." If the voice "holds within itself the life of the self," as Susan Stewart suggests, the utterance of the confessional poet is ostensibly the vocalization of a private, inner life (110). Millay and Sexton's audience often responded to the voice of these poets as much as to the content of their work, and I argue that criticism of modern expressive poetry such as that of Millay and Sexton should attend more closely to its aural traces.

In contrast with audio recordings of poetry that purports to speak in the voice of the poet, modernists often wrote and read in voices not ostensibly their own. Chapter four, "Impersonations: Poets, Preachers, Teachers, and the Re-Making of *God's Trombones*," examines an especially complex case of modernist poetic impersonation, one that resonated across the century on stage and in places of instruction—the school, the textbook, the community center, the church. James Weldon Johnson's intentions in *God's Trombones* (1927) were ethnographic and educational; as he put it, he sought to "fix something of the old-time Negro preacher" in his "negro sermons in verse" (*God's Trombones* 841). I place Johnson's recording of his poetry in conversation with contemporaneous studio and field recordings of African American preaching, and with Johnson's troubled theorizing of dialect writing, to demonstrate how Johnson "fixed" the preacher's voice in an effort to attune listeners to the artfulness of African American oratory. I then trace the outcome of his efforts by analyzing subsequent audio remakings of *God's Trombones* across the work's reception history. Johnson's example has many correlates in the modernist audio archive, and I close with a brief look at one of these: Arna Bontemps' audio compilation, *An Anthology of Negro Poets*.

Finally, in the book's epilogue, I consider what is at stake as the audio archive moves to the Internet, and in an appendix, I reflect on the pedagogical implications of listening to modernist sound recordings. I offer an annotated syllabus for a course, Poetic Voices, in which modernist recordings are primary "texts," placing on center stage problems of voice, authority, textuality, and reception.

PART I

IN THE STUDIO, ON THE STAGE

CHAPTER 1

MAKING POETRY RECORDS, REMAKING POETIC VOICES: CAEDMON AND THE LIBRARY OF CONGRESS

The dead art rescues the ephemeral and perishing art as the only one alive.

—Theodor Adorno, "The Form of the Phonograph Record"

Why did modernist poets get behind the studio microphone to record their work? I ask the question in this way because the studio recording implies a level of intent on the poet's part that most live recordings in the audio archive do not. Poetry readings and related events are usually recorded without the poet's input or assistance; indeed, after handheld tape players and, more recently, digital recorders in phones and cameras, it became easy to record the poet without her knowledge.[1] For field recordings, such as those ghostly, grainy voicings that Edison's protégés captured from Robert Browning and Alfred Lord Tennyson, the machine comes to the poet, who may or may not have an interest in the enterprise.[2] But to sit for a studio session, the poet must accept an invitation, adhere to a schedule, and speak into a machine; time must be given, poems must be read repeatedly, and all with the promise of modest remuneration at best (though there are exceptions, as we shall see). Perhaps unsurprisingly, modern poets' letters largely indicate their shared reluctance to enter the studio.

Be that as it may, most modernist poets—those whom we continue to read, as well as those we've essentially forgotten—did read in the studio, and it seems that their primary motive was to preserve a version of their work in their own voice. That is to say, the studio recording was a form of quality-controlled publication that archived the poem as the poet's voiced art. A closely related, second reason for studio recordings had to do with publicity; the recording was yet another way, usually at low cost, to disseminate one's work. Poets entered the studio for other purposes, such as to generate poetry through the coupling of voice and electronic technology, as has been documented by the critical writings of Davidson, Morris, McCaffery, and others whom I discussed in the introductory chapter. But my focus here will be the more pervasive modernist act of translating one's work from print to voice in a form that, from its earliest instantiations, purported to give the voice an afterlife.

Studio recording of poets began in earnest in the early 1940s, coinciding with advances in direct-to-disc recording, and took place primarily in universities and other educational institutions. The place and timing here are key, because many of the high modernist poets of the 1920s—Eliot, Pound, Moore, Stevens, and Williams, for example—entered the studio as established artists, and all were invited by members of a growing literary critical enterprise who considered them to be the essential voices of early-twentieth-century poetry. Among the largest and most influential of these recording projects was that of the Library of Congress, headed by the poetry consultant, a position that would later be recast as U.S. poet laureate. During his tenure as poetry consultant to the Library of Congress, from October 1947 to September 1948, Robert Lowell proved to be particularly skilled at building the modernist audio archive. With the disarming charm and regal authority that, for better or worse, were irresistible to many of his colleagues and acquaintances, Lowell persuaded over two dozen poets to take part in a recording project that had begun under his predecessor and mentor, Allen Tate, and had moved slowly until it met with Lowell's manic productivity. Lowell feted the poets and arranged for public readings, ushered them to the Library's recording studios, and along with a recording engineer and librarians Harold Spivacke and Robert Gooch gathered together much of what would be issued in 1949 as the first series of *Twentieth Century Poetry in English: Contemporary Recordings of the Poets Reading Their Own Work.*

There are several reasons why this series and Lowell's part in it are significant to scholars of modern poetry. The early history of the series is essentially the story of how advances in recording technology and the phonograph record enabled new ways of archiving, selling, and disseminating poetry—those three being bound up with each other. It is also the story of how the Library followed the New Critics' lead in endorsing a particular brand of modernist formalism, a brand that Lowell himself embraced and embodied early in his career. In this his first major public role, Lowell helped shape a version of the modern poetic voice that we continue to hear today, however unwittingly, in popular anthologies of recorded poetry, which often draw on the Library's archive.

Even as Lowell and the library were recording "representative" voices of twentieth-century poetry—as the catalog for the series proclaimed—another equally significant, if markedly different, recording project was about to begin (Library of Congress 3). It took place outside of the academy, and its purpose from the beginning was to capitalize on the poet's reading as a mode of intellectual entertainment. After a reading at the Ninety-Second Street Y in New York, Dylan Thomas was pursued—first on foot, then by phone—by Barbara Cohen and Marianne Roney, two young women hoping to record him in order to launch a new record label devoted to the spoken word. Under the slogans "A Third Dimension for the Printed Page" and "Speaking of the Best," Caedmon would make its own claims to shaping how poetry is heard, as well as *what* poetry *gets* heard. Over time, its catalog would prove more versatile and eclectic than that of any other producer of poetry recordings. By 1976, when Lowell recorded for Caedmon at his final reading at the Ninety-Second Street Y, Caedmon had acquired recordings from a range of sources, and its catalog included Gertrude Stein and Edna St. Vincent Millay, Frank O'Hara and Randall Jarrell.[3] But it was Dylan Thomas' voice and style—or, more to the point, how that voice and style were presented by Cohen and Roney—that would come to be most clearly associated with Caedmon and with commercial poetry recordings generally.[4]

In this chapter, with recordings of Thomas, Lowell, and Lowell's mentor, Allen Tate, providing historically coincident points of departure, I will take up the record as material artifact and consider the poem to be reproducible recorded sound, a product of far more than what Edna Millay referred to as the poet's "beautiful throat." Behind the illusion of the authentic voice, upon which much of the appeal of the recorded poet depends, is a host of stagings and, as technology advances, interventions and reformations. I will consider how the Library of Congress and Caedmon shaped the "voice of the poet" at mid-century, as well as why it mattered (and continues to matter) that the poet be the reader of his work. That is to say, if we accept the commonplace that poets are often not the best readers of their poetry, a set of values besides quality of performance must be operative in the practice of recording them. In the last part of this chapter, I will try to name those values, for they implicitly inform all of the recordings in the audio archive of modernism.

The Poets in the Library

In Saskia Hamilton's edition of Lowell's letters, there is a photograph of Lowell on the job at the Library of Congress (55). At his desk Lowell inspects a phonograph record from the series he has helped produce. To his right a turntable waits. His arm rests on a short stack of albums. He pulls the record from its sleeve, holding it gingerly by the leading edge. He looks tired, serious, studious. The dome of the capitol building, central and imposing, presides approvingly over the scene.

What does Lowell look at on the phonograph? Those of us who came of age before the advent of the compact disc will recognize Lowell's stance and gaze. The fragility of the 78 rpm disc, particularly in its earliest instantiations, left a permanent trace on the collective unconscious. Long after pliable acetate compounds replaced Vulcanite and other breakable hard rubbers, we handled phonograph discs as if they were china. And what is it that Lowell looks at? If the record were not new, we might assume that he inspects it for scratches, smudges, or dust. Not having the proper brush at hand, he would be tempted to polish the surface with his cuffs. Clearly, however, this is a new disc, and Lowell appears to be reading. The label is covered by the sleeve. His eyes are fixed on the spiraling grooves.

What kind of writing is it in the grooves that drew our and Lowell's gaze, a writing indecipherable without electronic prostheses, but nonetheless compelling? According to historians such as David Morton, Colin Symes, and Jon Picker, the material artifact of a recording session—beginning with the glass records of Leon Scott's 1850 phonautograph—was always treated as a sacred relic on which voice had been successfully inscribed. Scott's recordings could not be played back; Edison's later tinfoil recordings could, and as Lisa Gitelman has shown, people treasured these bits of foil, despite the poor sound quality and the fact that most had no way of playing back the recordings in their homes (158). All of these materials bore the ghostlier demarcations[5] of the master's voice. Or, to borrow again from Derrida's deconstruction of the privileging of speech, they bear the "worldly form" of the transient locutionary act.

The idea that sound recording constituted a form of writing, one whose traces were identical to the voice, is posited by Theodor Adorno in his 1935 "The Form of the Phonograph Record." Skeptical of the phonograph's potential for contributing to the advancement of musical composition, Adorno characterizes the record as primarily a storage device, though like many early listeners to phonographic recordings, he is awestruck by the potential of recordings to bestow an afterlife on performed music. Recording is a "process of petrification," he writes (56). But this process insures, ironically, that the sound event can be fully reexperienced, because the disc has been inscribed with the music's "curves, a delicately scribbled, utterly illegible writing" (59). It is in this writing, however illegible, that music "approaches decisively its true character," because the sound "that inhabits this and no other acoustic groove" is the sound of the music itself (59). This sound writing, he posits, is "true language" (59).

More accurately, however, the "scriptal spiral" on the phonograph record should be understood as a legible, material representation of the original sound waves. Before the sound is reproduced, the stylus must first read the ridges and angles of the groove. This is a reading aloud of sorts, for the stylus vibrates far beneath the threshold of hearing, and its vibrations generate an electrical current analogous in waveform to that of the groove. That current—that translation of the scriptal spiral—must be amplified (since the 1930s this has been done electrically) and transduced again, this time through the work of magnets and coils connected to a speaker cone, so that electrical impulses become the complex sine wave that we hear as the recorded voice of the poet. In my description, the frequent recurrence of the Latin "trans" suggests correctly that the voice is carried across several modes in the process of recording and replaying, each with a different physical manifestation. The writing on the phonograph is simply the most apparent, the most similar to the kinds of script we recognize. It is significant that the discs that revolutionized recording in the late 1930s were known as "transcription" discs, their acetate base being stable enough to hold the inscriptions and to withstand immediate playback, at least a few times. Because of their immediacy, they were also called instantaneous discs, a name that further elides the distinction between the sound event and its record, as if what we today call "real time" had been folded into the grooves.[6]

Tilting his record to catch the light, Lowell gazes at a writing in which inheres the voice of the poet, or so Adorno might have it. To what extent should that writing be looked at, magnified, and reproduced as part of the text of the recorded poem? Electron microscopy can render the scriptal spiral visible, if not legible (see figure 1.1). And as the "analog" in "analog recording" indicates, the undulations of the groove are analogous to the waveform of the voice that was recorded. We tilt the disc at the light as if our faith in what is there remains, as if we see the sound of the past and can read the scriptal spiral. But while it evokes metaphor—resonant hills and dales, echoing walls of a canyon—the consequences of this writing are dormant without the translating machine.

So Lowell tilts his record and is perhaps struck by what he cannot see. Much of what would be immediately apparent upon browsing a book of poems—lineation, rhyme and meter, the words themselves, even at a glance—is invisible. LPs would later provide some indication of a poem's length: there is a break where the scriptal spiral of one poem ends and another begins. But even this is hidden on the 78 rpm discs that Lowell investigates, for each poet's readings appear to be one, long track. The

Figure 1.1 Electron microscope image of record groove. Image created by Brian McIntyre and Chris Supranowitz at the Institute of Optics, University of Rochester, 2005.

converse of Adorno's hopeful "true language" might be anxiety about the difference between the printed and the recorded poem, a difference I will investigate in detail later in the chapter.

If Lowell felt any such anxiety, he never let it show. For his primary role was to sell the recording project's importance to his fellow poets, and he was clearly a successful salesman. From the photograph, it is impossible to discern what record he holds. But let us assume that it's one for which he bears some responsibility, a recording of a poet whom he'd invited to participate in the 1949 series.[7] Those poets included Conrad Aiken, W.H. Auden, Howard Baker, John Berryman, Elizabeth Bishop, Richard Blackmur, Louise Bogan, Witter Bynner, Katherine Garrison Chapin, e.e. cummings, William Empson, Robert Fitzgerald, Robert Frost, Horace Gregory, Randall Jarrell, Janet Lewis, Robert Lowell, William Meredith, Putnam Phelps, John Crowe Ransom, Herbert Read, Theodore Roethke, Delmore Schwartz, Karl Shapiro, Theodore Spencer, Stephen Spender, Allen Tate, William Carlos Williams, and Marya Zaturenska.[8] Lowell was tactical in his appeals to the poets to make these recordings. To Elizabeth Bishop, who disliked reading aloud and whose first round of recordings were disappointing, Lowell promised "some Jack Daniels" so that she could "start…off properly slugged this time" (*Letters* 93). In an ultimately unsuccessful appeal to Wallace Stevens, he pointed out that "with the exception of Pound (and he would if his strength were up to it and the government would let him out of St. Elizabeth's) you are the only important American poet who has not been recorded, we have Eliot, Frost, Williams, Moore, Ransom, Tate and Auden" (92). Because the recordings would be sold primarily by catalog and only by the Library of Congress, it must have been evident to Lowell and the poets that increased public exposure was an unlikely outcome of the venture. No attempt seems to have been made to package the records colorfully, though doing so was a common practice in the record industry by the 1940s. In both the 78 rpm and the later LP variants, the recordings were packaged in plain gray and brown albums, with biographical notes and transcripts of the poetry. But recording at the Library of Congress promised a relatively new kind of afterlife for the poet: not only a recording of her voice—a privilege enjoyed by very few poets before the Harvard and Library of Congress projects of the 1940s— but also being archived at the country's library. More immediately, as the letter to Stevens suggests, to be among the chosen for this project implied importance to American poetry, as adjudicated by Lowell.

What were Lowell's criteria for choosing poets? Importance, as Lowell's remarks to Stevens imply, could be claimed for a few. Among them, Tate and Ransom are the only two whose place would likely be disputed now, but given Lowell's own ambition to become important, it's unsurprising that he conferred that status on his earliest mentors. Fugitives and New Critics are represented heavily on the early series of Library of Congress recordings. Penn Warren and Winters recorded, and Aiken, Blackmur, Empson, Ransom, and Tate were among Lowell's invitees. Likewise, members of the so-called circle of Lowell are prevalent—Berryman, Bishop, Jarrell, Roethke, and Schwartz—and, broadly speaking, "formalism" is the poetics that, at the time of the recordings, everyone in these groups shares. The series thus essentially became Lowell's canon of mid-century poetry, read in the poets' own voices. Effectively, it was his first major project as arbiter of an academic poetry establishment of which he would be de facto leader for nearly three decades.

I want to qualify this, however, by noting that Lowell's chosen poets are far from univocal. If the 1949 series suggests that mid-century U.S. poetry—or, as per the title, "Twentieth Century Poetry in English"—is largely formalist, Lowell's readers offer up neither formalism alone nor a single brand of it. Moreover, poets have been grouped in such a way as to encourage comparisons.[9] Consider, for example, the albums that include

Allen Tate, who (as noted earlier) began the Library's recording project and, at this point in Lowell's career, continued to maintain a powerful influence on the young poet. As the Lowell photograph shows, the 78 rpm albums contained a series of sleeves, each with a record dedicated to a particular poet. Bundled together with Tate in album two of the first series were Paul Engle, Marianne Moore, John Gould Fletcher, and John Malcolm Brinnin: five records at $8.25. When the recordings were reissued on LP, the greater capacity per disc made new groupings necessary. Moore and Tate are paired on side one, and Louise Bogan becomes his opposite on side two.

That opposition is fortuitous and represents the variety within formalism that the series collected. I want to look at this pairing closely to illustrate how poetic voices on record tend to "speak" to each other, potentially regardless of the editor's intent. Tate and Bogan's friendship, initiated by Tate's interest in their common family history, had cooled after Bogan wrote a largely critical review of Tate's *Poems: 1928–1931* for the *New Republic* in March 1932. Bogan had characterized the Fugitives as too strident, derivative, and "vaguely philosophical" in tone, a group with overweening ambitions and mediocre abilities. Granting Tate "genuine poetic talent," Bogan argues that he has spent too little time apprenticing it ("Allen Tate's New Poems" 186). His poetry suffers from "determined incoherence," "preciosity," and "the spurious excitement of piled-up and complicated images" because, she implies, it is being made to carry the weight of his unrefined philosophy of what poetry should be (186–87). Bogan's criticism of Tate is trenchant, identifying the characteristics that would make his work increasingly unreadable. She recognized in Tate the habits of mind that would cause him, ill-advisedly, to discourage Lowell's experiments with personal writing in the early 1950s. Later, in response to an angry letter from Tate, Bogan further explained her objections to his poetry: "As you know, Allen, in a poem, not only can the feeling be in excess to the matter, but devices, crotchets, and all skilled traps for the unwary, can exceed. In short, these poems struck me as elaborate ruses, as poetic sophistry…" (*Letters* 63). Bogan and Tate are both formalists whose work is conceptually complex and densely figurative. But Bogan found Tate's work pretentious and emotionally empty, in need of honest expression and a refiner's fire.

It is in this last regard that her "The Alchemist," a short dramatic monologue from the 1923 volume *Body of this Death: Poems,* can be construed as a critique of Tate in its placement opposite his "Ode to the Confederate Dead" on the Library of Congress recording. "The Alchemist" works through an elaborate metaphor, in the manner of metaphysical poetry, to make a point that resonates with Bogan's criticism of Tate. Bogan's alchemy is an intellectual sacrament, carried out under the assumption that there are purer passions than those of the flesh. The speaker declares, "I burned my life, that I might find / A passion wholly of the mind" (*Blue Estuaries* 15). But distilled, the mind's passions prove to be fleshly, and the bread of this eucharist is "unmysterious" (15). If the alchemist here is a figure for the poet, as it is in the poem's main precursor text, Gerard Manley Hopkins' "Alchemist in the City," the poem declares the body to be the origin of poetic expressiveness. Passion begins in the "unmysterious flesh" before it is reworked by the will—or, as Bogan suggests of Tate, before it is overworked in "complicated images" in which the complexity itself becomes the object ("Review" 187).

What I am arguing is that by virtue of their placement on these records, Bogan's alchemist critiques Tate's imperious bard—perceptively, in my estimation. Whether this happens by design is less important than that it does so in effect, particularly when we take into account the contexts in which the album was assembled. Bogan had Tate right, even if her disclaimer in the letter—that she reviewed the book, not the man— seems disingenuous. Granted that as a genre the ode tends to excess, the bitterness and anger of Tate's most famous poem get diluted in overdetermined metaphors, which in turn communicate relatively simple and commonplace ideas. For example, that the dead eventually become part of the earth and sea seems to be the fundamental idea of Tate's extended description of how the "salt" in the blood of their decaying bodies "stiffens the saltier oblivion of the sea" (271). The sea becomes a flood, and as "we" the mourners in our "ribboned coats of grim felicity" attempt to make sense of the Confederates' problematic sacrifice, the flood recedes—or rather, disappears from the poem, and is replaced with the "unclean" bones of the dead, "Whose verdurous anonymity will grow" (271). The irony of greening, growing "anonymity" is intended to bite, but comes across as simply one more in a sentence clotted with ironies and adjectives. Tate's reading only reinforces the effect. Placed alongside Bogan's spare formality, Tate's lines are indulgent.

I have argued that importance, relevance to his own ambitions, and a commitment to formalism were the criteria implicit in Lowell's choice of poets for the Library of Congress series, and by focusing on Bogan and Tate, I have intended not only to show the variety within the formalism Lowell endorsed in his choices, but also to demonstrate how the groupings on the records effectively placed poets in conversation with one another. I want now to look further at this conversation between Tate and Bogan in order to address another important question about the recordings made under Lowell's watch: How do the poets sound?

Bogan and Tate are comparable readers of their work. Tate's languid reading carries an aristocratic surety, as does Bogan's, whose New England accent is the class equivalent of Tate's Kentucky gentleman. Both closely observe lineation and pauses, calling attention to form. The affective range of their reading is narrow. Bogan recites her lines clearly; her expression is measured, even in a potentially dramatic poem like "The Sleeping Fury." In this way her reading is similar to that of all the poets on the LP. Poetry, the readings imply, is serious discourse; its oral presentation should be neither theatrical nor understated. The voice of the formalist poet registers between these extremes.[10]

It would be wrong to suggest that there is no drama in the readings captured during Lowell's tenure at the Library of Congress. John Gould Fletcher bursts briefly into song while reading "Clipper Ships"; William Carlos Williams dramatizes the races of his "Yachts." Lowell was especially pleased to have persuaded Robert Frost to record in March 1948, and Frost had already developed his signature folksy voice. His performance of "Stopping By Woods on a Snowy Evening" orchestrates the poem's measured lyricism while voicing its apparent ease. In reading the title, for example, he pauses briefly after "stopping," but not long enough to become melodramatic. He then follows the lineation and punctuation exactly, observing end-stops and enjambment alike. He delivers the second stanza in nearly a single breath, until he arrives at the only full stop at the stanza's end, "the darkest evening of the year" (224). In contrast, at each comma in the final stanza, he breathes deeply, invoking silence and emphasizing the four end rhymes—deep, keep, sleep, sleep. Frost reads as if from a score or prompt text, and with few exceptions, this kind of dramatic reading is unusual among the poets in the 1949 series. For despite the different kinds of formalism, there is a similarity across the voices and reading styles on the Library of Congress.

The similarities in vocal quality derive from recording technology—in the 1949 series, its limitations. In their original state, all of the voices sound thin. Again, let's take as an example Tate's reading for the 1949 series, recorded on December 8, 1947. He read his "Ode" at a brisk pace, but as the longest of the poems he recorded that day, it consumed an entire side of the original 78 rpm discs. Like many monaural recordings, this one presents a crisp, dry soundscape largely as a result of a pre-stereo technical limitation: single track recording and playback. Such a soundscape favors Tate's sharp enunciation of plosives—for example, the /kt/ and /p/ in "strict impunity"—and his tendency to follow them with brief, empty pauses ("Ode" 269). Throughout the reading, Tate decelerates as he approaches full stops, and he allows his voice to trail on the final word before the punctuation.

What I mean to suggest by attending to Tate's voice as it is circumscribed by the monaural recording is that an audio poem is sometimes equal parts reading style and recording/playback quality. As technology advances, it becomes increasingly important to note how the voice of the poet has been engineered. Listening to a second Tate recording of the ode—in stereo, from a studio session at Yale in 1961—makes this clear. The Yale recording is stereophonic, giving a depth and breadth to the sound that contrasts with the flatness of the earlier monaural recording. More important, however, are the interplay of what sound engineers refer to as "warmth," "liveness," and "intimacy." In the Yale recording, "intimacy," or a sense of closeness to the speaker, is an effect of "warmth," or a higher level of bass or low frequency sounds relative to those in the mid-frequency range. On the Library of Congress recording, Tate was a tenor; on the Yale, he is certainly a baritone, his voice seeming much fuller and warmer than it had a decade earlier. Now, we might speculate that with age, Tate's voice mellowed, though many poets' recordings from late in their careers—Robert Frost's and Elizabeth Bishop's are key examples—demonstrate the opposite; the voice becomes thinner, raspier, even as the sound engineering allowed for warmth and depth. I want to suggest, however, that Tate's changes might have to do with differences in technology, not just anatomy. Because the 1960s saw the increased use of magnetic tape recording and studio editing, engineers could have bumped up the thermostat, so to speak, by suppressing mid-range tones in favor of the low range. Editing and stereo, as well as age, may have given us a baritone Tate.

That Tate's reading has been carefully produced is most evident in what is missing from his reading: breath. We rarely hear Tate breathe, and never deeply, even after he holds forth in such lines as

> You know the unimportant shrift of death
> And praise the vision
> And praise the arrogant circumstance
> Of those who fall
> Rank upon rank, hurried beyond decision—
> Here by the sagging gate, stopped by the wall. (270)

Aside from a brief pause and small inhalation after "death," Tate reads these lines without break and, it would seem, without breathing, not even after delivery, before he begins the next stanza. To a degree, a reader can create the illusion of breathlessness by pulling back briefly from the microphone and taking a short breath; radio announcers do this skillfully. But Tate's breath may also have been deleted during editing, a technique that was impossible when recordings were made direct-to-disc, as in the 1949 Library series. Unlike a live recording, on which a cough, shuffling pages, or a sudden bump against the microphone brings the poet's body into the soundscape, breath on the studio recording is the only physical trace of the poet besides the voice itself. Without the breath, the speaking voice becomes numinous; editing for this effect would prove to be essential for Caedmon, as I shall show later in the chapter.[11]

If the similarity across voices in the series may be partly attributed to limitations in recording technology, the relatively narrow affective range of the readings goes to the heart of a mid-century poetics that would come to be identified with the academy. I have suggested that the performances on these albums tend to be neither theatrical nor fully understated. While this does not indicate uniformity, as Frost's presence and the tension between Tate and Bogan illustrate, many of the poets' measured recitation honors formal difficulty and regulates emotional expressiveness. Writing about the late-twentieth-century academic poetry reading scene, Lesley Wheeler notes the intentional reserve and the evident suspicion of dramatization. In the Library of Congress recordings, we hear the initial institutionalization of this mode of poetry performance—literally, its aural codification. Performance is interpretation, and the shared idea among these readers seems to be that the poem should speak for itself, if in their voices.

No reading from the 1949 series illustrates this more clearly that T.S. Eliot's, recorded by Tate in New York in 1946. Studying T.S. Eliot's recordings of *The Waste Land*, Richard Swigg has demonstrated that Eliot changed his performance style, from the 1933 Harvard Vocarium recording in which he reads in character, to the later, more familiar Library of Congress recording. Initially, Eliot interpreted the multiple voices of his poem in a way perhaps best described by Virginia Woolf, "He sang it & chanted it rhythmed it. It has great beauty & force of phrase: symmetry; & tensity. What connects it together, I'm not so sure" (qtd in North 137). Listening to the poem before its publication, Woolf responds to the poem's variety of vocal registers as well as its apparent "symmetry." As if in anticipation of Brooks and Warren's theory of the inner tension of the strong poem, Woolf feels the "tensity" of the poem—or, more to the point, of Eliot's performance. Having not seen Eliot's typescript, Woolf cannot close read this Ur-text of the New Criticism. She cannot finally assimilate the diverse parts to a unifying idea for, having heard it only once, Woolf no doubt recognizes that discerning "what connects it together" depends upon the kind of repeated encounters and critical investigations that would become standard in criticism of the text. Such encounters she would soon get in working up an edition of *The Waste Land* for Hogarth Press. Nonetheless, Eliot's performance style indicated "symmetry, & tensity," and his 1933 recording gives us aural markers—dramatic vocal, tonal, and rhythmic shifts—by which to organize the recitation in our minds. These influence our interpretation. While the designed fragmentation, spacing, and allusiveness of *The Waste Land,* compounded later by the machinery of Eliot's footnotes, necessitate reflective reading—the work, that is to say, of the silent eye and an internal voice—the poem's polyphony, spoken aloud, engages the ears and mind in a process of rationalizing its dissonances. It is critical, therefore, that Eliot so dramatically shifted his performance style—for this and his other texts. The 1946 reading of *The Waste Land,* famously dolorous and intentionally monotonous, gives few aural cues. The language is, as it were, left to stand on its own. This later recording is consistent with the performance style in Lowell's group for the 1949 series: a style that is essentially the New Criticism on record.

Sound and vocal styles aside, the placement of one poem after another on the disc, with nothing to cue our listening experience but the change in poet's voices, is the sound-text equivalent to offering up the poem in isolation, as I. A. Richards had done in his poetry-teaching experiments reported in *Practical Criticism,* published, coincidentally, in 1949. To give us an experience analogous to that of his students, Richards prints thirteen poems without title, attribution, or any other identifying information, all of which he intentionally buries in a folded page in the appendix of the book. His students' written comments on the poems— what Richards calls their "protocols"—provide him with evidence that students rely on emotional response, processes of association, and prior knowledge to make sense of a poem, when better criticism would focus steadily on the form and content of the poem itself. Like Richards' isolated artifacts, floating in white space free of footnotes, the audio poem hangs in the air. The Library of Congress recordings never include oral commentary or an introduction of the poet, as live recordings often do and as many later studio compilations would; the albums do provide texts of the poems and biographical sketches that focus primarily on the poet's literary accomplishments, but these are necessarily separate from the audio poem itself. If we shuffle the paper aside and just listen, we encounter the poem unencumbered, as Richards would have it.

Except, I would argue, that the audio poem cannot be disentangled from the particular qualities of the reader's voice, no matter how deliberately controlled the performance style. Timbre, pitch, manner of reading: if the audio poem were fully analogous to the printed poem, these might be comparable to paratextual elements such as typeface and paper quality.[12] But there is nothing "para" about any of these in the audio poem— they are integral to the language and experience. In an early review of the

Library of Congress recordings, David Thompson includes Tate as one of three "excellent readers of their own poems," the other two being e.e. cummings and Theodore Spencer (92). An excellent reading, he maintains, is the result of skillful articulation and a "complete command of vocal variety" put to the service of the poem's intrinsic energy and values (92). From Thompson, it follows that in the best recorded verse, we assess the quality of the reading irrespective of the identity of the reader. Richards suppressed the poets' names because he calculated that knowing the author would influence the reader's reception of the work. A good poem speaks for itself, he implies. It follows, as Thompson would have it, that the value of the recording is measured by how true the reading is to the poem's voice.

But the New Critical stance does not square with the fact that in archiving the poet reading her work, the Library of Congress designated a poet's readings as historically significant, if not authoritative. The widespread practice of archiving poetry readings does the same. In an audio recording, the voice of the poet, regardless of her "command of vocal variety," and however engineered by technology, is the *same* as the voice of the poem. It is unsurprising that confessional and expressive modes enjoyed a revival concurrent with advances in recording technology; the advent of portable tape recording would be instrumental in the success and distribution of the Beats in the late 1950s. Among the poets in the 1949 Library of Congress series, Berryman, Roethke, and eventually Lowell himself would record primarily autobiographical verse, and as we shall see, the careers of Edna Millay and Anne Sexton turned on the listener's enchantment with the sound of their voices as they read intensely personal poetry. More dramatically than print, audio calls our attention to the poet as personality and maker.

Speaking of the Best

Commercial recording of mid-century poetry capitalized both on reading as performance and poem as poet's voice. This is clearest in the case of Lowell's popular contemporary Dylan Thomas, so much so that it is still impossible to read a Thomas poem without hearing it in the Caedmon Thomas voice. I write "Caedmon Thomas" because the voice on *Dylan Thomas Reading A Child's Christmas in Wales and Five Poems* is, as Sarah Parry has argued, clearly a hybrid of Thomas' charismatic performance and amplified brogue and Caedmon's recording preferences and sound editing (30). Unlike the Library of Congress or Yale Carillon or Harvard Vocarium, Caedmon privileged performance quality and, from the beginning, asked professional actors to read for its recordings. Thomas, as it happens, was a master poet-as-performer, whose readings at the Ninety-Second Street Y were the inspiration for Caedmon's founding. Thomas read for the recording on February 22, 1952, in Steinway Hall, an "in the studio" reading that took advantage of effects associated with live, stage recordings. In concert halls, sound engineers are concerned with the "early sound field"—that is, "the first few reflections of sound reaching the listener before the onset of a diffuse reverberant field" (Eargle 44). The early sound field is experienced subjectively as spaciousness, a feeling for how large the room is. In essence, one hears an echo, as in the Thomas recordings. However, on the 1952 Thomas recording, this echo does not fully produce the illusion of a live performance in a concert hall. There are no audience noises, and the echo of the empty hall has been minimized, such that Thomas' voice is given a kind of shadow or halo. When we listen to "Do Not Go Gentle Into that Good Night," for instance, we hear a poem spoken elsewhere, *not* in the room with us, and yet close at hand. This effect is heightened by the fact that, as Parry points out, we rarely hear Thomas breathe, because Caedmon edited out "all extra-linguistic bodily noises that poets might make in the course of a reading—hesitations, coughs, throat clearings, swallows, heavy breaths, mispronunciations, repetitions, and wavering amplitudes..." (30). As a result of such sound editing, coupled with Thomas' vatic deliverance, the poem becomes religious utterance.

Like Frost, Thomas treats the text as a score, with punctuation, line breaks, and meter indicating rhythm and tempo. In his reading of "Do Not Go Gentle Into That Good Night," Thomas observes different modes of punctuation with remarkable consistency. Commas at line ends receive a longer pause—usually by a full second—than enjambed lines, which also receive a pause, and stanza breaks usually elicit a three-second break. When these patterns shift, they do so in the interest of the overall tempo of the poem. For Thomas accelerates gradually, just as he raises the volume of his performance, such that both crescendo and accelerando reach a climax at "Wild men who caught and sang the sun in flight, / And learn, too late, they grieved it on its way" (128). There is a brief slowing and softening at this point in the reading, then a second climax with "Blind eyes could blaze like meteors and be gay, / Rage, rage against the dying of the light." Volume shifts coincide with modulation, such that across stanzas one through five there is an almost chromatic shift of key. Thomas' technique here prefigures Allen Ginsberg's in "Howl": a measured increase in tempo and volume, coincident with change of key. The result is that our attention is drawn less to the words themselves than to the intensity of expression—an effect the opposite of that sought by Eliot and Lowell's readers.

This is not to argue, of course, that Caedmon and Thomas are uninterested in our attending to the language of his verse. Rather, their performance preferences indicate an interest in how poetry signifies off the page. Thomas' reading of the final stanza is a case in point, emphasizing the painful emotional content. After he calls to his father, "there on the sad height," Thomas' voice fills with pain (128). The consonance of "curse," "bless," and "fierce tears" becomes a sibilant plea in Thomas' rendering, and the earnestness of the villanelle's final couplet is carried by the contrast of the hard and soft /g/ in Thomas' soft but emphatic enunciation of "gentle" and "good," "rage" and "against": "Do not go gentle into that good night / Rage, rage against the dying of the light" (128). Even more so than in Frost's reading, we are here to be affected by the sound of the poem in the poet's voice. Caedmon and Thomas' attention to the emotional sense released in sound—released by the poet's reading—is related to the aural craft of poets such as Edith Sitwell and Edna St. Vincent Millay and had its fullest expression in recordings by confessional poets; we will return to these relationships in detail in chapter three.

While Thomas' studio readings were foundational for Caedmon and, given Caedmon's success, essential to the shape of popular poetry recordings after the mid-century, after Thomas' untimely death, Caedmon continued to capitalize on the popularity of his readings by issuing LPs made from live recordings by the BBC and on stage in the United States. Extraneous noises and commentary play an integral role in these recordings, as the liner notes to *An Evening with Dylan Thomas Reading His Own and Other Poems* indicate. Having described Thomas' notorious bohemianism, his lateness and drunkenness, the notes conclude:

> For some, this unique recording of one of these typical evenings will be nostalgic. But beyond that, it is a historical document of a particularly intimate kind, caught by a close microphone which picked up his funny quips as quickly as he dropped them. Probably even the audience didn't hear them all, but the microphone (unintimidated by his unkind comments about it) faithfully captured everything—the lonely man on stage and his dazzled, loving, but essentially strange and transient audience beyond the footlights.

The language here, which situates our listening, repays close scrutiny. The recording is called "historical," which gives it objective value for those interested in literary study; elsewhere on the album, the writer proclaims that "All who have written of Dylan Thomas' recordings agree that the voice holds the absolute key to his works," which are "those of genius." Interestingly, the recording is also called a "document," as if it were written, a text for our instruction. At the same time, it is "intimate"—as it had been for Millay, and would be for Sexton—because it puts us so close to the source. The role attributed to the microphone is critical: faithful and disinterested, it represents the man as he was. Where sound editing leaves off, annotations pick up. Caedmon here chooses to present Thomas unedited, as it were, in order to further the case it had always made: the poet's own voice is the voice of the poem.

Thomas spoke of this on a September 29, 1949, BBC broadcast called "On Reading Poetry Aloud"; the transcript was published in *Quite Early One Morning,* and Caedmon included the broadcast recording on *An Evening.* Thomas comments on reading aloud and performs "There Was a Saviour," "If My Head Hurt a Hair's Foot," and "Poem in October." His remarks are characteristically disingenuous, a ballast to his full-throated declamation of his poetry. Reading aloud is interpretation, he claims, if "that is not too weighty a word just for reading them aloud and trying to give some idea of their sound and shape" (167). What is being interpreted are the "original impulses" or "the first impulse that pumped and shoved" the poems along (167). Impulse, pump, shove—the rhythms that initiate poetry are rough and sexual, and when the poet reads aloud, he attempts to reenact those rhythms. Memory will fail him, Thomas suggests, but the physical act of reading aloud calls forward "inner meaning" (167). Having suggested that the full history of a poem is latent in the text and that the poet's reading can express it, Thomas issues a disclaimer: that he cannot "agree whole-heartedly" with what he's just said. He goes on to caution against the Scylla and Charybdis of reading aloud: the tendency to "mawken and melodramatise" or, contrastingly, to offer a detached "condescending undersaying" of one's poems (167). That he stands most in danger of the first, he freely admits, knowing that it will be "only too clear" to his audience.

Thomas' irony here is part of his performance, intended to indicate self-awareness in spite of his romantic attachment to melancholy and expressiveness. Contrasting sharply with the understated style of the formalist poets and the tongue-in-cheek of W. H. Auden, whose work he grudgingly admired, Thomas' readings had been characterized as mawkish and overblown.[13] For example, Andrew Lycett reports that Kingsley Amis considered Thomas the "epitome of a bombastic, old-fashioned style of poetry" (315) and that Louis MacNeice, who produced many of Thomas' BBC broadcasts, compared his voice to an organ (236). While critics of Thomas' style were in the minority, it is nonetheless true that Thomas held to a manner of reading in the line of "elocutionism," a mode of oral interpretation we'll consider in detail in chapters three and four. This appears not to have been deemed a liability by Thomas' listeners, many of whom would have been schooled in the theory that, as Yeats claimed of his rendering of "The Lake Isle of Innisfree," a poem should not sound simply like prose read aloud. Nonetheless, it means that much like the relatively narrow range of variation across reading styles in the Library of Congress recordings, Thomas' readings have a signature quality that marks any poem he performs. That quality can prove elegant and meaningful, as in his reading of "Do Not Go Gentle Into That Good Night." It can also flatten out differences between poems. Caedmon recorded him reading many of his favorite poets, from Shakespeare and Milton to Louise Bogan and Robert Graves. The two poets he read most frequently, Yeats and Auden, become strangely similar when filtered through Thomas' voice. The understatement and black humor of Auden's "As I Walked Out One Evening," for example, are lost in Thomas' performance, in which the poem comes to resemble one of his many lyrics on time's dominion. In his late romanticism, Thomas is closer to Yeats than Auden. In reading "Lapis Lazuli," however, he follows the same arc as when he read "As I Walked Out," building up to a climactic intensity at "On all the tragic scene they stare" and slowing to poignancy with the final repetition of the refrain. Yeats and Auden have not only been "Caedmonized," but also "Dylaned."

I have argued that the *Twentieth Century Poetry in English* project, especially under Lowell's leadership, favored modern formalist poets and presented their voices in ways commensurate with the New Criticism. At the same time, with Thomas as its star, Caedmon indicated the continued vitality of a kind of Shelleyan romanticism, in which poetry is an unbidden hymn sung with unapologetic vigor. It is too simple, however, to suggest that the Library of Congress and Caedmon projects merely replicate differences between modern and romantic, depersonalized art and poetry as cult of personality—differences outlined in such modernist credos as Eliot's "Tradition and the Individual Talent." In the audio poems in these admittedly divergent recording projects, points of convergence in voice and poetics are often striking, as I learned by deforming the poems electronically. I digitized and wove together recordings of Thomas and Tate, whose recordings I have so far set up as opposite, to create a third audio poem in the two poets' voices. I aligned Thomas' 1952 Caedmon "Especially When the October Wind" and Tate's 1947 Library of Congress "Ode" such that Tate's first offset couplet—"Dazed by the wind, only the wind / the leaves flying, plunge"—coincides with Thomas' final refrain ("Ode" 270). The duet version proves difficult to transcribe accurately, given the limits of representing a sound event in print. But the print version does expose points of convergence. Note that in the following transcription, phrases on the same line across columns are to be read simultaneously. Separate lines in the middle column are to be read successively, one following the other more rapidly when the column is aligned left:

<pre>
                        Like the blind crab
                        Especially when the October wind
                        Dazed by the wind
                                    Some let me make
    Only the wind   You
                        Of autumnal spells
                        The leaves
    Flying   The spider tongued
                        Plunge
                        And the loud hill of Wales
                        You know
                        With fists
    Who have waited by the wall   of turnips
                        Punishes
                        The twilight
                        the land certainty
                        of an animal
                        Some let me make you
                        Those midnight
    Restitutions of the blood   of the heartless
                        Words
                        You know
</pre>

Thomas and Tate declaim authoritatively, Tate with aristocratic assuredness, Thomas with the frenetic voice of a prophet. The sound alone evidences this, but it is written into the language of the duet, especially the repeated knowledge-claims. The poet declares that "You know," that he intends to "make you" by force ("You know / with fists") or by spell. The incantatory elements of the two readings are reinforced by the interplay of sibilants and liquids, especially in the initial lines of this section.

With the second stanza of his "Ode," Tate becomes more insistent, raising his voice and speeding the lines. Here I overlaid Tate with Thomas' 1952 Caedmon "Do Not Go Gentle Into That Good Night," a poem thematically similar to Tate's, but with a much more sentimental, earnest attachment to its subject. Immediately apparent is the extent to which both poets seem to command us. Alongside the dead soldiers, we are the "you" in Tate's ode, as he calls to us, "Turn your eyes to the immoderate past, / Turn to the inscrutable infantry rising / Demons out of the earth they will not last" (270). Likewise, we become the "you" alongside Thomas' father in the famous villanelle, raging against the end of day and life. Heard as duet, Thomas' repeated "rage, rage" draws out the anger of Tate's invocation of battlefield names, "Shiloh, Antietam, Malvern Hill, Bull Run." Thomas is the campy counterbalance to Tate's affected naturalism, his melodrama a ballast to Tate's understated seriousness in such troubling lines as, "The hound bitch / Toothless and dying, in a musty cellar / Hears the wind only" (271). However, the duet generally tends toward fusion: the two seem to take on each other's rhythms, and their voices trail off together. In sound and sense alike, this duet is a sermon, true to the hieratic character of the poets and their work.

Aside from the common ground that this deformance uncovers beneath examples of the Library of Congress and Caedmon projects, it brings into perspective the dual nature of the recorded poem. Bogan recording "The Alchemist," Frost reading "Stopping By Woods," Thomas' readings of his work, or Eliot's variations on *The Waste Land*—each is on the one hand an artifact intimately tied to the author and to the mechanical processes of vocal production and sound recording that rendered it; while its link to print is critical, at least in the many instances in which print precedes audio, the recorded poem registers signifiers, such as timbre, pitch, and tempo, unavailable to its print variant. Moreover, it requires a translating machine, a mediator between listener and text. In short, the recorded poem is in many ways tightly bound both to its point of origin and by its materiality. On the other hand, as the poem is being played back, its making is, effectively, reenacted, carried out in real time. It is an utterance in process of becoming, permeable, irruptive, and loosely bound. In short, if the recorded poem is an artifact to be studied, it is also an event in sound in which we may take part.

Robert Lowell on Record

In the final section of this chapter, I want to return to Robert Lowell, whose own recordings we have yet to consider. They're significant to the argument of this chapter because like Lowell's poetics, his mode of reading changed dramatically over time, such that his recordings embody a range of modernist sounds. On March 20, 1946, Lowell read in the studio for Harvard Vocarium, recording "The Quaker Graveyard in Nantucket"; on December 8, 1976, near the end of his life, he read at the Ninety-Second Street Y and was recorded by Caedmon. These recordings, punctuating Lowell's long, diverse career, link the academic to the popular, the formalist to the confessional, the staged-studio to the live-on-stage reading.

I have suggested that in the 1952 Caedmon recordings, Dylan Thomas' voice sounds "elsewhere." Even at his most eschatological, Robert Lowell on record from the mid-century never sounds elsewhere. As with Tate, when we listen to Lowell's early recordings, we're never in doubt that the spoken poem is tethered to a written text, not only because the album provides us with print versions of the poetry (significantly, the Thomas recordings do not), but also because complex metrics and rhyme scheme, syntactical density and allusiveness point us toward print. Reviewing *Lord Weary's Castle* for the *New Yorker*, Louise Bogan described Lowell's work as "violent, tightly packed, and allusive," a poetry that operates at "a high pitch of baroque intensity" (29). The description is apt for "Quaker Graveyard" and could easily be applied to Tate's "Ode," for both poems are written to be close-read. If "Do Not Go Gentle Into That Good Night" is an utterance from beyond channeled through the vatic poet, Tate's "Ode" and Lowell's "The Quaker Graveyard in Nantucket" are voiced variants of a *writing* we are not allowed to forget came first.

Unlike Tate, however, Lowell delivers long sections of his poem in a kind of plainchant, and in this way is closer in spirit to Thomas than to the Tate recordings. Listening has a mesmeric effect that carries us forward, allowing the sheer density of words to signify beyond the specific imagery. A waveform of his reading of part five of "Quaker" illustrates a typical pattern (see figure 1.2, which shows a waveform of Robert Lowell reading "The Quaker Graveyard in Nantucket").

Figure 1.2

This waveform, generated from Lowell's Harvard Vocarium reading, graphs the first ten lines of part five of the poem, with its disturbing images of an eviscerated whale.[14] In Lowell's reading, the pitch—represented by the up and down motion of the wave—and the tempo—represented by the length of the segment—remain relatively constant. Where the horizontal white line is thinnest, Lowell pauses very briefly at punctuation, as at the question mark after he asks whether the sailor's sword will "sink into the fat" of the whale (16). Rarely does Lowell seem to take a breath—he reads the ten lines in thirty-five seconds—and he never raises or significantly lowers his voice. The reading moves inexorably forward, like the brutal work of flaying that it depicts, and the entire arc of Lowell's densely textured metaphor is subsumed into long, essentially monotone swaths of sound. Hard consonants are especially prominent—the "bones cry for blood" and the lance "hacks the coiling life out." Similarly, "fall," "fat," "Jehoshaphat," "flail": the many repeated /f/ sounds give a breathy heft to the reading. In a letter to Babette Deutsch, Lowell later claimed that rhythm had been essential to composing the poem: "I grew drunker and drunker with the sea. I put all my chips on rhythm, more than I have ever done since" (*Letters* 245). If intoxicating, the rhythm of Lowell's reading is less like the sea than the chanted Latin mass that Lowell heard regularly while composing the poems that would later be collected in *Lord Weary's Castle.*

Lowell's recitation here would be difficult to best; in his tone, volume, pacing, and rhythm, he skillfully interprets the textual features that carry the poem's mood and meaning. Recall Adorno's claim that sound recording is "true language," and Thomas' that the poet reads his work in order to "put across his own memory of the original impulses behind his poems." While one can imagine another reader just as skillfully rendering "Quaker Graveyard," Lowell's recording suggests an analogy from music, when composers perform their own work. Rachmaninov performed and recorded his pieces. We may prefer Horowitz or Ashkenazy, but the composer's performance is his attempt at fully realizing his intent, so Rachmaninov's recordings are important data in the study of his compositions. Granted that musical notation depends on performance in ways that the text of poetry does not, poets read, and we listen and record, in part because the text alone does not fully embody the poem as speech and sound. The poet's reading is therefore more than an elaborated variant; it is an authorized (not to say authoritative) interpretation, analogous to the composer's performance.

In his later, live recording of "Skunk Hour," the final poem in his most influential book, *Life Studies,* Lowell deliberately uses the public reading as a scene of interpretation. Not only does he gloss specifics in the poem, a common practice at poetry readings, he also reflects on particular commentaries and on criticism generally. His remarks and his interestingly varied recitation of the poem suggest his mastery of the two mid-century modes we've encountered in this chapter.

Lowell prefaces his reading by describing "Skunk Hour" as his "most popular poem." He tells us that his first popular poem was "The Drunken Fisherman," followed by "The Quaker Graveyard." The problem with reading a popular poem, he says, is that "you see the poem too often, and also your approach is not equaling it. However, I do like this one..." Much of this is typical of poetry readings—an apologia for giving the audience what it wants to hear, and an apology for what may turn out to be a disappointing recitation. More unusual is the extent to which

Lowell goes on to interpret the poem for us. The opening description of summer's end in Maine is typical, he tells us, of his "perverse deterministic, pessimistic way," in that Maine is depicted as "going downhill." Of course it *is* going downhill, he quips. In this disarming manner, Lowell defends the perspective of the poem's opening and makes light of the determinism that is his nemesis in "Skunk Hour." Lowell next tells us about the poem's shift to a "secular dark night of the soul," in which he watches lovers in their cars—watching lovers from a distance being an idea he took from Whitman's autobiography.[15] "This makes me desolate," Lowell explains.

Turning next to the poem's ending, he comments on efforts at critical interpretation of the imagery:

> Now people have interpreted this different ways. My old friend John Berryman, the late John Berryman, said that the skunks are a catatonic vision of frozen terror, but Dick Wilbur said they were cheerful [snicker] emanations of nature. [Audience laughter] That's the advantage of writing in an ambiguous style. [Audience laughter] There's one line even critics don't understand, seemed easy to me, "a red fox stain covers Blue Hill," I just meant it was sort of a reddish fall color, the fox color. There's some amazing interpretations, that I was thinking about the Spartan boy who held a wolf under his coat and let it gnaw his chest to pieces without making a sound. [Laughter] There's nothing about that Spartan boy in this! Only, one thing more, I suppose they don't exist anymore. There was something called a Tudor Ford, t-u-d-o-r, and it meant "two doors." Ford was being very Elizabethan. [Laughter] It's dedicated to Elizabeth Bishop. (*Robert Lowell Reading*)

Fellow poets Berryman and Wilbur offer conflicting but reasonable interpretations, and I would argue that Lowell refers to them not simply to get a laugh—though getting laughs is part of his strategy here—but to contrast them with the "critic," whose ludicrous interpretation is typical of his tribe. Lowell embraces poetic ambiguity, the inner tension that Cleanth Brooks considered to be essential to the lyric, but he wants us to understand that sometimes a fox is just a fox, a Ford simply a Ford. The notion is calculated to put an audience at ease with not fully understanding a poem, literary critics being necessarily overly zealous in their search for meaning, as Lowell, Berryman, and Wilbur would all agree. It follows that Lowell would end his preface with a footnote that simply defines "Tudor Ford." He has already told us how to think about the thematic arc of the poem and how to reckon with the ambiguous conclusion: like Keats and his Shakespeare, be comfortable with indeterminacy. As Bishop would later claim, the best questions about a poem have simply to do with the facts; all other queries must be answered by the poem itself.[16] Having been a leader in the mid-century marriage of poetry and criticism, Lowell skillfully practices sleight of hand, interpreting his poem while casually denying the possibility of interpretation. In this case, the poem is what it says and what the poet-critic says about it.

Lowell's reading then bridges the two styles that I've identified with the mid-century Library of Congress and Caedmon. The opening in Maine and the closing with the mother who "will not scare" (191) are attentive to lineation and syntactic rhythm; they are emotionally restrained but not flat. Stanzas five and six, Lowell's "secular dark night of the soul," have the quality of a confession: slightly agitated, brooding, and finally resigned with "nobody's here" (192). This confessional quality coincides with the entry of the first-person pronoun in stanza five, "I watched for love-cars," and is carried forward through the shift to present tense with "My mind's not right," then subsides with the shift of focus away from the "I" in stanza seven. While the accuracy of the term "confessional" has been repeatedly questioned, from Lowell's own distaste for it to Thomas Travisano's analysis of its shortcomings in *Midcentury Quartet* (1999), it does capture the quality of Lowell's performance of the self speaking its suffering and disillusionment. In the reading, Lowell chooses not to return to this confessional mode in the final stanza, with the return of the "I." Even as he stands "on top / of the back steps," we are to take in the entire scene and Lowell's carefully derived connection of self, breath, and the mother skunk. The scene is symbolic, he has implied in his preface, and thereby richly ambiguous. There can be no other answer to the nihilism of "nobody's here."

Because Lowell is an apposite reader, listening to his performance opens up the poem's possible moods, rhythms, and pace. It is significant that the Ninety-Second Street Y reading was recorded in 1976, over two decades after Lowell's work at the Library of Congress and Caedmon's "discovery" of Dylan Thomas. For poetry recording in the intervening years had diverged widely from these mid-century models, and perhaps the most relevant for Lowell were those in which illness was dramatized, as in the recordings of Anne Sexton we'll take up in chapter three. For now, I will simply propose that Thomas' success at Caedmon and, shortly thereafter, the success of confessional poets on record are linked by the vocal performance of suffering and the poets' evident intent to convey personal trauma. Reading "Skunk Hour," Lowell hesitates to participate fully in this. His prefatory remarks objectify the "I" of the poem, placing it as an earlier avatar of Lowell that can be examined and explained, as Lowell does. At the same time,

Lowell embodies that earlier "I" when he reads the poem, such that "I myself am hell; / nobody's here" (192) has the same lugubriousness and exhaustion as Thomas' "Though I sang in my chains like the sea" (180). Overall, that is, balance seems to be Lowell's approach in the 1976 reading—a balance between the poem and the "I," the voice of the poem and the voice of the poet.

★   ★   ★

In the process of comparing the mid-century recording projects of the Library of Congress and Caedmon, I have argued that several factors shape what we hear as the voice of the poet: technological limits and advancements in sound-editing, the choice of poets and arrangement of poems on an album, the qualities of the poet's voice and her manner of reading. I have suggested that these two projects differed radically, that the Library of Congress under Lowell promoted varieties of formalism associated with the academic establishment, whereas Caedmon built its success on the neo-Romantic poetry and performances of Dylan Thomas. However, I have also shown that mid-century formalism inadvertently pushed against its own limits when works such as Lowell's "Quaker Graveyard," Bogan's "The Alchemist," or Tate's "Ode" were moved from page to disc and tape. In those states, the poem and the poet are heard as one and the same, a fact of sound recording that Thomas fully exploited. In one of his last public readings, recorded by Caedmon, Robert Lowell carefully balanced confessional expressiveness with the kind of ironic distancing of the self that was essential to New Critical poetry on record.

Sound recording alters—and enables imaginative alterations of—even such print-bound work as Tate's. Poetry on record is the inscribed voice of the poet, circumscribed by the technology and experienced as a series of aural effects. Earlier, I claimed that the poet's reading should be considered an authorized, if not authoritative, variant of her work. I invoked the discourse of textual bibliography because the value of these recorded poems lies primarily in their status as part of the author's oeuvre, no more or less significant than editions and revisions overseen by the author. When Lowell made records of others, he shaped the story we tell of mid-century poetry. When he spoke into the microphone to create the scriptal spiral, he made an audible variant of his poems that is remade each time we play it.

The mid-century projects of the Library of Congress and Caedmon are significant to the study of poetry on record because they define a horizon of expectation for a vast range of voices in the modernist audio archive. Caedmon and Thomas placed value on the quality of performance and the personal appeal of the poet. The effects of this approach to disseminating the poet's voice will be the topic of chapter three, when we consider vocal connections between Edna Millay, Anne Sexton, and the audience for voiced modernism. By contrast, the Library of Congress recordings under Lowell—and, for that matter, the poetry consultants who followed him—embody in their sound and materials the values of an increasingly academic poetry establishment that had its origins in modernist formalism. Eliot, Lowell, Tate, and Bogan's readings, while hardly uniform, share in an effort to make the poem speak, as distinguished from speaking through the poem. This has important implications for considering the question "who speaks?" when we listen to the modernist poem, and that question comes into play particularly in the recordings from chapter four, when I consider an important modernist experimentation in voice impersonation. But in the next chapter, we will examine artifacts from the other major category of the modernist audio archive, the live "on stage" recording. We will focus on an especially resonant genre of live poetry recording—the "occasional" recording—in which the connections among poetry audio, the literary critical establishment, and the poet's voice play a central role.

CHAPTER 2

POETS AND CRITICS LIVE AT THE FORUM: THE OCCASIONAL RECORDING AND ELIZABETH BISHOP

Sometimes I find it terribly embarrassing. I avoid all the readings I can.

—Elizabeth Bishop, in conversation with Susan Howe and Charles Ruas

Unlike studio recordings, such as the Library of Congress and Caedmon projects investigated in the previous chapter, the numerous live recordings in the audio archive of modernism were ruled largely by serendipity, a source equally of their immeasurable critical value and, at times, their frustrating unevenness. Reel-to-reel and cassette recordings from the 1950s forward occasionally suffer from sound distortion and weak microphones, and even high-quality reproductions cannot amplify the poet's voice above chiming clocks, slamming doors, and barking dogs—all of which play a role, for instance, in a 1971 recording of Allen Ginsberg, the first half hour of which I have tried in vain to make audible. The fact is, however, that most live recordings are listenable, and they contain a wealth of data that could greatly enhance our understanding of how public events shaped modernism.

What to listen for, and how to describe what we hear, are the primary challenges to scholars interested in archival audio. On the subject of the live recorded performance, Charles Bernstein writes, "The audiotext, in the sense of the poet's acoustic performance, is a semantically denser field of linguistic activity than can be charted by means of meter, assonance, alliteration, rhyme and the like (although these remain underlying elements of this denser field)" (*Close Listening* 13). Bernstein's ear is trained on the poem as sound—what he calls an "audiotext," what I have referred to as the audio or recorded poem. Close listening to the audio poem per se and trying to represent the sound and experience played important roles in chapter one, as it will throughout this study. However, in this chapter, I want to extend Bernstein's claim about the audiotext to include the commentary, conversation, and ancillary sounds that situate the recorded reading. For I argue that these are integral to the experience of close listening and to the artifact's literary historical value.

As I noted earlier, most archival recordings capture staged readings, and it is these performances that have been of principal interest to critics. Assessing the history of the U.S. poetry reading, Lesley Wheeler notes that despite the innovative practices of such groups as the Beats, members of the Black Arts movement, and, more recently, advocates of slam poetry, the dominant mode of presentation since the 1950s has been remarkably, some would say lamentably, consistent: the poet alone at a lectern reads from his work to a small audience in a lecture hall (127–36). Commercial recordings of live readings usually delete all but the poet's actual reading, and even digital archives, such as poets.org and the recently developed Essential American Poets project, have tended to err on the side of isolating the poet's voice. However, I want to suggest that some of the richest sources of material for the study of poetry on record are unedited tape and online audio of events that celebrate or commemorate a poet's work. I will refer to these as "occasional" recordings.[1]

In general, occasional recordings come in three forms—the recorded forum among poets and critics to appraise a poet's work, often a new publication; the formal reading or lecture in honor of a poet, often to recognize a lifetime's achievement; and the anniversary commemoration or memorial service, which combines elements of the other two. The public, unrehearsed nature of these events binds them, such that even the most scripted bring together disparate voices and elicit strongly felt commentary. As I hope to show, when critics and poets gather to discuss another's work and read from it, poetry performance and reception are fully integrated in the recorded artifact.

To anchor my analysis of this large subset of live poetry recordings, I will closely examine examples of the three kinds from the life and work of Elizabeth Bishop. Bishop's ambivalent relationship to poetry performance makes her an important foil to many of the poets in this study, and her avowed resistance to poetry criticism challenges not only some of the voices alongside hers on these occasional recordings, but also the mid-century poetry establishment led by Lowell and sounded in the previous chapter—an establishment that, ironically, embraced her work long before her position as a canonical modernist poet was secure. Her conversations "at the forum," her readings and commentary at a Lowell commemoration, and the discourse at a memorial service held in her honor by poets, critics, and friends shed light on the essential features of the occasional poetry recording. At one level, my analysis of the recordings is intended as a model of how to work with these kinds of materials, and as is my practice throughout this study, I will consider the recordings alongside print texts, manuscripts, letters, and critical writing. But I also propose that Bishop's example demonstrates that the occasional poetry recording has a vital role to play in the reception study of modernist poetry.

Bishop at the Forum

On April 19, 1977, Elizabeth Bishop read and discussed her work with poets Susan Howe and Charles Ruas on Howe's Pacifica Radio broadcast. The occasion was the recent publication of Bishop's *Geography III*, a slim volume that contained some of her greatest work and was to be the last collection published in her lifetime. During the one-hour session, Bishop reads "The Moose" and "Crusoe in England" from her new book, as well as "The Man-Moth," "Brazil, January 1, 1502," and "At the Fishhouses." Following her readings, she, Ruas, and Howe cover a range of topics, from poetry performance to her influences. Just as the style of her readings calls into question the goals of performance, many of Bishop's comments during the conversation are disarming, if not deflating. She often resists questions of analysis and appraisal, even though her life and work are the ostensible subjects of the interview. Bishop's manner has to do in part with her admitted shyness and distaste for public readings, as we shall see, but I want to argue that "resists" is the operative verb here. For subtle resistance is the theme of this recording—of what Bishop says, how it resonates in the forum, and how it defines her perspective on the vicissitudes of reception.

Reading in public, whether informally, at a poetry reading, or for a studio recording, had always vexed Bishop. In her first letter to Robert Lowell (August 14, 1947), she mentions the "dreadful" results of her being recorded at Harvard, though she jokes about the process—"like a fish being angled for with that microphone"—and writes admiringly of Lowell's recordings (*One Art* 147). While Bishop's reading could never be fairly described as "stammering elocution"—as she describes the reading of an imagined performer of Hemans' famous "Casabianca"—it is often flat and breathless, the latter an effect of asthma brought on by anxiety (Bishop, *Poems* 5). An avowed introvert and compulsive reviser, Bishop dreaded reading aloud. The public reading took away the possibility of revision, and in an academic setting, it exposed the poet to the scrutiny of scholars. Or so Bishop felt:

> I absolutely hate reading my work aloud under any circumstances. The first time I gave a reading I stopped for twenty-six years. Harvard is a terrible place for reading; they are famous for being cold and you feel your voice getting deader and deader. The further west you go, the better the audiences, because they're not showing off. The nicest audience I ever had was children (at the American school in Rio). They asked such good questions, like, Why did you choose this word instead of that. Simple, practical things, which is the way you write, of course. (Monteiro 113)

The circumstances of Bishop's Pacifica session offer a greater degree of mediation between the poet and her listeners than the Harvard reading she recalls with dread—she and the Pacifica radio audience are invisible to each other. Her primary listeners are the sympathetic Howe and Ruas, who are gathered with her in the radio studio. Notwithstanding these favorable circumstances, Bishop's choice of "The Moose" and "Crusoe in England" as opening poems seems risky. While these have become two of the most critically acclaimed poems from *Geography III*, the common wisdom at a poetry reading is to begin with short works and work up toward difficulty and length. Granted that Howe's audience was likely a select group of poetry enthusiasts, who may have tuned in for the purpose of hearing Bishop's new work, the poet's slow, quiet performance tests attention and patience.

If, as I claim, Bishop's choice of poems resists the common wisdom, positioning her against the exigencies of performance, her laconic reading suits the desultory journey recalled in the form of "The Moose." The poem describes a bus trip across Nova Scotia and New Brunswick toward Boston, the simple sites and conversations among passengers along the way, and the unexpected appearance of a moose on the "moonlit macadam," which forces the bus to stop briefly (173). The opening four stanzas, each six lines long, are constructed of a series of adverbial clauses that postpone the entrance of the bus into the text even as they imitate its journey. The clauses closely delineate the landscape—watery, red with silt, dotted with clapboard buildings. In a sense, Bishop's pacing here is as appropriate to the subject as Dylan Thomas' was in "Do Not Go Gentle Into That Good Night," and not unlike that consummate performer, Bishop observes long pauses at stanza breaks, effectively creating a series of aural vignettes. But staying sharply attuned to those vignettes is challenging, for Bishop's poem, like the long bus trip, continues in this methodical way, the landscape moving slowly by until night falls and we reach the woods.

At this point, fourteen stanzas into the text, sounds replace sights, and the principal content of the poem becomes voices. As the one who over-hears, Bishop does not attempt to imitate the locals who quietly converse. Hers—her poem's—is not the tactically de-personalized voice of Eliot's LOC recordings, but it *is* a voice that beyond observing stanza breaks, deploys few dramatic techniques. Bishop resists drawing attention to her voice as performative or to the poem as performed sound. However, despite her anti-performative stance, Bishop indulges in one instance of theatricality in the following stanza:

"Yes…" that peculiar
affirmative. "Yes…"
A sharp, indrawn breath,
half groan, half acceptance,
that means "Life's like that.
We know *it* (also death)." (172; Emphasis in the original)

Before the second "yes," she gasps—a "sharp, indrawn breath," a locu-tionary act that Bishop associates with the Maritimes and cannot resist echoing. Given the nature of Bishop's recitation, the gasp comes as a surprise, but it punctuates the connection here between sudden breath and a knowledge of death, and it foreshadows the startled exclamations of passengers when the moose appears—exclamations that, unsurprisingly, Bishop chooses not to voice as such.

What I mean to suggest here is that Bishop's anti-performative read-ing of "The Moose" is at once an unscripted rendering of the text and an opening gambit against the demands of public readings—demands that, as we shall see, became a major topic of the Pacifica conversation. Her reading occupies a space outside of the mid-century mode of the LOC recordings and the dramatic style of Dylan Thomas. Though far from self-consciously performative, Bishop's reading accomplishes somewhat incidentally a form of resistance most often associated with avant-garde performance poets. Arguing that the sound of the poetry should test our expectations, Charles Bernstein laments that "many poetry performances tend to submit to, rather than prosodically contest, the anesthetized speech rhythms of official verse culture. Indeed, one of the effects of chatty introductions before each poem is to acoustically cue the per-former's talking voice so that it frames the subsequent performance" (*Close Listening* 16). Lowell's Ninety-Second Street Y reading seems to fit this characterization: commentary that pre-interprets the reading and forestalls criticism, plaintive vocalizing that marks line endings with an unresolved cadence, orchestrated moments of epiphany. While Bishop has been claimed by "official verse culture" (by which we may assume Bernstein means the line of Lowell and proponents of mainstream MFA poetry programs) *and* its opponents—notably here, Susan Howe—her reading doesn't fully submit to either program. Bishop does seem to honor the text, and yet that sudden gasp, the irruption of Bishop's placid reading, suggests that "The Moose" would lend itself to a far more dramatic interpretation. In other recordings of "The Moose," Bishop does not gasp, but does, on the other hand, modulate her voice slightly to indicate different characters. What I mean to suggest is that Bishop does not hew to a style in this recording or subsequently—she has, I would argue, chosen not to choose. That is to say, she simply reads—insofar as any poet can manage this—risking inconsistency, depending on her voice and the text to carry her, and counting on our willful attention to hear the meanings of sound and sense.

I have claimed that the theme of the Pacifica forum is resistance, and during Bishop's interview with Howe and Ruas, this is evident in what Bishop says about performance as well as in how she performs—as poetry reader and as a participant in the discussion. Halfway through the interview, Ruas asks about the tension between being a "private person" and the need to perform one's work. The exchange is worth transcribing in full:

CR: You're an extremely private poet and private person as well. I was wondering what you think now of people who take their poetry and perform them [*sic*], literally, not quite in the troubadour traditions...

EB: Well, they even have music in the background, some of these people. I haven't heard very many readings. I don't like to give readings and I don't like to go to them. And at friends' readings I get very upset, so I try not to go to readings of people I like very much... there are some people who are naturally actors as well as poets, and some aren't. Cummings, for example, was one of the few people—I've heard him read only twice—but he had a beautiful voice and he acted out his poems but it was not embarrassing, he was wonderful. But sometimes I find it terribly embarrassing. And I avoid all the readings I can.

CR: What do you think? That your work, for example, should be read silently?

EB: Well, I think I'm wrong, I'd prefer to read it to myself. I know that all the good arguments are on the other side, but actually I prefer to read it to myself, mine and other people's, too. It is supposed to be read aloud, should be...

SH: You get nervous, I know what you mean, about a reading. It's all these things, I get nervous that the poet's going to make a mistake, an audience is going to walk out, or they're going to be bored.

EB: [Describes hearing Marianne Moore read at the New York Public Library] To my surprise, Mayor Lindsey began by reading a poem that I wrote about Marianne Moore some years before. It was so strange, and there I was with people eating their sandwiches around me...

CR: But, for example, Robert Lowell reads with a great deal of flair.

EB: I haven't heard him read in quite some time, though he's read some of my poems, and he reads them very well. I was taken from school once with a friend to hear Edna St. Vincent Millay read in Boston, and we both hated it. One of our teachers, a very nice woman, took us, we didn't like to tell her, we were very polite and lied about it, but we didn't like it a bit. But we were very snobbish little girls, of course, very high-browed, very snobbish. That was the first poetry reading I ever heard.

CR: You mean you didn't fall under her spell?

EB: Oh, not in the slightest! And then Archibald MacLeish came to Vassar while I was there, that was the second reading I heard, and I couldn't bear that either. He's a very nice man...

SH: I have Wallace Stevens on a record and he sounds wonderful. When you listen on a record, he sounds just incredible.

CR: Well, so does Edna St. Vincent Millay on her record, she actually sounds very nice.

EB: Well, I was in the Library of Congress job that they give a poet every year or so, in 1950, and we were making records, all these recordings, and it was before tape, they just made the disc. So I heard an awful lot of them, and maybe that's why I got tired of hearing readings. Also, at that time, all the women's records sounded absolutely terrible, and maybe they didn't have such good controls. I knew one or two of the women, and I knew their voices, and reality didn't sound like that, they almost all sounded very bad. And I had to, I sat with Dylan Thomas while he made records, and I sat with Robert Frost and Mrs. Morrison while he remade his records, he was such a perfectionist, he did them over two or three times, maybe that's why I got tired of hearing... (Bishop, Interview)

This exchange establishes embarrassment as the primary risk, even the inevitable outcome, of the public reading, both for the performer and for the poet who attends. Carrying forward from the dichotomy that Ruas sets up between the private person/poet and reading in public, Bishop and, later, Howe concentrate on being embarrassed for someone else— anticipating her mistakes, worrying about her reception, or questioning her aptitude as a performer. Bishop sets up extremes that position poets on stage as either "natural" actors such as e.e. cummings or pretenders who rely on factitious display—those who "even have music in the background," a likely reference to Anne Sexton and Her Kind, though there are many possibilities by 1977. It is embarrassing, she implies, when poets pretend.

Embarrassment for another causes us to withdraw, to turn aside and place our attention elsewhere in an effort to escape from confronting the source of discomfort. What begins in empathy retreats from it and disconnects.[2] Bishop's embarrassed response to the public reading is less a reasoned critique than a somatic defiance, which then reinforces her insistence on letting the poem speak and keeping the poet and critics silent. The link between performance and embarrassment is so strong for Bishop that she cannot seem to break it, even when Ruas and Howe offer alternative approaches to the question of public reading. Ruas attempts to shift the conversation to reading per se: should poetry like hers be read silently, a provocative question in light of the poems with which she began the broadcast. Howe brings up recordings: when one listens on record, as opposed to in a live audience, one might be better able to enjoy the sounds of the poet's reading. We are left to wonder what Bishop thinks, for she continually returns to scenes of embarrassment: hearing her "Invitation to Miss Marianne Moore" read by the mayor of New York, having to be polite despite the embarrassing performances of Millay and MacLeish, being embarrassed for the women whose voices "sounded absolutely terrible" because of poor recording techniques. Perhaps Bishop, as the "private poet and private person," cannot resist externalizing a deeply felt anxiety. Having enjoyed just enough economic privilege that she could for many years avoid teaching and giving readings, being on stage has, for her, no relevance to making poetry, even if it is a practical necessity for many poets.

Nancy Miller has argued that the reader's embarrassment at authorial spectacle in personal writing is "a sign that it is working," because the reader has confronted the contingency and materiality of subjectivity (24). Bishop's embarrassment betrays a sharply limited perspective on poetry performance, and beneath her blush lie her own fears of the vulnerability of the self on stage. However, I want to argue that Bishop's anti-performative stance, to which embarrassment is a contributing factor, ironically places her in a strong rhetorical position in the forum with Ruas and Howe. Bishop frequently but politely dismisses questions about her relationships with other writers. She arrived in Key West after Hemingway, she avers. She rented a cottage to Charles Olson but she "can't say [she] likes his writing"; she lived in Greenwich Village at its heyday but she "didn't know anybody." Bishop speaks of her early indebtedness to Marianne Moore, but claims that she never wrote like Moore because she couldn't make herself work hard enough. While Bishop does engage in a lively discussion of South American writers, she primarily offers anecdotes about her experiences, avoiding Howe's efforts to draw conclusions about her perspective on translation and her debt to non-U.S. schools of poetry. I propose that with this evasive, sometimes disingenuous, mode of response, Bishop does perform, but just not according to the rules of the occasion. She undermines a goal of the forum: to draw conclusions, however provisional, about the poet's influences, allegiances, and ideals. Offering advice to a young poet, Bishop encouraged her to read all of a non-twentieth-century poet's work, then read all of a modern poet's work, along with the letters of both. But, she claims, "I always ask my writing class NOT to read criticism" (*One Art* 596). At the forum, Bishop seeks to avert critical inquiry because of its imperative to arrive at an interpretation, just as she is skeptical of poetry performance because of how, in her estimation, it stands to restrict or obfuscate the poem. Her skepticism of performance falls in line with that of the mid-century formalists, but her manner of reading lacks even the reserved performativity of Lowell or Bogan. Moreover, her resistance to Howe and Ruas' questions is consistent with how she positioned herself outside the alliance between modernist poetry and criticism—an alliance inscribed in the Library of Congress project and fully institutionalized by the time of her Pacifica interview. Even though this forum itself takes place "off-campus" and seems essentially congenial, Bishop slips away whenever Howe or Ruas try to nudge her toward a claim.

In a 1987 essay-review of *The Complete Poems*, Helen Vendler argued that Bishop's work resists conclusiveness, preferring "closure in questioning, loss, or inscrutability" (838). Predating by over a decade Bishop's seemingly secure status as a major modernist poet, her Pacifica session offered listeners an elusive image of Bishop; it is an example of a poet's reception in flux, in the making. In that respect, the Pacifica session is typical of recorded forums. They are inconclusive by nature, their informality allowing for give-and-take, speculation, and opinion that rarely survive the revision and editing of a published essay. They include a reading from a poet's work, which always generates discussion of how poems sound and how they might best be performed, and, as in the Pacifica session, they put poets in dialogue with the critical ideas—and sometimes with the critics themselves—that frame the reception of their work. In her conflicted relationship with performance and criticism, Bishop betrays a concern for reception that will surface again in another example of an occasional poetry recording, her commemoration of Robert Lowell, to which I will turn next.

Bishop Commemorating

In the year following Robert Lowell's death, Elizabeth Bishop offered two public remembrances of the poet and their friendship: a reading at Harvard on March 1, 1978, and the publication of "North Haven," first on illustrated broadside, then in the December 11, 1978, *New Yorker*.

I want to compare these two literary events and link them with Bishop's private ruminations on how to remember Lowell in "North Haven." In effect, this series of events constitutes a short chapter of literary history. The theme of the Lowell reading—a version of what Lawrence Lipking, following Mallarmé, designated the "tombeau"—is "remembering"; we see it in Bishop's choice of poems and her commentary. More to the point, Bishop begins a public dialogue with her late friend on the question of why and how to remember, a question that will be central to "North Haven."

Given what we've established about Bishop's relationship to performance, the circumstances of the Lowell memorial reading must have been particularly dreadful to Bishop: a public reading at Harvard for its most celebrated poet, and for a friend whose significance in Bishop's life could not be overestimated. On the day of the reading, she wrote to Ashley Brown that she "wish[ed] the next two days were over with!" (*One Art* 620). The results of Bishop's "remembering Robert Lowell" reading, however, were hardly dreadful, providing as they do a public prelude to the private ruminations that led to "North Haven."

As planned, Bishop reads a program "half Cal, half me"; though there are twice as many Lowell texts, Bishop reads two of her longest poems and shares a number of anecdotes (Poetry Reading). If her choice of long poems in the Pacifica session posed a challenge to the occasion, the rationale of her choices here is fundamentally topical: all of the poems investigate remembering. She begins with two of Lowell's "family elegies" (Ramazani 22) and a poem on death—"Death from Cancer," "Mary Winslow," and "Where the Rainbow Ends." She then reads four poems in which Lowell reflects on his struggles with mental illness, poems with recurring figures of psychic death and resurrection: "Waking in the Blue," "Home after Three Months Away," "Skunk Hour," and "Thanks Offering for a Recovery." Her reading betrays no sign of her anxieties about the event; her voice is not shaky and tentative, as it had been in her recordings from the 1940s.[3] Be that as it may, her voice is thin and weak, often raspy on this occasion. As in the Pacifica readings, she resists dramatization. Even when a line of verse seems to call for verve or bite—for example, Lowell's echo of Milton's Satan, "I myself am hell" (*Collected Poems* 192)—Bishop's delivery is restrained. When Bishop reads, complex verse becomes conversational, offered in the same genuine, unaffected voice as her commentary and anecdotes.

Her mode of delivery is therefore consistent with the Pacifica readings, and I would argue that at the Lowell memorial, the mode takes on an added significance. For throughout the service, it is the poetry, as opposed to Bishop's running commentary, that carries forward the conversation on death and remembering and that, subtly, critiques Lowell in ways that will come to fuller fruition in "North Haven." In effect, poetry here is a form of criticism—the only form that Bishop will endorse. Bishop limits her comments primarily to elucidating the sources of poems—information on St. John's Day celebrations, for example, to explain "The Armadillo"—or defining words such as "bibelots" and "azulejos." Indeed, when Bishop deviates from this strategy, she gets into trouble. She prefaces her reading of the "mental illness" poems from *Life Studies* with an uncharacteristically interpretive comment:

> And these poems, the first two I'm going to read, are very sad because as you probably all know he had very tragic breakdowns from time to time. But what was wonderful about him was the way he recovered from these things always, and always started writing again, and wrote magnificent poetry very soon afterwards. (Poetry Reading)

Neither "Waking in the Blue" nor "Home After Three Months Away" is "very sad." On the contrary, Bishop's conversational style of reading brings out the humor of the lyrics. Her voice lightens noticeably in the ironic third and fourth stanzas of "Waking," where Lowell's fellow inmate at the asylum "swashbuckles about in his birthday suit" and where Lowell quips that "There are no Mayflower / screwballs in the Catholic Church" (Lowell, *Collected Poems* 183–84). Similarly, Bishop almost laughs at the image of Lowell's daughter helping him with a shave in "Home." But notice Bishop's phrasing in her prefatory comment: "these poems…are very sad *because* [emphasis mine]" of what the audience "probably" knows about Lowell's illness and its attendant traumas. Bishop acknowledges that the biographical circumstances here may affect our reception, but as in her reflections on her childhood and her writing during the Pacifica session, she insists on a spatial, temporal distance between the life and the poetry. The "magnificent" writing came "afterwards," after recovery and at a safe remove, emotion recollected in tranquility. Control of the materials prevents embarrassment of the kind that Bishop dreaded for the poet on stage, and while the actual circumstances that lay behind "Home" and "Waking" could be "sad" and embarrassing, Bishop's performance reflects her belief that Lowell managed the content with a keen eye for the humorously absurd and the effectively sentimental.

"Each of Miss Bishop's readings counts," proclaims Monroe Engel when he introduces the poet, and I would argue that what "counts" most at her Lowell reading is her choice of poems, rather than her reading itself (Bishop, Poetry Reading). Lowell, Engel tells his audience, is a poet "whom we have not yet begun to know how to be without," and as I've suggested, the poems that Bishop has gathered address the problem of being without. The sequence opens with the two elegies for Lowell's Winslow grandparents. In both, precise, sometimes unflattering details about the Winslows and their Boston environs are infused into the mythic image of Charon rowing to their bedsides to ferry them to Hades. The Charles flows into the river Acheron; Boston and Lowell's ancestors become part of a "familiarized" classical mythology. Bishop greatly admired what she called Lowell's "family life" poems,[4] but his tendency toward the mythopoeic is challenged by the poem with which Bishop closes her reading, "Santarem." Bishop stands at the "conflux of two great rivers" and rhapsodizes on the "idea of the place." Isn't it like the Garden of Eden, she asks; don't many "literary interpretations" spring readily to mind when the poet dreams of rivers? Such interpretations, she argues, dissolve in the "watery, dazzling dialectic" of the rivers' confluence. If Lowell's mythic narratives anchor memory in classical structures, Bishop's "dazzling" rivers erode the sand beneath them. Memory flows—it is unstable ("watery") and destabilizing ("dazzling").

What, then, will be the nature of poetic remembering? "Santarem" begins "I may be remembering it all wrong": the ethics of accurate representation are often at odds with the demands of art and the friability of memory. As Thomas Travisano has noted, Bishop repeatedly calls attention in the poem to the tenuousness of her authority: was it two rivers or four that, as Bishop writes, "sprung / from the Garden of Eden"? (190). Bishop was troubled by Lowell's poetic license in his "family life" poetry,[5] and even in her commentary during the Lowell reading, she cannot resist pointing out examples of, on the one hand, completely accurate representation and, on the other, "exaggeration," as she calls it. Bishop, of course, was not opposed to the artful revision of memory, nor did she hold that the past could be delivered with objective accuracy, as is evident in "North Haven." Rather, her worries about the tension among art, memory, and accuracy are the best evidence of her belief that poetry could matter, that it could affect real people and real lives.

That effect is one subject of "The Armadillo" that seems especially salient in the context of the Lowell reading. In the poem, she upbraids the "too pretty, dreamlike mimicry" of the St. John's Day ceremony, and at the Lowell reading, she comments that despite its beauty, the practice of sending up flaming prayer balloons often caused damaging fires and fatal accidents. This is a comment she often made about "The Armadillo." But the poem is hardly a Calvinist sermon against excess. On the contrary, it mimes the very beauty that it chastens; after all, what can be more "dreamlike" than a baby rabbit transforming into "a handful of tangible ash / with fixed, ignited eyes," or what more "too pretty" than "the paper chambers flush and fill with light / that comes and goes, like hearts"? Beautiful things can cause pain; "The Armadillo" is itself "too pretty, dreamlike mimicry" despite the moral of its final stanzas. By that same token, pain can give rise to beautiful things; out of Lowell's desperation comes "Skunk Hour," a poem dedicated to Elizabeth Bishop and, according to Lowell, inspired by her "Armadillo." Bishop was troubled by the potential grief that Lowell's confessional poetry could cause family and friends, but she was equally persuaded that art depends upon the revisiting and revision of painful memories. This is evident in the poems she chose to read at the Lowell commemoration, and it is essential to the development of "North Haven."

Bishop composed "North Haven" during the months following the Lowell service. She often devoted many years to single poems, putting them aside then circling back for more revision, but she focused intensely on "North Haven" over these few months.[6] There are nineteen separate drafts, including her last-minute changes on the *New Yorker* proofs. Alluding to Bishop in his masterful study of the modern elegy, Jahan Ramazani has argued that "the 'One Art' of the modern elegy is not transcendence or redemption of loss but immersion in it" (4). If the final version of "North Haven" depicts Bishop immersed in loss, it does so because Bishop herself had moved beyond the loss through the art of writing; her drafts trace memory's textual history, which is to say memory's differentiation in the service of mourning *represented*.

"North Haven" began as a short sketch in one of Bishop's notebooks; because the sketch is undated, it may have preceded Lowell's death. It shares no language or imagery with the many drafts from the spring and summer of 1978, but its first lines contain the final poem's interest in the intersection of landscape and personal history. It begins by repeating, "Before any of our history / Before any history that we can say / belongs to us," then shifts to images of a seaside picnic, mentioning clam-bakes and lobster. At the heart of each version of the poem is the question of how the landscape inscribes personal history and how, thereby, meditation on the "blue frontiers of bay," the flowers, and the birds of North Haven conjures memory. In this respect, "North Haven" rests squarely in the tradition of the pastoral elegy, working as it does in the "contrast between the idyllic pastoral and the intrusive reality" of a loved one's death (Sacks 3). The drafts, however, show Bishop moving into the position of observer not only of the pastoral landscape but also of Lowell. Helen Vendler lists among Bishop's poetical "attitudes" a "cold capacity for detachment" ("Poems" 838). In "North Haven," Bishop becomes increasingly dispassionate, I would argue, to become more artful in the rendering of her memory.

Let us assume that Lowell is Bishop's partner in the plural pronouns of the manuscript sketch. "Our," "we," and "us": the manuscript draft is addressed to Bishop and Lowell as one and sets the stage for a poem about "our" history. Compare this to the later, typescript drafts, in which "our" occurs only once. Over the course of revision, Bishop essentially distances herself from Lowell by moving toward a deliberate structuring of the poem around its personal pronouns: from "I," to the single "our" of stanza three, to the "you" of the final two stanzas. That Bishop had this progression in mind is clear from the poem's drafts. The penultimate stanza, in which "you" tells Bishop about discovering girls, moved several times before settling down in the eighth draft. Thus the elegy creates the illusion of a logic to Bishop's grief. First the "I" observes—the bay, the flowers that hint at Lowell's former presence—then her observation of nature conjures a memory of "our" time at North Haven and leads to the insight that nature "repeats herself, or almost does," an insight that finally brings Lowell ("you") fully into view for the "I" to scrutinize.

Bishop also significantly altered how we would see Lowell in those final stanzas. In the first typescript of the poem, the final stanza began, "But you have gone for good, but our / poems stay." Among the changes that Bishop wrote in the margins is "the" to replace "our," again distancing the speaker from Lowell. More tellingly, she runs the last sentence through several distinctly different variants: "Dear, you can't change," "My dear, you cannot change," "And you, my dear, can't change," and ultimately "Sad friend, you cannot change." The sentimentality of "my dear" is wisely traded for "sad friend," a simple but touching characterization of Lowell and of her relationship to him. Across all these variants, however, "can" is the helping verb; in death, of course, Lowell is unable to change. But Bishop's combination of present indicative and direct address equally implies that in his essential sadness, Lowell never could change. The "can't" of the final sentence contrasts with the "won't" of the sentence that precedes it. As the drafts show, Bishop was equivocal about whether the "words" (sometimes "poems" in the drafts) "can't" or "won't" change. Critics have noted that Bishop is gently teasing Lowell here for his incessant revision, even after publication. But she is also giving to the "words" a will that, in death, Lowell no longer has; perhaps the words *could* change, the grammar implies, but they won't. Furthermore, by deciding on "words" instead of "poems," Bishop tacitly acknowledges that the poems have a life of their own; in her estimation, the words are fixed, but the poems are fluid. Lowell may be unable to "derange, re-arrange" his poems, but what might the poems do without him?

The answer to that question, I would argue, is a source of anxiety for Bishop, which is evident in the elegy's preoccupation with continuity and change, control and loss of control. On the one hand, Bishop's gradual shifting to a more dispassionate perspective gives her command of her subject and allows her to critique her "sad friend," however gently; as Herbert Marks writes, "the final line of the poem…is poignant but also a bit patronizing, concealing, but only barely, an unnerving hint of triumph" (202). This distancing is particularly apparent in Bishop's revisions of stanza five, "Years ago you told me…," easily the most worked-over of the poem. Until the latest drafts, its sympathy for Lowell verges upon the sentimental, suggesting that life never allowed Lowell to have fun, which one version of the poem describes as an "elemental good." Later drafts and the published version are ironic about Lowell's complicity in his own misery—and, by extension, Bishop's complicity in *hers*. "Fun" is given scare quotes and Bishop is clearly rolling her eyes at the intellectual contempt for it: "('Fun'—it always seemed to leave you at a loss…)." You never had much interest in fun, she implies, but that amounts to another loss.

On the other hand, Bishop's increasing control of her language and, thereby, her representation of memory lead her to rhetorical claims about "change" and "loss" that the subtext and imagery of her poem contradict. As I've noted earlier, her choice of "words" in the final line begs the question, "but will the *poems* change"? If "revise, revise, revise" was Lowell's refrain in life, just as it was Bishop's in composing the elegy, his death and the poem's publication put an end to revision, but only the revision that the author controls. In the third and fourth stanzas, the natural images that Bishop records are presented as repetitions of the past, signs of its eternal return. But the poem goes on to argue that Nature's repetitions are an "almost," for in fact they are revisions. More importantly, Bishop's vision of them is, literally, a second seeing; that the buttercups, clover, vetch, and so on have "returned" is an illusion of art. The flowers and birds at North Haven this year are different from the last; this year's sparrow can change his song, but neither he nor his song is necessarily the same as last year's. Lowell has died: he cannot change his poems. Bishop has sent "North Haven" off to the *New Yorker* and can no longer revise it. But Lowell's poems, Bishop's "North Haven," can (will) change over time among readers.

Earlier, I argued that Bishop's anti-performative stance derived in part from her resistance to fixing a reading of the poem, just as her behavior during the Pacifica interview was elusive, a form of resistance to the imperatives of critical reception. Precisely because they are "on the stage," these live events test the limits of the poet's control over her reception— hence Bishop's aversion to them. However, while Bishop would allow the poem to speak, rather than speak for it, she did so because of her questionable assumption that the poem holds its meanings, just as the poet keeps her self private, eluding critical scrutiny. As she discovers over the course of drafting "North Haven"—a course that begins, I argue, in the Lowell service—"The words of a dead man / Are modified in the guts of the living," writes Auden in his elegy for Yeats (Auden 81). Bishop's approach to this sentiment is less direct than Auden's.[7] But I would argue that in "North Haven" she has begun to recognize a characteristic of texts and reading that Fish famously describes in "Interpreting the Variorum": that interpretive communities (re)write the text. Bishop knows that her elegy will not simply "repeat," it will be revised. In her desire to stabilize text and memory, Bishop is drawn toward an illusion, the unending present of lyric time, but pulled back into what Paul de Man called "the actual temporality of experience" (225). In the final stanza, death ushers in permanence, but the subtext of much of the poem is that permanence and continuity are illusions—*lyrical* illusions. Nowhere is this clearer than in the opening stanza, which Bishop deliberately italicized and set apart from the rest of poem. The stanza suggests timelessness, an eternal present, that in combination with the painterly accuracy of the imagery situates us in an aestheticized, lyrical space; in a letter to Frank Bidart, Bishop claimed that the stanza was meant to evoke "intensely quiet meditation" (*One Art* 624). However, the very position of the stanza calls attention to its artificiality, all the more so when we realize that Bishop moved the stanza all around the poem before setting it in the first position. Similarly the stillness of the stanza was the result of revise, revise, revise; what "is so still"—the day, the spruce, the bay—changed significantly as the poem developed. So the very landscape of this unmoving island altered as Bishop re-collected it for the purposes of art. What is to prevent the art, the poem, once it passes out of lyrical time and into the "actual temporality of experience" from doing the same?

Famously, Bishop was slow to make her work public—hesitant to read it aloud, cautious about publishing it before she had exhausted the possibilities of revision. She recognized, though she hesitated to acknowledge, that once a poem entered the public sphere, it began to change. In an interview with George Starbuck near the end of her life, Bishop recalled reading "Roosters" many years after it was published: "Some friends asked me to read it a year or so ago, and I suddenly realized it sounded like a feminist tract, which it wasn't meant to sound like at all to begin with. So you never know how things are going to get changed around you by the times" (Monteiro 89). Poetry, in its mutability over time, is analogous to memory, and no one better than Bishop understood the protean nature of memory—"I may be remembering it all wrong" she announces through "Santarem" at the end of the Lowell reading. "Life and the memory of it," she explains in "Poem," run together in art;

she and her uncle may have looked at the same landscape "long enough to memorize it," but landscape and memory are changeable, and Bishop's "look" at her uncle's painting results in a remaking: the poem. A similar remaking happens in "North Haven," for the Robert Lowell of that poem is an artifact, interpreted by Bishop, up for interpretation now by her readers. It is that revision, the reader's, that Bishop wished to forestall. Indeed, she dreaded it, as she dreaded reading aloud. Bishop wanted to believe in the permanence of the poem, in the integrity of the object as in itself it really is. "The words won't change," she promises her sad friend, in what we might understand as a white lie. For their meanings, as components of poetry and memory, surely will.

Bishop Commemorated

At the poetry forum and as reader and commentator at a commemoration, Bishop struggled with how a poet's life and work are appraised and who frames the terms of the appraisal. Turning now to the final kind of occasional recording—the recorded memorial service—I want to consider the initial moment of posthumous reception, when the poet's voice has been silenced, and others begin again to sound its importance.

In "At the Fishhouses," Bishop declares that "our knowledge is historical, flowing, and flown," dynamic and, simultaneously, situated (*Poems* 66). Memories, like poems and the island of North Haven, are both "anchored" in specific historical moments and "afloat in the mystic blue" (188). When the poet becomes historical—that is to say, when she passes into memory—she takes on the condition of memory and knowledge, which is the condition of text, material in its temporal habitations, variable in its specific meanings. Poet and text are polymorphous, though each new body retains some imprint of the first embodiment. Consequently, reception theorists generally agree that the initial reception of a poet should be given special attention, but that it does not fully delimit the poet's subsequent histories. "The way the work is received by its first public," writes Janusz Slawinski,

> and hence understood, interpreted, evaluated, considered perhaps as unreadable, rejected, or simply unnoticed—determines its primary semantics and demarcates the beginning of its existence in literary history. [But a] text's encounter with its first public is not to be identified with the irreversible "immobilization" of its semantics, or the preempting of its fate. As the work circulates both in time and space among new and different reading publics, its primary semantics undergo modifications that are sometimes far reaching...the text gradually acquires new readings and

interpretations which somehow follow it on its way among its readers, or on occasion totally insulate it. (522)

I want to extend Slawinski's formulation to include the poet as well as her work, and I want to suggest that despite the constraints of convention, memorial readings and services can be instances of revaluation, signaling a turn in a poet's reception, even as the "main stream of reception history flows by without a sound" (525). In the case of the Bishop service, I certainly cannot claim that what transpired had a direct impact on the subsequent reception; however, as I hope to show, the participants' efforts to offer up an interpretation of Bishop's work and life represent a mode of reception that has, in effect, become the "main stream of [Bishop's] reception history." What I will argue, therefore, is that like the forum and the commemorative reading, the memorial offers insight into the *shaping* of reception, for we become witness to processes analogous to those in Bishop's drafting of "North Haven." Furthermore, as a public event, the recorded memorial archives a greater range of voices than most texts or events to which we would normally turn for reception artifacts. We hear the critics and fellow poets, but we also hear the family, the friends, the congregation.

What image of Bishop emerges from the Harvard memorial service? To answer this question, we must first decide which aspects of the service are worth attention. For instance, there are a number of awkward moments during the course of the hour, some of them humorous. John Ashbery hasn't arrived when it is his turn to speak, so Robert Fitzgerald comes to the podium, clearly agitated, and exclaims, "I'm sorry to be advanced in this way." There are problems with the microphone, voices catch and tremble, a siren wails as Helen Vendler reads George Herbert. These moments would seem worth including in a short story about the event, and even in a critical account, they remind us of its human quality.[8] But more pertinent to Bishop's reception are the hymns, the readings of poetry, and the commentary on her work and personality. In the following pages, I will argue first that the content of the service anticipates an important theme in Bishop's posthumous reception; I will then go on to suggest that the readings and commentary create, in effect, an eclectic, annotated Bishop "text."

The service begins and ends in song. Congregation and musicians together contribute four hymns. During her time at the podium, Frani Muser reflects on Bishop's love of hymns, "congregational hymns, rugged American songs like good New England granite," and while her description doesn't truly fit "There is a Balm in Gilead," it accurately describes a Bishop favorite, "A Mighty Fortress is Our God," which occupies a central position in the service just as it does in "At The Fishhouses."[9] What do we make of the prominence of hymns in this otherwise secular service? The question could be asked of Bishop and her oeuvre, in which Protestant ethics factor significantly, despite Bishop's agnosticism. Muser's "rugged" and "New England granite" suggest an answer. The child in "Sestina," the young Elizabeth in "In the Waiting Room," the melancholic voice of the end of "Over 2000 Illustrations and a Complete Concordance": repeatedly in Bishop's poetry, the cold reality of life is the "element bearable to no mortal," and yet bearing up—being "back in it," fully and with clear vision—is what Bishop's poetry professes. Running parallel with the theme of suffering and perseverance in her poetry is a quality of restraint, which manifests in her diction and her personal humility, and which meets its opposite in her lifelong bout with alcoholism and the guilt that attended it. In diction, as well as the pull and tug between indulgence and restraint, she is most like her favorite poetic precursor, George Herbert. Herbert's and Bishop's Protestantism intersect at the memorial service, as we shall see when we come to Helen Vendler's reading of "Love Unknown." But for the moment, suffice it to say that the hymns are more than mere nods to Protestant ritual. On the contrary, they tacitly acknowledge the role of Protestantism in Bishop's personal and poetic development.[10]

Several hands went into the making of the service. Participants include Alice Methfessel, Robert Fitzgerald, Robert Giroux, Anne Hussey, Frani Muser, John Ashbery, Octavio Paz, Frank Bidart, Helen Vendler, and Lloyd Schwartz. The service is loosely structured: each speaker offers comments and a reading, and the quality of delivery and the mood and content of the remembrances are as diverse as the individual interests and biographies of the participants. In their comments, several of the speakers stick to personal anecdotes. Ashbery's recollections are quirky and elusive, centering on two encounters with Bishop at hotels. Muser remarks on admiration for "the Bishop" during their Vassar days, and, in the only sad moment of the service, Giroux tells a poignant story of attending a production of *La Bohème* with his niece. Giroux notes that Bishop had been an opera fan, recounts a humorous story of attending an opera with Bishop and the Lowells, then ends with the *La Bohème* anecdote. Giroux recalls that his niece cried at the death of Mimi, and when her mother came to pick her up, she was still crying. "What's wrong?" her mother asks. "Oh mama, I was having such a good time. But Mimi died."

Giroux ends there without comment. This moment in the service recalls the understated simplicity and sentiment of "Sad friend, you cannot change." I would further argue that Giroux's representation of Bishop as "Mimi," like Bishop's representation of Lowell as "Sad friend," is an example of the grief-work that Freud identified in the "fort-da" episode and that, subsequently, literary critics have found operative in the elegy. In his history of the English elegy, for example, Peter Sacks applies Freud's fort-da to the work of the elegist. Freud's fort-da is an account of a child learning to "represent absence" through imaginative work similar to that of the elegist. An object or idea over which the child has some control replaces the deceased, but ironically that object does not merely restore presence; it also signifies absence. This process, which tells us as much about the mourner as the mourned, is also evident in the elegist's work with tropes and language.[11] We've seen it at work already in Bishop's tributes to Lowell, both at the reading and in the drafts of her elegy. Personal memories become public representations of the poet, whose very work was to represent.

At the memorial service, the connection between Bishop's biography and her poetry is overtly drawn by Helen Vendler. Vendler relates three occasions on which Bishop demonstrated her characteristic "kindness to the young." The stories are simple: Bishop grants an interview to a student newspaper despite the inconvenience it will cause her; she invites a young Radcliffe poet to tea; on the day of her death, she tries to contact a young scholar who has confused two of her poems. She wants to save him from embarrassment, Vendler explains. These "nameless, unremembered acts of kindness and love," Vendler concludes, show a side of Bishop that is, "reflected as well in the poetry, that is [to say] that she knew the emotions of human beings and their sufferings." Vendler's remark anticipates a fundamental assumption of McCabe's book-length treatment of Bishop's "poetics of loss," that "One mourns for life in order to live it, to understand its limits. Elizabeth Bishop knows this. She also knows that writing helps us raise and recall our losses so we can move ahead" (1). Following Vendler and McCabe, I am inclined to augment my reading of "North Haven" and suggest that Bishop's personal knowledge of suffering intensifies her sympathy for Lowell—the sympathy that she painstakingly restrains over the course of drafting the elegy. In the end, "North Haven" is a product of Bishop's campaign for control of her materials— the landscape, Lowell, the words—and of her mourning.

In presenting Bishop as a poet whose life is a window on her work, the memorial service echoed a theme of the Pacifica session—where, as we saw, Bishop never allowed it to develop—and forecasted the shape of things to come in Bishop's critical reception. While there was relatively little published criticism of Bishop prior to 1980, interest in her life and work increased dramatically shortly thereafter, possibly influenced by the publication of her letters and, as Dana Gioia has argued, the rise of gender and women's studies. A review of Bishop's posthumous reception indicates that, as at the service, Bishop's life—her childhood, her sexuality, her friendships, and travels—has played a significant role in numerous studies of her poetry and influence since the early 1980s. This is true of the psychoanalytical criticism of Susan McCabe, of Brett Millier's literary biography and essay on alcoholism, and of David Kalstone's influential work of biographical criticism, *Becoming a Poet* (1989). More recently, in *Midcentury Quartet* (1999), Thomas Travisano has carefully examined the personal relationship between Bishop and Robert Lowell. He argues not only that "Bishop's work anticipated Lowell's, both in technique and subject matter"—a claim that Lowell himself would have endorsed—but also that her poetry fits Diane Middlebrook's definition of "confessional," though he rejects the "confessional paradigm" in favor of reading Bishop and others as "primarily engaged, not in acts of self-revelation, but in an ongoing exploration of the problems of selfhood in a postmodern world" (67). Critical examination of those "ongoing exploration[s]" involves bringing biography to bear, cautiously, as is evidenced by Travisano's analyses of Bishop's poetry.[12] Other recent critics posit a more direct link between Bishop's work and life. For example, Kit Fan reads "Crusoe in England" as a "reticently autobiographical poem that explores Bishop's return to Boston after the exile in Brazil" (47), and Timothy Materer examines the autobiographical impulse in Bishop's and James Merrill's poetry. At least one critic, Bonnie Costello, has called into question the biographical tendency in Bishop criticism, though her concept of the "impersonal personal" does not deny its essential validity as a mode of response that much of Bishop's verse calls forth.

Remembering Bishop, in short, seems to be a critical part of how we read Bishop despite the fact that, unlike Dylan Thomas or Robert Lowell or, as we shall see, Edna Millay and Anne Sexton, Bishop limited her time on stage and before the microphone. Foucault predicted that the author, as a "function" of our readings of literary discourse, would disappear in light of post-structuralist understandings of culture and meaning; there would be other "systems of constraints" on how we make meaning of text, but the "author" would no longer prove useful. It seems unlikely, however, that the author will disappear so long as we read in order to connect with or re-collect the writer—a purpose for reading that obviously stands behind commemorations and memorials, but is also implicit in the vast majority of literary criticism. The identity of the author, and our identification with her, are essential components of gender and postcolonial critiques, as it was to psychoanalysis and Marxism. We may argue about what constitutes the "author" or "poet"—it should become clear soon enough that my own argument is indebted to a Foucauldian understanding of the subject as a discursive construct—but the very act of turning to a Bishop poem *because* it is a Bishop poem assumes that there is something "Bishop" to be constructed in dialogue with that poem— its language, form, ideology, voice. At the Lowell reading, an audience comes to hear "Lowell"; at a Bishop reading, "Bishop." That the body of the poet has passed on seems merely to open up possibilities for the poet to speak through another.

Balancing the anecdotes at the memorial service are readings of prose and poetry, with occasional commentary on Bishop's poetics, particularly her observational acuity. In effect, the combination of biographical notes, literature, and critical commentary generates a text, an annotated selection of Bishop's work. The text is bound temporally by the historical event, the memorial service; despite its unique material manifestation, a cassette tape, the text behaves much like a printed memorial edition (e.g.) of Bishop's work. That is to say, commentary seeks to frame a "reading" of the selected literary pieces, which in turn interact with each other intertextually. Following Sharon Cameron in her work on Dickinson, and Anne Ferry in hers on the nature of the anthology, I want to attend closely to the choice of poetry/prose and to the order of things in the memorial text, even though the gathering necessarily lacks the authorial oversight we could assume in the LOC and Caedmon recordings of the last chapter. For the choice and order are instrumental in the participants' construction of the author—in the remembering of Bishop.

Derived from the service, these would be the contents of the memorial text:

1. "Recipe for Combating Low Spirits" by Sydney Smith
2. excerpt from final chapter of *Charlotte's Web* by E.B. White
3. "Manners (for a Child of 1918)" by Elizabeth Bishop
4. "Twelfth Morning or What You Will" by Elizabeth Bishop
5. "A Miracle for Breakfast" by Elizabeth Bishop
6. "Objectos y Appariciones" by Octavio Paz, with translation by Elizabeth Bishop
7. "Love Unknown" by George Herbert
8. "The Moose" by Elizabeth Bishop
9. "Sonnet" by Elizabeth Bishop

Pathos, made acute by its connection to images of childhood, threads together much of the text's content. Alice Methfessel's reading from *Charlotte's Web*, like Giroux's tale of his niece and *La Bohème*, invites a sentimental response; the famous children's novel ends with the pig, Wilbur, remembering Charlotte as he watches her babies sail from her nest. Furthermore, the passage anticipates Vendler's descriptions of

Bishop's "kindness to the young" and sets up (serendipitously) Robert Fitzgerald's reading of "Manners (for a Child of 1918)."

Neither Fitzgerald's commentary nor the poem he chooses could be accurately described as "sentimental." But Fitzgerald reads "Manners" as if he were telling a children's story: his manner is conversational, and he gives voices to the characters. According to his introductory comments, the poem is meant to demonstrate that Bishop "loved the oddities and the beauties among things seen and heard. And in her poems they were subject to a serene ordering, as in the little poem that I would like to read…" Among Bishop's poems, not least those in the memorial text, "Manners" does seem "little"—a simple work, thematically and poetically. However, as we've seen with "North Haven," the ease or serenity of the narrative belies the labor of the "ordering." Fitzgerald's "serene ordering" is an incisive description of Bishop's process.

The memorial text goes on to pay tribute to Bishop's influence on post-modern poetry; Ashbery credits "A Miracle for Breakfast" with inspiring his experiments with sestinas. It also presents her as translator; Paz offers a tribute to Bishop as "a truly modern artist." But the many ideas of Bishop that circulate in the service—spiritual and musical, empathetic, modernist and complex—coalesce in Helen Vendler's introduction and reading of "Love Unknown." That poem becomes a center of gravity on the recording.

Bishop's relationship with Herbert is well known; I use "relationship" deliberately here to highlight her personal as well as intellectual connection to the poet of Little Gidding. Shortly after the tragic death of her partner, Lota Soares, Bishop received a copy of Herbert's *Selected Poetry*, edited by Joseph Summers, a friend and Herbert scholar. In a letter (September 23, 1967), Bishop thanks him for his "beautiful little Herbert book," praises his introduction, and writes, "I've been reading some of the poems again, too—some even help a bit, I think" (*One Art* 469). Bishop found Herbert consoling, at least "a bit," and in an essay on the two poets, Summers draws on unpublished correspondence to demonstrate that Bishop admired Herbert's tormented but steadfast faith in the face of pain and loss. The Bishop-Herbert relationship, founded on a shared sense of loss, stands behind Vendler's inclusion of Herbert in the memorial text. But her choice of "Love Unknown" adds another layer of meanings—and text—to the service.

Vendler chooses the poem because Bishop had chosen it. "Love Unknown" was paired with Bishop's "In the Waiting Room" in a curious coffee table book from 1974, *Preferences: 51 American Poets Choose Poems from Their Own Work and from the Past*. According to the editor of the volume, the poet Richard Howard, *Preferences* was the brainchild of the photographer Thomas Victor. Inspired by his collection of photographs of the modern poets, Victor suggested that poets identify "poems of their own they preferred, and with them poems from the past, poems from before 1900, from the entire range of poetry with which they felt their own poems sustained some interesting relation, even the relation of contradiction or challenge..." (Howard X). Vendler mentions *Preferences* and "In the Waiting Room" before reading "Love Unknown," so that Bishop's preference becomes a context for the reading, and "In the Waiting Room" an intertext.

Vendler reads "Love Unknown" clearly and with careful attention to prosody; I make note of this because along with Fitzgerald's, hers is the only untroubled reading during the service, though unlike his, hers does not attempt to dramatize the poem. In this respect, Vendler reads in the manner of Bishop, deepening the analogy between Bishop and Herbert that is set up by the placement of "Love Unknown" among Bishop's works. Vendler's reading consoles, even as the content and message of the poem challenges. Written in dialogue—arguably the most accessible of literary forms—the poem constructs a dense allegorical machinery in which the suffering of the good soul is rationalized. The speaker, a renter who tries to improve the lands that he holds, complains to a friend about suffering at the hands of his lord; the friend takes the side of the lord and demonstrates how suffering can be construed as salubrious. "In the Waiting Room" is similarly conversational, in that we are the friend to whom the speaker recounts her puzzling experience. Pain is pivotal in Bishop's poem, as it is in Herbert's—specifically, pain's surprise. In "Love Unknown," the speaker offers a sacrifice to his lord "to warm his love, which I did fear grew cold" (31); but the speaker is shocked when the lord's servant snatches his heart and throws it in the "scalding pan" marked "AFFLICTION." The physical pain is redoubled by its being unexpected and, moreover, emotionally charged. Aunt Consuelo's physical pain in "In the Waiting Room" is redoubled in "Elizabeth," who is surprised into traumatic identification with adulthood, womanhood, and humanity each in its fleshly weakness. "What took me / completely by surprise," she admits, "was that it was me: / my voice, in my mouth." Like the speaker of "Love Unknown," Elizabeth confronts herself, disoriented and frightened, on the other side of surprising pain.

While these similarities present themselves when "Love Unknown" and "In the Waiting Room" are placed in dialogue—as they are, I'm arguing, not only in *Preferences* but also at the service, by virtue of Vendler's invoking the anthology and reading Herbert in the manner of Bishop—two differences between the poems are worth consideration.

First, Bishop's poem is no allegory, unlike her more strictly "Herbertian" lyric, "The Weed." "Love Unknown" is presented as a personal account; while narrative in structure, it is memory filtered through lyric just as "North Haven" is. Despite this generic difference, I want to suggest that in the cases of these two lyrics, personal account and allegory have a similar goal: the representation of a universal experience. The "I" of "In the Waiting Room" is analogous to the speaker of "Love Unknown" insofar as we readers are meant to identify with them.

The second difference has to do with endings. "In the Waiting Room" offers no consolation to the suffering Elizabeth. There is in the end no freedom from her sense of misery (to borrow from Samuel Johnson's definition of "console"). She is "back in it" after her epiphany, back in the waiting room and the troubled world, though compounding her vexations is the question of who she is. By contrast, Herbert's poem ends in blessed assurance. "Your Master," the friend explains, "strive[s] to mend, what you had marr'd" (67). The point of suffering is to render the sufferer "new, tender, quick" (70). It seems unlikely that Bishop believed this, and yet by pairing "Love Unknown" and "In the Waiting Room," Bishop creates an irresolvable, epistemological tension. If experiences of suffering bind past and present, what Bishop and Herbert make of suffering suggests their historical difference. On one level, Bishop was attracted to Herbert precisely because his poetry attests to a faith that, as a modern, she considered inaccessible. "I'd been thinking that it was the hymn-singing Baptist backwards...village life," she wrote to Summers, "that made me so susceptible to Herbert in the first place" (qtd in Summers 48). To claim that suffering has a divine origin and rationale is "backwards," but to come through suffering "new, tender, quick" must have seemed a hopeful prospect to Bishop.

So, returning to the memorial service, we arrive at the question of Vendler's choosing to read only the Herbert. Whatever the intent of her choice—whether she *could* have chosen to read both is of course questionable, given time constraints—the effect of the Herbert alone is hopefulness, and specifically a hopefulness that follows from the heavy intellectual and emotional work represented in the poem. Elsewhere, Vendler has argued that Herbert is "above all a poet of named emotionalities," that the "realm of the sacred and a reason for devotion" do not "touch the essence of Herbert" ("Herbert and Modern Poetry" 84–85). In her estimation, he shares Bishop's complexity and all of Bishop's strengths, adding to them an "ease in convention," by which she seems to mean a facility with conventional forms and tropes that allows him to exploit them fully and happily. In the conventional setting of the memorial service, "Love Unknown" resonates where "In the Waiting Room"—with its resistance to consolation—would seem dissonant.[13] Perhaps ironically, given Bishop's modernity and her relationship to criticism, it is a critic's reading of a seventeenth-century metaphysical poem that seems to tie together the diverse strands of this memorial recording. Effectively, "Love Unknown" has become a Bishop poem in the anthology, resonating with her life and work as it is commemorated.

★   ★   ★

The features and interworkings of these three Bishop recordings are representative of occasional recordings in general. Subject to the choices of multiple participants and to the particular contingencies of the event, such recordings offer multiple points of entry; loosely organized and unedited, these artifacts invite speculative practices that can open critical paths. I have been treating an ephemeral recording of Bishop's memorial service as a text—specifically, as a kind of anthology. Occasional recordings, like all live recordings with multiple participants, lend themselves to this approach. Doing so here sheds light on a paradox that Bishop confronted in "North Haven": that the materiality of poet and poem fix them in history, that the immateriality of memory and poetry unfixes poet and poem. Lowell is inscribed on the landscape of North Haven, but "North Haven" is unstable as an inscription of Lowell, just as Bishop's memory of him necessarily was.

The occasional recording amplifies the importance of reception study to the practice of close listening, not least because it is the product of efforts, whether well-intended or unintentional, to define and historicize. In the Pacifica recording, we heard Bishop's resistance to the drive for conclusions essential to critical inquiry. Her performance style, I argued, implies a preference for the "flowing" to the "flown," but her attempt to stabilize her and Lowell's reception betrays the same anxiety that surfaced in her conversation with Howe and Ruas: that embarrassment and—worse—loss follow from a poet's relinquishing control of herself and her words to the critic. To achieve the status of the poet who is read, interviewed, critiqued, and memorialized is to become subject to the vicissitudes of reception. How Bishop is remembered at the memorial service is the result of a confluence of memories, loosely channeled as it were by the order of the service, and now filtered through my own interest in reception history and occasional recording.

In these Bishop examples, recordings of the forum, the commemoration, and the memorial service, like the publication of "North Haven," are attempts to stabilize memory through acts of textualization. Such is the archival impulse that underwrites the recording of ephemeral occasions. But as Bishop pointed out, while the words remain, the poetry changes when it enters the public sphere. In this respect, the occasion on record is no less a "literary event" now, as it is replayed and rethought, than it was at its inception.[14] For at any such occasion, just as at any scene of reading, poet and poetry are rewritten by communities of readers, gathered to appraise, mourn, or celebrate, gathered to remember.

PART II

IN FIRST PERSON, IN ANOTHER'S VOICE

CHAPTER 3

AUTHENTICITY AND AUDIENCE: MILLAY, SEXTON, AND VOCAL CONNECTIONS

One of the most readily recognizable symbols in U.S. commercial culture is the RCA Victor dog, who sits by the cone of a phonograph and listens to "His Master's Voice." Persistent, he remained at attention throughout the twentieth century, seemingly regardless of evolutions in sound quality. For whether monaural or in stereo, some essential feature of his master's voice had been caught in the recording.[1]

Although it is clear that sound technologies shaped the voice of the poet, the recorded poem seems to hold the poet within it. "The voice," writes Susan Stewart, "with the eyes, holds within itself the life of the self—it cannot be another's" (110). The primary marker of identity is not the content of speech but the quality of sound unique to the speaker. Dylan Thomas claimed that that sound inhered in the text and was released upon a poet's reading; Adorno and Lowell imagined that it had been cut into the spiral of the audio disc. "To address sound in poetry is to invoke a body," Wheeler claims, "whether the body belongs to the poet, the audience, or both" (23). I want to extend that claim, adding that to listen to poetry in the poet's voice is to seek a connection to the poet. This is a desire that underwrites the audio archive of modernism, regardless, it seems, whether the voice proceeding from the machine is self-identical with the poet.

Because voices are unique to specific bodies, vows must be spoken by the one making the pledge, confessions by the one asking for mercy. The voice comes into the room and into the mind, urgent and intimate; even when the sound is mediated by technologies, a sense of immediacy is integral to the experience of listening. Confession may well be a "ritual of discourse," as Foucault argues, and vows a set of prescribed claims in a ceremonial performance, both vows and confessions being contingent on the witness of an audience (*History* 2: 61). But the artifice of ritual and performance does not preclude authenticity; it is the means of actualizing it. Of the confessions of alleged criminals, for example, Foucault writes that the mass of textual documentation gathered by the penal investigation is outweighed by the confession of the accused himself, first in voice, then in writing (*Discipline and Punish* 37–38). Both events are staged, the writing being a second-order performance of the oral confession that ends in an artifact. A recording would do just as well, perhaps better, given the intimacy of the vocal connection to the accused.

In writing about recordings of Elizabeth Bishop, I suggested that while Foucault's concept of the author-function is useful in accounting for the relationship between text/poet and reception, it does not preclude the humanist impulse to seek out the Bishop poem (for example) as Bishop's or to hear the poem in the author's voice. The same holds true for the confession as Foucault helps us understand it. The voice speaks to us convincingly because of the ritual, not in spite of it, though the ritual would be undermined if the voice of the confessor proved to be another's, the signature a forgery. The balance between performance and authenticity, between the voice as performed sound and the voice as the unique sound of a self, was especially critical to the success of modernist poets on record who worked in expressive modes—modern, lyrical poetry "in first person" that has been variously categorized as personal, confessional, and testimonial. Lowell's reading at the Ninety-Second Street Y, I argued, betrayed the influence of such modes on his former style of presentation; recordings of Thomas were staged in a way that created warmth, bringing him into the room with us even as sound editing and his hieratic style made his voice other-worldly. However, none of the poets I have so far considered surpassed Edna Millay and Anne Sexton in their use of voice in performance as a means of connection to an audience. Millay's listeners described hearing her read as an intimate experience, and in the first part of this chapter I will show how Millay helped create that experience by her skillful performance of an aesthetic I call "the beautiful throat," taking a phrase coined by Millay. That aesthetic, revised in important ways, continued to flourish in the work of Anne Sexton, whose poetry on record will be the focus of the second half of this chapter. Sexton's "living voice," as one of her listeners put it, was a product of her reading style, her popular reception, and her carefully crafted, female "I." Millay's and Sexton's works demonstrate that modern expressivist poetry was most successful when heard, and it follows that studies of these works should focus more intently on their aural traces.

Millay's Beautiful Throat

In the poetry of Edna St. Vincent Millay, presentation is perhaps not all, but it is supremely important. Throughout the 1920s and 1930s, when Millay's fame was ascendant, her poetry arrived in beautiful packaging: there was her tantalizing persona, at once cheeky gamine and brooding romantic; there were artfully crafted editions of her poems, always featuring that most cultivated of lyric forms, the sonnet; and there was her voice, which her would-be lover Edmund Wilson described as the source of her authority with her audience. Traces of that voice remain in recordings that Millay made of her work, and in the notations of many of her listeners who tried to describe her sound and her style of reading.

As Lesley Wheeler demonstrates, Millay "encodes performance insistently within printed poetry and dramatically performs poems that represent sound in visual terms" (58). Millay's work, as Wheeler puts it, is "sound-saturated" (59). By that same token, Millay's reception is filled with descriptions of her voice and its effects. Millay's voice was as familiar to her contemporaries as her "extraordinary good forehead" and "mysterious mouth." What role, therefore, should listening to Millay—on record, situated in a horizon of expectations set by her original listeners—play in our current understanding of her persona and poetry? I will address this question by beginning to construct an audible Millay from the various remaining traces of her voice. I will consider Millay's references to the qualities of her voice, and analyze public reactions to her readings. These provide an essential context for understanding Millay's reading style, the arrangement of poems on her recordings, and the critical differences between listening to Millay "then" versus "now." I will argue that Millay and her audience shared an aesthetic, encapsulated in the phrase "beautiful throat"—an aesthetic of performed sincerity mediated by the poet's expressive voice.

There is a famous photo of Millay as a young poet, standing beneath a magnolia tree (figure 3.1). Gazing pensively away from the camera, she is rapt in sentimental melancholy. In her biography of Millay, Nancy Milford tells the story behind the photo. On her way back to Vassar College, Millay had stopped in the city to visit Mitchell Kennerley, whom she had met through Witter Bynner and who would eventually publish her first books of poetry. Kennerley arranged for her to be photographed by Arnold Genthe, an arrangement that flattered and thrilled Millay. Milford quotes a letter that Millay wrote to her family in which she describes the photograph, drawing special attention to her beautiful throat: "Besides having beautiful hair, an extraordinary good forehead in spite of the freckles, an impudent, aggressive, & critical nose, and a

Figure 3.1 Edna St. Vincent Millay at Mitchell Kennerley's house in Mamaroneck, New York, 1914.

mysterious mouth…I have, artistically & even technically, an unusually beautiful throat" (qtd in Milford 117). Millay wants her family to notice the line of her neck, perhaps the cast of light and shadow—the art of portraiture and the artfulness of her beauty. But her choice of words here is significant. She draws our eyes down from the forehead to the "mysterious mouth," then fixes our gaze on her "throat." Sensuality and mystery find their source in the mechanisms of voice production.

Like Adorno's scriptal spiral, the physical manifestation of sound in its range of hills and valleys, nonetheless silent without the phonograph, Millay's beautiful throat is a synecdoche for the poet as sensate machine of sound production. The voice of the poet, Millay continually reminds us, begins in a body; beautiful poetry, she wryly implies, is produced by a beautiful body. Many of the modernists who read for Lowell and the Library of Congress were at pangs to deny such bodily connections, despite the fact that record and tape erased the boundaries between the poem and the poet's vocal production. If Louise Bogan's carefully articulated, artfully restrained reading of "The Alchemist," for example, effectively isolates the poem, complementing its presentation on the LOC albums, Millay's readings tend to do the opposite—breathy, at times breathless, they issue from a body nearly in distress in its urgency to speak the words. Years after the Kennerley photograph, Millay dedicated her sonnet sequence *Fatal Interview* (1931) to Elinor Wylie, a poet and friend who died December 17, 1928. In the epigraph, sound, word, and life are contingent upon breath—in Millay's lines, literally air in the "throat" (ii). But thinking of Wylie, she claims, takes her breath, leaving her "bereft" of air and sound alike—leaving her wordless (ibid.). Perhaps the word of grief has formed in the poet's mind, but the unspoken word is "nothing"—it is an absence. In composing this epigraph, Millay doubtless had in mind a letter from Elinor's second husband, William Benet, in which he described Elinor's dying in his arms: "She died as I lifted her, I know. Death was in her throat" (qtd in Milford 308). What indicated that "death was in her throat"? A gasp, perhaps, or a gurgling, and it's significant that Millay chooses to make the dying poet's throat "bereft" of sound as well as air. We know a poet is dead by her silence.

We know she is alive by her affective speech, her declaiming of the self. In the epigraph, Millay speaks of being speechless in an act of empathy for Wylie. Her voice connects the "I" and the "you." If, to paraphrase John Stuart Mill, the lyric is an utterance that is overheard, Millay's whispered verse was a lyrical act. Benet overheard her, and surely others did also. It may be that Millay knew they would (over)hear, that she self-consciously performed the role of the poet; this would certainly follow the logic of her career, in which, as Wheeler writes, "she performed the poetess, but paradoxically she also performed authenticity, as twentieth-century audiences would increasingly require" (45). As Mill would have it, the intent to publish was no impediment to genuine expression so long as "no trace of consciousness that any eyes are upon us...be visible in the work itself" (349). An actor, Mill claims, fails when the audience detects that he knows he's acting. However, Millay's audience tests Mill's thesis and the supposed tension between genuineness and performance. It sought the poetess, embodied in Millay, whose vocal performances were considered expressions of the genuine.

In her study of the relationship among the modern lyric, professionalism, and sincerity, Susan B. Rosenbaum argues that commitment to the poem as sincere self-expression has not necessarily been at odds with a writer's active construction of a public, professional self (6–7). "Claims to sincerity," Rosenbaum writes in an analysis of Jane Tompkins' "Me and My Shadow," "are textual, mediated, conventional, theatrical, and yet also promise something more, a hinge to the 'real' author's experiences and feelings" (230). Millay's audience heard in her voice the fulfillment of that promise: access to the poet herself. Millay's reading tours began in January 1924, shortly after the November 1923 publication of *The Harp Weaver and Other Poems*. As would become customary, her first tour took her across the country. Daniel Mark Epstein writes that the tour of many U.S. towns and cities "was grueling but profitable. She netted more than two thousand dollars. Millay was delighted by the size of her audience and their enthusiasm, amazed by how many people had read her books and how many readers knew her poems by heart" (182–83). Millay made a similar tour after publishing *Buck in the Snow* in 1928, the last stop on that tour being the Brooklyn Academy of Music on December 17. Before going on stage, Millay learned of Wylie's death, and chose to read exclusively from Wylie's verse. In the 1930s, Millay's tours anticipated print publication; this was true of her promotion of both *Wine From These Grapes* (1934) and *Huntsman, What Quarry?* (1939). Even without the radio broadcasts of her poetry in the winter of 1932–33, Millay's voice carried her poetry to the public.[2]

What did that public see and, more to the point, what did it hear when it attended a Millay reading? In a letter to Edmund Wilson, Hubertis M. Cummings described a Millay reading in Cincinnati: "The slender red-haired, gold-eyed Vincent Millay, dressed in a black trimmed gown of purple silk, was now reading from a tooled leather portfolio, now reciting without aid of book or print, despite her broom-splint legs and muscles twitching in her throat and in her thin arms, in a voice that enchanted" (qtd in Milford 182). Black trim, purple silk, tooled leather…enchanting packaging, enchanting voice. Less than charmed by Millay's throat, Cummings is nonetheless so enchanted that he works a curious alchemy on her eyes; famously blue, they were gold on that night in Cincinnati.

Descriptions of Millay's reading often dwell on the topic of enchantment; indeed, the word "charm" appears nearly as often among the letters and reminiscences of her audience as the word "beautiful," their adjective of choice. Millay's enchanting style distinguished her among fellow poets and lecturers at a reading at Bowdoin College in May 1925, where she participated in the Institute of Modern Literature, a celebration of the centennial of Hawthorne and Longfellow's graduations in 1825. The program boasted a host of literary luminaries: Robert Frost, Carl Sandburg, Irving Babbitt, Willa Cather. On the program, Millay is called "poetess, author of 'Renascence,' 'The Harp-Weaver and Other Poems,' etc." Interestingly, as the only other woman on the slate, Cather's title is not gendered—she is a "novelist, author…" As "poetess," Millay wears the mantle of Elizabeth Barrett Browning and Felicia Hemans. Charm precedes her. Gendered female, it is what her audience expects from the poet of "Renascence." Millay read from her poems at 8:15 on the evening of May 5, then facilitated a roundtable conference the next morning at 10:30. A cover article in the *Bowdoin Orient* from May 13, 1825, offered one perspective on her readings:

> Edna St. Vincent Millay who spoke last Tuesday evening, intrigued her listeners—held them spellbound as she read her poems with a touch of Frost's "Vocal Imagination." She amazed them with her versatile genius and the beauty of her poetry. And when she had finished acting a play of hers—acting it in a clever, fascinating, and inimitable way—the audience left their seats reluctantly. ("Robert Frost")

Allowing for the excesses of undergraduate journalism, the language points to a supernatural effect—amazement, intrigue, being "spellbound." In his essay "Understanding the Sound of Not Understanding," Jed Rasula argues that the intended effect of an "oracular declamatory" mode of reading aloud—the mode in which Millay read—is enchantment (236–37). Meaning, in fact, becomes subordinated to the sensual effects of the spoken word in ways that we noted in Dylan Thomas' readings, which followed Millay's by nearly thirty years and are closely akin to hers stylistically. A crucial difference, however, is that Thomas' persona, unlike Millay's, became a liability; his alcoholism led to frequent cancellations and compromised his personal appeal. Millay's listeners responded to the sound of her voice in ways that suggest unbridled adoration of her persona, and her biography only seemed to amplify interest and strengthen the connection between poet and audience.

I have been arguing that in her public performances, Millay was positioned as feminine, and that she traded on this in staging a persona and crafting a voice that enchanted. Among the poets on record we've encountered so far in this study, Millay is hardly alone in self-consciously staging gender. Thomas speaks as the man of feeling, whose voice shudders as he urges his father to a masculine "rage against the dying of the light." Lowell's commentary on "Skunk Hour" effectively distances the vulnerable man in the poem from the authoritative poet at the microphone. Famously, perhaps infamously, Bishop refused to be included in anthologies of women's poetry, a refusal she addressed in the Pacifica interview. "At that point, that was a feminist stance," she claims, because she associated the categorizing of women's poetry with a poetess tradition that ranked women below men. She acknowledges that by the 1960s and 1970s, feminism had redefined the category "women's poetry," but "I felt I couldn't change my point of view. It's still the same" (Bishop, Interview). As we have seen, gender became an essential component of Bishop's posthumous reception, despite her efforts during her lifetime to deflate critical approaches that read her work not only through gender, but also biography or politics. Among the various stagings of gender in the audio archive of modernism, Millay stands out not because gender played a role in her persona and reception, but because the ostensibly feminine charm of her voice so effectively communicated a poetics of sincerity to such a wide constituency.

Among Millay's listeners, there were a few who objected to what we might call her uses of enchantment. After Millay's reading at Bowdoin, a second news report in the *Bowdoin Orient* mentions charm in its title— "Miss Millay Charms Hearers With Readings From Poems"—but the undergraduate reporter Lawrence Leighton claims that he has not succumbed. He argues that Millay has essentially duped "a predominately masculine audience." Her "femininity, charm, graciousness, good acting" are a "subtle drug." Many, he implies, have gotten addicted, from the dean of the college to critics and the public who would dare compare the poetess to "Byron himself." He admits that her voice "was beautifully musical," but finds her "cadences" monotonous. Leighton, in short, describes a form of intoxication, a siren song—sexy, beautiful, "feminine," and insincere. Leighton's objections are rare in Millay's reception, as is the distinction he draws between her voice and her style. Many compared Millay to Byron. Like her romantic precursor, Millay embodied an ideal of the poet and the poetic. She was intentionally feminine, enchanting, and dramatic, as he was masculine, melancholy, and daring. Her private life was for public consumption, and she skillfully balanced the ironic lightness of "Only until this cigarette is ended" and the leaden seriousness of "Renascence." To suggest, however, that the act was insincere is to miss the point. Millay and Byron *were* their performances of themselves.[3]

How can we know the dancer from the dance? To Millay's audience, her voice and reading style embodied an ideal of the poetic. "It is a joy," wrote a Ms. Janet K. Smith in 1933, "to hear the poems of Miss Millay read in her own fascinatingly distinctive voice and with her own simple and moving presentation of them" (Smith). Millay reading is described throughout the letters and reminiscences of her audience as simultaneously simple and dramatic, formal and informal, natural and theatrical. "It's simply intoxicating," one of her listeners remarked in a December, 1932 letter to Millay, "Don't, don't ever change, and become stiff or formal or eloquent...You sound so real, so natural, so—so very much alive..." (qtd in Milford 367). How can we square this listener's "so real, so natural" with Edmund Wilson's description of her "deliberate grand manner," a description that likely rings truer to our ears (*The Fifties* 556)? Millay's highly stylized mode of presentation was "natural" insofar as it was the voice that one would expect a poet to have. Millay's audience listened for "the voice of the poet," and naturally what they heard was poetic. As Elizabeth Clark said of Millay, she had a "poetic way of talking" (qtd in Milford 371). " 'It [her voice] was dramatic, lifting and falling without anything forced about it," wrote one ardent fan in December, 1932, "she was a person who made one believe, in her presence, that there is a muse. And Edna was visited by her' " (368). Millay's voice gave her "presence," and its drama and incantatory lilt were evidence to her listeners that she embodied the muse.

Millay's poetic way of talking drew thousands of people to their radios on Sunday evenings during the winter of 1932–33, when she gave eight readings on NBC.[4] In response to the broadcasts, Millay was inundated with letters from enchanted listeners. According to Margaret Cuthbert, who produced Millay's broadcasts and collected the fan mail, the poet and NBC received fifteen hundred letters, a selection of which Cuthbert painstakingly transcribed.[5] "Many people who had never bought radios did so to hear Edna Millay's broadcast," Cuthbert writes, "The letters asked nothing. Poetry opened the hearts of the people and they wrote as they felt. Some were too personal to include [in the typescripts]. They told Miss Millay their life histories. Their letters showed how starved people are for the real thing." By the "real thing," Cuthbert appears to mean a genuine experience of the beautiful, in which the genuineness and the beauty are beyond question. "Your broadcast on Sunday evening," wrote Lewis Sisson of New York, "gives the tired and bitter world the balm of belief and beauty. It is so sorely needed, this kind of religion...Again permit me to thank you for the splendid contribution you are making in acquainting our nation with truth and beauty in your works." Beauty inheres in Millay's works, but also in her voice. "Your voice came over beautifully," "she has the most beautiful voice in the world," "I thought your voice the first night was like lovely music," "Your voice has just gone—it was very rich and beautiful tonight": nearly every letter testifies to the beauty of Millay's voice.

A few attempt to define this beauty. For Julia Irene Logan of Sioux City, Iowa, "it was a delight to hear a voice so human—not to speak of the round vowels, distinct consonants and open tones." A beautiful voice is in part the result of effective elocution, which many in Millay's audience would have studied in school, as we noted in chapter one. In *Shores of Light*, Wilson dwells at length on Millay's /r/, "different from the harsh or slighted r's of the American regional accents" (750). Millay's consonants and vowels, however, are not customarily the focus. Rather, beauty has most to do with what Logan describes as the "so human" traces of emotion, especially sorrow. Writer and activist Floyd Dell, an early champion of Millay's work, writes in his autobiography that he "became acquainted with the girl poet as a human being," and that her "reciting voice had a loveliness that was sometimes heartbreakingly poignant" (301). To be human is to experience sorrow; to articulate that sorrow beautifully is to be a poet. As is often the case, Edmund Wilson movingly sums up the experience of listening to Millay read her work:

> What was impressive and rather unsettling when she read such poems [as "Elegy"] aloud was her power of imposing herself on others through a medium that unburdened the emotions of solitude. The company hushed and listened as people do to music—her authority was complete; but her voice, though dramatic, was lonely. (*Shores* 750)

The voice transmits the self, and it does so with "authority." But despite the connection to an audience, the voice—Wilson intends a synecdoche here, I believe—remains "lonely." It is irony we will see repeated in the performances of Anne Sexton.

If Millay felt alone—and perhaps being in the studio booth, as opposed to on stage, reinforced a sense of distance—her audience felt drawn to her. Whether over radio or at a poetry reading, Millay's listeners talk of enchantment and the beautiful. "Her voice haunts me," wrote listener Frances Trams from Joliet, Illinois, "like the passion for beauty." And whether Millay is present in body or in embodied voice, listeners describe the experience as intimate. Mary Slaughter's remarks are typical: "I feel all of your radio audience was drawn very close to you by your sweet informal way that binds hearts close together in a bond of truth and trustfulness...You drew us very close to you Miss Millay. I shall anxiously await your next readings." The closeness, the binding of hearts, the eagerness for the next meeting: Slaughter's letter describes an assignation. Millay's radio audience imagined that she spoke directly to them; it was, Slaughter continues, "as though she had known you all the time, and had written her poems about or for you." As Cuthbert notes, listeners seemed starved for this kind of intimacy, a poetic intimacy. A listener Evenlyn Hilberg writes of her "prosaic life," of the "luxury it would then be to iron" while listening to Millay. Others describe isolation and destitution and their hope that, as a Mrs. Snow proclaims, when a "new deal" comes to fruition, they can afford to buy Millay's books. In the meantime, they will meet her faithfully each Sunday by the radio.

While it would seem important to distinguish between reactions of an audience that was present at a Millay reading and those of a radio audience, what is remarkable is the consistency of response that one finds across these very different scenes of listening. In her cultural study of radio, Susan Douglas demonstrates how the phonograph had set the stage for radio: the notion of a disembodied voice and communion with an absent other linked the two scenes of listening.[6] Similarly, as we have seen, the audience at poetry readings and by the radio focused intensely on the qualities of Millay's voice and elocutionary style. For the listener in each setting, the voice was paramount.

Millay's Beautiful Throat Now

Millay's work is encountered now almost exclusively in print text. Wheeler's study of Millay's voice—the most comprehensive of any in criticism of the poet's work—focuses primarily on print traces of Millay's sound. But what happens if we listen to recordings of Millay?[7] Millay's "deliberate, grand manner" sounds inauthentic today—a parody of seriousness at best, maudlin and histrionic at worst. Yet the language of the letters and memoirs we've been examining—a language of lovers, a language of sincerity—clearly indicates that the vocal techniques we might consider artificial drew Millay's audience in. In this section, I will examine differences between listening to Millay "then" versus "now," and argue that the reception of Millay's readings provides an essential context for close listening.[8] This has important implications for listening to many recordings in the audio archive, especially those in which sincerity is conveyed through a performance aesthetic best encapsulated in Millay's synecdoche, the "beautiful throat."

In that aesthetic, which is expressed most completely in the first-person lyric, the poet uses voice as an emotional instrument, calling on the full capacity of breath, pitch, enunciation, and tempo. We are always aware of the poet as speaker, whose eloquence is *made* genuine in performance. Recordings of Millay are audible inscriptions of the beautiful throat aesthetic, which equates beauty with poignancy, values sincerity, and considers the poet's voice an authentic register of her feelings. Millay and her audience shared this aesthetic, and it is encoded in her reading of sonnet 11, "Not in a silver casket cool with pearls," from *Fatal Interview*. Millay's reception reestablishes a former "horizon of expectation" for our listening (Jauss 25). This is serious, dramatic art, though the drama is "natural," welling up from the soul of the poet speaking. In the sonnet, a woman declares that the sincerity of her love is evidenced by the simplicity of her offering—"love in the open hand" as opposed to a "silver casket cool with pearls" (*Selected Poems* 122). Millay declaims the sonnet passionately, reading with vibrato throughout, though her reading is inflected in ways that guide our attention to specific words and poetic effects. In both recordings of the sonnet, Millay strikes hard on the opening syllable of several lines, emphasizing her replacement of iambs with trochees. This effectively creates a pattern among certain words and lines. The repeated "not" of lines one and four become anaphora and are further knit together by Millay's open-mouthed /o/ in not, knot, and the "locked" of line three. Trochee and short vowel, emphatically enunciated, contrast with Millay's softer, elongated long o and r-controlled vowels; cool, pearls, blue, girls—all are drawn out in long, breathy sweeps. Millay's elocution, in short, dramatizes the speaker's hard-nosed declaration of her difference from "other girls" and her softer, more sincere offering of love in the open hand. The importance of sincerity is the final message of the poem and the reading.

That sincerity, however, brings me back to the question of then versus now. Millay's audience understood Millay to be the speaker of the sonnet, not just its reader. The note of sincerity at the sonnet's end was authentic, all the more so because Millay had spoken beautifully; recall the words of one of her listeners—"you sound so very much alive." But is it possible that in its overt artifice, Millay's reading serves to *distance* her from the lyric's speaker? Listening now, when an ironic performance of such a lyric would carry greater appeal than a sincere delivery, I am inclined to hear irony in Millay's reading of the sestet. After all, even as the speaker scoffs at the material tokens of love that other girls offer, she declares her love in the artificial beauties of sonnet form and imagery. Millay's affectations in this sonnet reading are Wildean, a mask of earnestness that should cause us to question the poem's propositions and Millay's sincerity. Heard in such a way, Millay's pauses in her readings of line seven and the final line of the sonnet are pregnant with irony. In line seven, she stops briefly before "Semper fidelis" then raises her volume melodramatically, as if such declarations of faith are cause for skepticism. She declares her "love in the open hand" as different, and we would expect her to deliver the final couplet, the sonnet's resolution, with sincerity. But "Look what I have! And these are all for you" is read with a cloying sweetness, in imitation of a child, an effect that is especially clear in the earlier recording, when Millay's voice was younger (122). It is as if in proclaiming her difference from other girls, the speaker has worked herself up into an overdetermined declaration of her sincerity. Her cry "Look what I have!" becomes no less suspect than the brazen "Semper fidelis" that she ridicules.

Note that among contemporary critics, I am not alone in detecting irony in Millay's theatrics. In her essay "Uncanny Millay," Suzanne Clark argues that "masquerade functions as critique" in Millay's poetry— critique, that is, of the very gendered subject positions that Millay's lyric speakers take (5). So how do we reconcile these contradictory readings, my and Clark's ironic Millay with the sincere Millay of the early-twentieth-century reception? Referring to the moment that a text enters circulation, Jerome McGann speaks of poetry as a literary event, bringing our attention to the historicity of material text, specifically its social element. The event consists of the poem, poet, readers, and materials of production, all taking place, or perhaps more precisely, *making* place in the ever-unfolding history of the text (*Beauty*). McGann's concept of the literary event was critical for Charles Bernstein, whose focus on the text as performance I discussed in the introduction, and following these critics' lead, I have argued that in essence, the recorded poem is reconstituted, re-voiced, each time we play it. It follows that Millay's reading of sonnet 11 necessarily differs in meaning now versus then. Listening to Millay on record involves holding in tension two opposing aesthetics, one that appreciates Millay's theatricality *as* theatricality and Millay as artful poseur, and another that understands Millay as sincere poet of the beautiful throat. Of the two, the sincere Millay will prove to be the most difficult listening for us today. In his reception histories of sentimental poetry, McGann has further argued that modern "high culture" criticism generally holds sentimentalism to be "something of an embarrassment—at best a topic of academic interest, at worst a perceived threat to the practice of art" (*Poetics* 1). Millay's reception is critical to our listening today because it provides an important historical check on our tendencies either to dismiss her sincerity as an "embarrassment" or to search for evidence of irony in her performances to the exclusion of taking seriously the aesthetic of the beautiful throat. Millay's audience, which spanned academic and popular culture, took the aesthetic seriously, and to appreciate Millay's influence, we must entertain the possibility that the speaker of sonnet 11 *is* Millay, full-throated and heartfelt as her listeners passionately believed.

Listening to Millay now involves not only careful attention to how she reads and to the horizons of expectation set by her aesthetic, but also to the sequences of poems in both the broadcast and studio recordings and to such paratextual elements as liner notes. A poet's arrangement of her poems, as Neil Fraistat and others have argued, provides an important framework for intertextual interpretation.[9] We've seen a version of this in operation already, in the interplay among poets and poems on the Library of Congress recordings. Millay took full advantage of it in her radio broadcast, beginning with the popular devout poem "God's World," and ending with the dark sonnet 52 from *Fatal Interview*—beginning, therefore, with devotion and ending in eros gone awry. Even when we can be less certain of her control over arrangement, sequences of poems on her recording repay close scrutiny. Given her involvement in the details of her book production, Millay likely had a hand in the arrangement of her original RCA recordings. These consist of four 78 rpm long-playing records and include a sequence of several later poems: "For Pao-Chin," "The Anguish," "I Must Not Die of Pity," "To the Maid of Orleans," and "Where Can the Heart Be Hidden in the Ground." This grouping seems especially important in light of the album's liner notes. The notes repeatedly draw connections between Millay's biography and her poems, and the "For Pao-Chin" sequence is used to illustrate "how deeply, from the very outset of her poetical career, she was affected by social conditions, social maladjustments and injustices" (Millay, RCA). The notes suggest that Millay's readers do not associate their favorite poet with politics.

In fact, the opposite was true. Millay's protests of the Sacco and Vanzetti trial in 1927 and her support of American intervention into the war with Germany in the late 1930s were widely publicized. Milford reports that after the fall of Poland in 1939, Millay participated in a radio broadcast called "The Challenge to Civilization." Introduced as an "American possession" who "contrary to most poets...does not live in the ivory tower," Millay concentrated her remarks on the importance of maintaining civil liberty and free speech in a time of fear (Milford 434–35). She closed with a reading of "Underground System" from her new book *Huntsman, What Quarry?* A warning against the dangers of complacency, the poem declares that "Ease has demoralized us, nearly so" (*Selected Poems* 179). Millay imagines life as a field undermined by moles; the surface appears stable, but collapse is inevitable and rejuvenation unlikely. Reading to a country wavering about entering a war that was ravaging Europe, Millay takes on a prophetic voice in the service of intervention. By the time the United States entered the war, civic activism was part of her public persona, though her political verse, most notably in *Make Bright the Arrows* and in the pages of the *New York Times*, had fared poorly with the critics. In the following year, the radio broadcast of "The Murder of Lidice," which Millay had written hastily at the request of the Writers War Board, would receive a great deal of attention in the press. The verse drama recounts the destruction of a Czechoslovakia village by the Nazis in June 1942. Nearly two hundred men were summarily executed, and the remaining population was extradited to concentration camps. The text was published in a variety of formats, as Mike Chasar's recent research indicates.[10] But most of the critical reviews of the poem and the broadcast echoed the *New York Times* and Millay's own reservations: "Not a great poem, not her best poem, but one which finely serves the time, the medium and the intention" (Hutchens). These overtly political poems appeal to the sentiments, as Jo Ellen Kaiser has argued, but Millay herself dismissed her political poetry, written with (as she put it in a letter to Cass Canfield) "an ulterior motive, such as, for instance the winning of a world war to keep democracy alive" (*Letters* 329).

Perhaps because of Millay's forays into what the *Times* called "shoddy political stanzas," the RCA album notes want to redeem her as "unacknowledged legislator" without recourse to overtly political verse. Consequently, the notes maintain that the "For Pao-Chin" sequence deals in a poet's reactions to "the suffering of humanity in the world," and the evidence inheres not in any historical reference, but in Millay's emotive performance. For instance, the final poem in the sequence, "Where Can the Heart Be Hidden in the Ground," seeks to justify the speaker's romantic desire for oblivion, and Millay's rendering is impassioned, even angry. Millay's voice becomes almost shrill as she inveighs against eternal life: who would want to hover in a ghost's form, speechless and helpless, above an anguished earth, she asks. As in the verses Millay whispered over Wylie, the imagery here connects the poetic voice to a desperate body. The poet after death would be a "stuffless ghost...wretching in vain to render up the groan that is not there" (*Selected Poems* 155). Millay reads the line without irony in her "deliberate grand manner," ripping across the /r/ sounds of "wretching" and "render." The poem ends quickly as Millay's voice, enervated, dwindles to the final word, "alone."

Emotional excess and exhaustion in this poem and reading indicated to listeners *then* that Millay was "deeply...affected" by injustices in the world. The Caedmon reissue of the recording on a single 33 1/3 rpm LP retains the "For Pao-Chin" sequence and reprints the notes, further confirming that it is an intentional grouping. But on the reissue, the sequence precedes the final "Elegy" on side two. This shift is significant, for it effectively repeats a pattern that we saw in Millay's 1932 broadcast—a movement from hope to pathos, from light to darkness. Each side of the

Caedmon recording begins with a long, affirming narrative poem from Millay's youth—"Renascence" on side one, "The Ballad of the Harp Weaver" on side two. By contrast, each side concludes with a lyric in which hope has been fully compromised, the final sonnet from *Fatal Interview* on side one, and "Elegy," an early lyric that Millay wrote in memory of a fellow student at Vassar, on side two. So the very sequence of poems on the Caedmon reissue signifies that the poet has been "deeply affected."

Among these, Millay's readings of the sonnet and elegy are typical of the beautiful throat aesthetic, what her listeners described as "poignant." Millay reads the sonnet with an air of foreboding, her voice trembling, imitating the agitation and grief of the goddess Diana, who searches in vain for "mortal Endymion" (*Selected Poems* 143). In the last couplet— "Whereof she wanders mad, being all unfit / For mortal love, that might not die of it"—Millay slows the pace, accentuating the irony that the goddess cannot fully experience "mortal love" because she cannot "die" with her mortal lover (143). Even the immortals, according to the sonnet, cannot forestall the despair that awaits anyone who loves. Millay ends the album with a still bleaker message. The final lines on side two, which conclude "Elegy," a poem written for a friend of Millay's from Vassar, signal the silencing of a poet's voice. Millay proclaims that the "music of your [D.C.'s] talk" had the power of restoring the earth in which her friend now lies, but then ends with a curiously worded lament for the silence imposed by death: "All your lovely words are spoken. / Once the ivory box is broken, / Beats the golden bird no more" (*Selected Poems* 34). "Are spoken" has several meanings. It can be read as past tense— that there will be no more lovely words because they have already been spoken—or as a simple equation—that the lovely words are the spoken ones, which are now lost with the speaker's death. An optimistic reading is also available, which says the lovely words are always being spoken, granting immortality. The poem's last image, however, closes off this possibility. The breath that produces words is the wind off a golden bird's wings, and death has loosed the bird from the "ivory box" that contained him. In the poetic anatomy, that "ivory box" is of course the throat.

While delivering the final line of "Elegy," Millay pauses dramatically before darkly intoning "no more." In the silence that precedes those words is the anticipation of sorrow, and resignation to it follows in the low electronic hum and hiss of the LP. The final effect of listening to Millay is melancholy of the kind described by Dell, the "heartbreaking poignancy" that forged intimate bonds between her and her listeners.

That, at least, is the effect indicated by the reception. Whether we *feel* the effect today is, as Edmund Wilson suggested, another matter. Ever

Millay's paramour and advocate, Wilson found himself in the minority at a dinner on June 29, 1958, with Harrison Dowd and Djuna Barnes:

> Harrison Dowd was less loyal to Edna than I should have expected him to be—thought some of her short poems were good, didn't care for the way she read her poems: too much of the elocutionist about it. There is something in this, and it is the reason that some people find her records embarrassing; but she and her poetry meant, and still mean, so much to me that I don't mind it at all. Besides, this deliberate grand manner united them. (*The Fifties* 555–56)

Dowd was an actor who had starred as Pierrot in the debut of Millay's *Aria Da Capo*, March 1920. Troubled by Dowd's disloyalty, Wilson is nonetheless unsurprised that her readings could be considered embarrassing. Embarrassment, as McGann suggests, is the fundamental high culture reaction to sentimentalism, specifically to its affectations. It was Bishop's reaction to hearing Millay, though it was her reaction to listening to most poets perform their work. Listening to Millay now, in an academic setting, where the beautiful throat aesthetic has appeal principally as camp, most of us will begin from a place of embarrassment—the place where Dowd ends—and move back to the sentimental through our attention to reception history. We may not, however, feel connected to Millay by her voice, as Wilson does. For Wilson operates from the opposite vantage point. He can appreciate Dowd's embarrassment, but in the final analysis, he succumbs to Millay's effects because he feels her poetry, especially upon hearing her read it.

The crucial element in Wilson's sentimentality is his sense of intimacy with Millay. "Meant, and still mean" alludes nostalgically to a relationship consummated in Millay's "grand manner," in that her manner "united" poet, poetry, and Wilson. As we've seen, many of Millay's listeners from the 1920s through the early 1940s felt a similar intimacy with the poet, who came to their towns and into their homes and read for them. She was a public figure, indeed the people's poet. It is perhaps that lack of intimacy that will always compromise our listening to Millay, though her reception can bring us closer to her than her voice alone.

"A Reincarnation of Edna St. Vincent": Anne Sexton and the Beautiful Throat

Before turning to how the beautiful throat changed later in the twentieth century, I want to sum up its essential characteristics and purpose as I have so far defined them. It is, I have argued, an acoustic aesthetic—a performance style and an expressive poetics that rely on acoustic sensations generated by the poet's vocalization of her work. It assumes that theatricality facilitates sincere expression and, unlike the stylized delivery often dismissed as "elocutionism," it presupposes a mutual desire for intimate contact between poet and listener. While the semantic content of the poem in such a performance is critical, so are the particular resonances of the poet's voice—the voice of the poet as an "I" whom the listener seeks to know. I want to suggest that Edna Millay mastered this aesthetic, and that her voice resonates among expressive poets in the audio archive of modernism.

Based on their performance style, there are many poets whose recordings cluster around Millay: Dylan Thomas, Sylvia Plath, and John Berryman, for example, all of whom combined controlled self-disclosure with carefully wrought vocal performance. But a pivotal voice is Anne Sexton, who was self-conscious about her connection to Millay, but whose performances put self-consciousness to the service of sincerity and remade the beautiful throat. In the context of the late 1950s and early 1960s, Sexton's version of the aesthetic challenged the narrow vocal range practiced by the academic modernism of her mentors. Like Millay, Sexton marshaled the physical effects of sound, and it is this, as much as her charged subject matter, that created her "voice" and persona.

Shortly after she joined Robert Lowell's poetry workshop at Boston University in September 1958, Anne Sexton wrote an anxious, typically effusive letter to her mentor, W.D. Snodgrass. Intimidated by classmates and instructor alike, Sexton exclaimed, "I shall never write a really good poem. I overwrite. I am a reincarnation of Edna St. Vincent" (*Letters* 40). At one level, "overwrite" implies unnecessary excess, and Sexton's anxiety suggests that in the academic poetry establishment, "Millay," whose work she had admired in her youth, was a metonym for the emotional excess associated with being a poetess. One can imagine that Sexton has been told to revise in the interest of understatement. But in Sexton's "overwrite," there is also an echo of Edmund Wilson's complaint that Millay read in a "deliberate grand manner." To overwrite, in this sense, is to call attention to one's artifice and to the work as a performance. It is to allow excess and expect to be indulged. When Millay, for example, intones "no more" breathlessly at the end of "Elegy," or Dylan Thomas' voice trembles on the last "rage" in "Do Not Go Gentle Into That Good Night," those sounds are meant to strike us; they are as essential to the aesthetic of the beautiful throat as traditional prosody and emotive content. In the studio, the Library of Congress project narrowed the range of vocal performance to reflect the preferences of mid-century formalism. On the stage and in public, Bishop sought to minimize what she considered to be the risk of speaking one's self and attempted transparency in her performance. The skepticism of Sexton's mentors notwithstanding, the acoustics of her readings and the deliberate theatricality of her "beautiful throat" are an essential means by which her poetry speaks. She took advantage of the fact that the voice affects the body of the listener, whether it caused a tremble of delight or, as with Bishop, a blush of embarrassment.

As with Millay, Sexton's reception sets a horizon of expectation within which we can effectively listen to her performances, for it was in negotiation with her audience that Sexton refined her persona and vocal style. In her recent, book-length study of Sexton's work, Jo Gill considers the exchange between reader and poet to be an essential part of Sexton's poetics. She argues that we should "understand the confessional text not as the compulsive expression of the prior experience of the author, but as a gesture which achieves its meaning and status as confession only in the process of being received or read" (19). Confession assumes an interlocutor, whose listening and response authenticate the "I" and its speech. As with Millay, Sexton's audience sought a connection with her as a person whose life and concerns interested them. Referring to Sexton's unpublished lecture notes from Colgate University—notes that Sexton titled "Anne on Anne"—Gill reports that Sexton asked her students to read her poetry, write questions, then imagine the answers "Anne" would give. In this way, Gill writes, the students

> authorize her in a process which replicates that by which the confessional persona is constructed by her audience. Sexton develops this idea further by suggesting that the "Anne" who is both the subject and the object of the lectures is not only a construction of her present audience, but also a product of her previous and potential audiences. (27)

That Sexton cultivated a persona in conjunction with her audiences is clear. However, she held this performed self in tension with a belief in an essential self, just beyond the reach of her public, no matter how personal her writing or unguarded her self-presentation. As she understood it, the voice proceeded from this deeper self.

It is worth recalling at this point Michael Davidson's concept of the "poetics of presence." As I noted in the introduction, Davidson maintains that the Beat writers used recording technology to affirm an essential self, carried in the voice and captured on tape (99). Audience serves a similar purpose in the beautiful throat aesthetic, although an important distinction needs to be drawn, one clarified by Sexton's example. In her work, the voice connects poet and audience, and the self is made vulnerable. But for Sexton, what becomes "present" is a likeness, over which she maintains greater control than her listeners. Consider, for example, how Sexton always introduced her readings. Cigarette in hand and perched on the edge of a chair, she began by proclaiming that she would read "Her Kind" first, so that listeners would "know just what kind of a poet I am, just what kind of a woman I am. And then if anyone wishes to leave, they may do so" (qtd in Gill 26). The comment implies she'll lay bare her essential self, as poet and woman, but she does so—if she does so—in an extended metaphor. In the poem, the kind to which she belongs is a "possessed witch," a "lonely thing, twelve-fingered, out of mind" (18). But as she reads, does she still belong? As if confessing a past transgression, Sexton casts her refrain in the present-perfect—"I have been her kind." Similarly, the metaphor positions Sexton as an observer who describes the witch, then attempts to classify her among women, "a woman like that." Her taxonomy, she suggests, is speculative, for a "woman like that is not a woman, quite." As Sexton ostensibly opens herself to her audience, she speaks of a past self, a possessed witch, that is woman but not quite woman. Vocal presence signifies a self that recedes behind layers of metaphor and discourse.

I want to suggest that this staging of a self and, more to the point, of the elusiveness of identity even to the speaker is what made Sexton's claims seem authentic to her audience. Speaking poetically of herself, Sexton was seemingly within reach but fundamentally mysterious. Whereas the operative terms in the reception of Millay's voice were "charm" and "beauty," the sounds of Sexton's beautiful throat were variously heard as incantations and seductions. Alicia Ostriker has called Sexton's readings of "Her Kind" a "seduction of the audience." Ostriker maintains that "Sexton's vocation as a poet was determined to an extraordinary degree by an assumption of and dependence on readerly empathy," which she gained by encouraging her readers "to respond personally to the poetic fiction of a direct address expressing need, hope, pain, joy, anger, and despair, calling on our love and sympathy, or attacking us for our indifference and neglect" ("Seduction" 9, 14). "Seduction" is a troubling metaphor for Sexton's methods, implying as it does the reader's initial stance of skepticism and resistance, followed by her relinquishing of agency. It nonetheless captures the erotic undertones of Sexton's performances, much as "enchantment" points us to the element of mystery that Sexton cultivated in her version of the beautiful throat. Following a reading in June 1968, Sexton wrote about her stage persona to Paul Brooks, her editor at Houghton-Mifflin. Brooks had evidently spoken to her about being mesmerized by her performance, to which Sexton replied that "of course I am a witch, an enchantress of sorts and have already been worshipped and hung and in the same order" (*Letters* 325). She goes on to agree with Brooks that poetry "is an oral art" and that after she's gone "only the page" will carry her—recordings, perhaps, notwithstanding.

In those recordings, we hear a version of the beautiful throat that, like Millay's, calls attention to self-expression as a performance, but that replaces full-throated emotiveness with darker tones, as in her readings of "Her Kind."[11] Very early in her career, in 1959, Sexton was recorded reading this poem in Boston; much later, in 1974, she recorded the poem in the studio for Caedmon. Aside from differences in quality that we may attribute to the venue and technical advances, Sexton's readings differ principally in the degree to which she dramatizes the lines, the later sounding like the work of the more seasoned performer, who has a greater command of vocal range and breath. To some extent, Sexton's style of reading invokes Millay and shares qualities with Sexton's contemporary Dylan Thomas. For example, before her first intoning of the refrain, "I have been her kind," she pauses and lowers her voice; then, after another pause, her volume increases abruptly with the opening of the following stanza. Silence is essential to Sexton's dramatic effect, a technique made visible in waveforms of her reading (see figure 3.1, which shows a waveform of Anne Sexton reading "Her Kind").

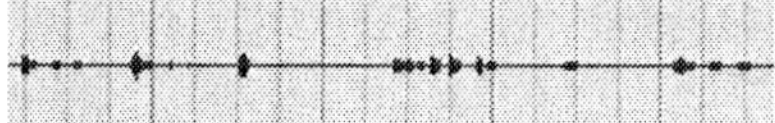

Figure 3.1

This image, based on the Caedmon recording, represents the following lines: "lonely thing, twelve-fingered, out of mind. / A woman like that is not a woman, quite. / I have been her kind" (Sexton, *Selected* 18). The valleys of the form represent the commas, line breaks, and full stops in the poetic lines. If we think of the image as three clusters of hills, each corresponding with a line of poetry, "quite" is the isolated peak between the second and final cluster. As I suggested earlier, Dylan Thomas makes the same use of pauses and silence in the Caedmon recording of "Especially When the October Wind"—the lowering and slowing at the end of the first stanza, the abrupt rise in volume of "Some let me make you..." In both cases, it's as if having acknowledged a dark truth, the poet unleashes energy for the next series of painful observations. As in Millay's reading of "Elegy" and "Renascence," we are always aware that "Her Kind" is a performed text, not only because Sexton's reading is unapologetically dramatic, but also because she draws attention to her text's formal shape. For example, when sounded, the dispersed /ind/ rhymes punctuate the refrain and reinforce the poem's rhetorical mode, proclamation. However, unlike Thomas or Millay, irony is a counterweight to earnestness in Sexton's performance. Here, as in many of Sexton's readings, the breathiness and vibrato of the beautiful throat have been exchanged for a sharp, almost acidic voice. Her most disturbing claim—"A woman like that is not ashamed to die"—is delivered with quiet, frank assuredness.

In listening to Millay, I suggested that intensity conveyed by pace and dynamics was as important to the beautiful throat as the content of the text being performed. This is equally true of Sexton's performance of "Her Kind," which is an aural example for a theory of rhythm she communicated in a 1974 interview with Barbara Kelves. While she considers "images" most important, since they carry the poem's "story," she says that she works hardest at rhythm because it is synonymous with "the feeling, the voice of the poem, and how it will come across, how it will feel to the reader, how it feels to me as it comes out" (101). Feeling, for Sexton, is what connects poem, reader, and poet, and, significantly, she treats the poem's rhythm, feeling and voice as synonymous. In this equation, it is not so much the vivid content of "Her Kind"—the "possessed witch," the flames, the cracking ribs—as the flow of speech that invokes enchantment.

For Sexton, as with Millay, the physicality of voice complements an expressive poetics, one that, through the reading, seeks intimacy between audience and poet. Sexton's reception can be roughly divided between an academic literary culture that approached her largely through print and held her persona in suspicion, and a popular audience that connected with her at readings and felt she spoke to them—often, for them. I want to review, briefly, this divided reception, not to classify Sexton a popular poet misunderstood by the academy, but to reveal the ways in which the reception registers sound—how Sexton was heard and not heard.

Having determined upon poetry as a profession, Sexton sought and received the support of the most influential establishment poets of mid-century, though that support was rarely unqualified. A typical example can be found in a December 1961 letter from Robert Lowell. In response to Sexton's request for his impressions of *All My Pretty Ones,* Lowell writes that the poems are her "version of my *Life Studies* style," but that this derives "from similar experiences not imitation..." (*Letters* 393). He claims that the faults in the book are "unavoidable human limitations," but then lists several that betray his skepticism of Sexton's abilities. For example, the work suffers from a "monotony of tone," and Sexton tends to let "everything in too easily" (393). While there may be some merit to Lowell's critique, it is predicated on a poetics of understated expression—ironically, given the extent to which he was placing his life on stage by 1961. Lowell's criticism portends similar commentary in an infamous review of *All My Pretty Ones* by James Dickey, in which Dickey declares that

> It would be hard to find a writer who dwells more insistently on the pathetic and disgusting aspects of bodily experience, as though this made the writing more real, and it would also be difficult to find a more hopelessly mechanical approach to reporting these matters than the one she employs. (Qtd in McClatchy, *Artist* 106)

Dickey had made similar remarks about *To Bedlam and Part Way Back* in a review that Lowell no doubt knew. Lowell is not offended by Sexton's subject matter, but like Dickey he questions her technique and, patronizingly, suggests that for many of the poems, "all one can say about them is they are Sexton and therefore precious" (*Letters* 393). Poetry and poet are identical in this formulation; what makes the poems "precious"—that they *are* Sexton—also gives Lowell permission to dismiss them.

Implicit in Lowell and Dickey's critiques is skepticism of a poetry that achieves its fullest expression when staged in the voice of the poet. Recalling a 1961 reading by Sexton at Amherst College, William Pritchard is troubled by the fact that an audience might be responding to Sexton herself, rather than her poems. Pritchard describes the reading in his review of Sexton's letters, a review he titled "The Anne Sexton Show." He introduced the poet "to a packed room of awed students who applauded her wildly. She read with spellbinding intensity, to the extent that one wasn't sure just what one was responding to—the poems?—or something else—the life that was all tied up with them?" (Pritchard 390). Again, the reading is depicted as a scene of enchantment. But Pritchard's review is largely contemptuous and sexist, predicting that Sexton will be read less and less, only by a "few unhappy college students, probably female ones" (391). Moreover, like Dickey and, to some extent, Lowell, Pritchard is predisposed not to take Sexton seriously because her voice is too appealing. Reading with "spellbinding intensity" is, ironically, a liability. Pritchard's comment is symptomatic, I would argue, of the institutionalization of a relationship between audio poem and print text that we saw developing in the Library of Congress recordings in chapter one. Print is primary, audio is supplementary at best, and when the reading turns us to the poet, the poem will be lost. It's an ironic position, as we've seen, given that even its staunch advocates recorded their work, and the recording makes the poet's vocalization the primary object of inquiry.

In the commentary of the academic poetic establishment, the supposed tension among the Sexton persona, subject matter, and serious poetic craft would become a major theme. Sound often plays a role in the way critics characterize the problem with Sexton's work, but rarely is it the sound of her poetry as we hear it on record. Reviewing *All My Pretty Ones*, for example, Louise Bogan argued that "to describe fully the dark conflicts of the self without slipping over into the shrill voice of confession or the sobbing note of self-pity requires high control at every conscious and unconscious level" (qtd in McClatchy, *Artist* 126). "Confession" is necessarily "shrill," and "pity" egotistical, for Bogan assumes that a melodramatic soundscape is the borderland of expressive poetry. The spatial metaphor is revealing: Sexton will fail if she slips from the place of "high control." Sexton's performance of "Her Kind" clearly evidenced "high control," but the evidence Bogan seeks is a style that, as M.L. Rosenthal wrote, "purifies" pain (qtd in Colburn 69–70), much as Bogan's alchemist tried to burn away passion. Beside the measured, depersonalized performances valued by academic modernism, Sexton's beautiful throat sounded histrionic, despite her vocal control. Not until the early 1970s, with the growing strength of feminism, did critics consistently write in defense of Sexton primarily on the basis of her daring openness—her supposed lack of restraint. Sandra Gilbert, for example, defends the flaws of *The Death Notebooks*, claiming that Sexton "probably had to cultivate self-absorption, speak in a deliberately naïve or flat tone, risk sentimentality and cuteness, in order to achieve the triumphs of this new collection which, by narrowly skirting melodrama, wins through to a kind of grandeur" (qtd in McClatchy *Artist* 164–65). Gilbert, like Bogan, describes melodrama as a soundscape and the beautiful throat aesthetic as risky in its theatricality and preoccupation with the poet's self. Interestingly, Gilbert maintains that Sexton has succeeded, however "narrowly," because of her indulgence.

Gilbert's apologia for *The Death Notebooks* provides a point of departure for listening to Sexton's recordings from the volume. I have suggested that the darkness and irony of Sexton's performances recast the beautiful throat aesthetic, but Sexton was equally capable of voicing sincerity unapologetically, in the manner of Millay. Her 1974 Caedmon recording of "The Fury of Sunrises" from *Death Notebooks* is a case in point. The poem tracks the gradual progress from darkness—the night's and that of speaker's spirit—to light. It is constructed of a long series of short lines, mostly single, highly descriptive images that have struck the speaker. In Sexton's voice, the poem is clearly cast as an expression of personal experience, but the performance demonstrates Sexton's mastery of her voice as instrument. Reading slowly, marking each end-stop, Sexton modulates the key signature downward in the scale three times in the first eight lines—at "darkness," "the yellow mouth," and "no stars."

She then reverses the modulation, moving upward, accompanied by a crescendo that complements the birdsong she hears:

> the birds in their chains
> going mad with throat noises,
> the birds in their tracks
> yelling into their cheeks like clowns. (*Selected Poems* 214)

While Sexton identifies with this maddening birdsong, she does not ventriloquize it. She pauses after the birds, and beginning at "the stars gone," repeats the modulations and dynamics of the opening. However, with each repetition of "lighter, lighter," which serves as a refrain in the poem, Sexton's voice lightens and her tempo increases. Her technique, I would argue, is intended to pull us closer and to raise us up with her. From darkness and a wish for oblivion, she resolves "not to die, not to die" at the climax of the poem, which coincides with the full break of day. The conceit of the poem is that the speaker's faith is reaffirmed not by the drama of sunrise but by how the light brings back into perspective the pleasures of the quotidian—preparing for breakfast, taking out the dog. Sexton's reading does not so much "cultivate self-absorption" as encourage our "absorption" into the experience of another self.

The gender of that self played an important part in how Sexton's beautiful throat was heard. Janet Badia, in a comparative study of Sexton and Plath's reception, notes that critics such as Irving Howe and James Dickey positioned the "Plath-Sexton reader female, diagnos[ed] her as depressed and sick, and assess[ed] her as an uncritical consumer of bad literature" (241). Whereas many of Sexton's outspoken academic critics diminished her achievement along gender lines, just as they had framed Millay as poetess, Sexton's popular audience tended to do the opposite. For Sexton's popular reception consistently depended on her successful performances of the "Anne" whom Jo Gill portrays in the classroom, the "Sexton" whom Lowell dismissed as "precious," and the enchantress whom Pritchard bridled at: that is, the bold and sexually active middle-class woman, unafraid to speak with "spellbinding intensity" (to borrow from Pritchard) about her experiences as daughter, mother, and wife. As Jane Hedley writes in an essay on Sexton, Lowell, and gender, Sexton's "transgressiveness involved not only her themes or subject matter; it also had to do with the positioning of her poems' aggressively female speakers" (96). Sexton's popular audience embraced her "aggressively female" persona, which was as much a creation of her poetry readings—her look and her voice—as it was of the published poems.

Like Millay, Sexton performed for sold-out audiences and received hundreds of letters from fans, and these letters have been closely analyzed in an essay by Janet E. Luedtke. Noting that the majority of the letters were written by women, Luedtke demonstrates that Sexton's female correspondents read or heard her work as "testimonial":

> [her correspondents] regard it as a testimonial—the striking, affective presentation of one person's story that is meant to be appropriated by the listening community as their collective story. The listener/reader does not simply empathize with the confessing "witness," but instead re-produces the text internally so that the words become the listener's own. And, as the teller experiences catharsis and transcendence by the process of speaking, so does the listening community who "speaks" with her communally. (175)

The reaction Luedtke describes is precisely that sought by Sexton's "Fury of Sunrises" performance. In response to Sexton's vocal effects, we appropriate the experience as our own. Luedtke further observes that in their immediacy, intimacy, and unbridled expressiveness, many of the letters record "visceral reactions to Sexton's work [that] demonstrate its power to effect a catharsis" (177). The model of the testimonial contrasts with Ostriker's "seduction," for the audience and the testifier have entered into a contract. To hear Sexton testify is to hear a version—perhaps a more vibrant, articulate version—of one's own experience of joy or suffering, of pain indulged or overcome. The difference between the metaphors chosen by Ostriker and Luedtke may be explained by the difference in the audience they imagine. Ostriker's is for the most part high-brow and academic, dominated in the 1950s and 1960s by men and by suspicion of the beautiful throat. Luedtke's audience is middle-brow and middle-class. Like the listeners who responded so enthusiastically to Millay's performances, they attended a Sexton reading eager for a personal connection.

Earlier, I claimed that Sexton believed in an essential self that remained just out of reach of her audience. Her readings are a pose, but one developed in the interest of sincere expression. By her own admission, performance caused her to question her ideal of an unmediated self.[12] Deeply involved in psychoanalysis throughout her career, Sexton's was a Lacanian dilemma. A recorder was often her mirror. Diane Middlebrook reports that a basic component of Sexton's therapy was her review of audio recordings of her sessions in order to objectify the self who professed and confessed during analysis. Such close listening was frustrating and painful, often confirming Sexton's fear of being inauthentic. Similarly, when Sexton recalled her performances, she spoke the language of regret and embarrassment. In a letter following a successful reading, she writes apologetically to Snodgrass that she "is a little bit of a ham and I can't seem to cut that out" (*Letters* 163). This regret over self-display contrasts with her claims elsewhere that the performance is merely performance, that it is just a way to "make your living reading…dead and old poetry" (150). Sexton's dismissal of the reading, however, seems defensive, an affected disdain, typical of many poets, for putting art on display. Display was essential to her poetics, as to her success on tour, and Sexton's art of self-display seems often to have ended in emotional trauma. In an interview with Barbara Kelves in 1974, Sexton claimed that giving a reading took "three weeks out of [her] life," first because of her anxieties about the performance, and then because the reading itself was always "a reliving of the experience" in the poem (*No Evil Star* 108).[13] That a reading could be a "reliving" suggests the extent to which Sexton approached reading her work as though it were a script for performance. As Sexton describes it, a reading is at once an act—she is "an actress in [her] own autobiographical play"—and an authentic, even traumatic, return to the scene of suffering that gave rise to the poem (108). That is to say, the reading is a replay of suffering and a resurrection of past selves. It is a re-actualization of a life latent in the poem.

On the subject of the "actual" in performance, Richard Schechner distinguishes between mimetic and actual performance art. Schechner writes that from Aristotle forward, art has been considered to be "the process of transforming raw experience into palatable forms" (6).[14] In traditional and avant-garde performance, by contrast, art is actualized in the performance itself, shared by actors and audience. "Modern Western theatre," he writes, "is mimetic, reactualizing on stage what has occurred elsewhere. Traditional theatre, and again I include the avant-garde in this category, is *transformational,* creating or incarnating in a theatre place what cannot take place anywhere else" (emphasis Schechner's; 119). According to the criteria that Schechner develops here, a poetry reading should be considered mimetic, "reactualizing," and insofar as Sexton's "reliving" suggests repetition, her confessions on stage or record would be scripted acts—to cite Foucault again, variations within a "ritual of discourse." As we saw in her readings of "Her Kind" and "The Fury of Sunrises," the performance is carefully orchestrated—so much so, in fact, that Sexton reads with remarkable consistency over time. However, recalling Jean Luc Nancy's theory of listening, I would argue that "re-actualize" does not adequately account for the presence of an auditor or interlocutor as the reading is carried forward—or repeated in the playing of an audio recording. Sound connects speaker and listener, such that Millay and Sexton's audience professed an authentic experience of engagement with the poet. What Sexton may have experienced as a reliving was, effectively, an actualization from the point of view of reception.

This suggests a different interpretation of Sexton's anxieties about read-ing, one that recalls Elizabeth Bishop's. The poem of private experience, however "cooked," becomes the raw material of self-actualization when the poet speaks it to her listeners. The private self is immaterial, literally, while the poem's content, the poet's look and voice, and audience's interac-tions recreate Anne Sexton. Near the end of her life, Sexton wrote a vitri-olic attack on the poetry reading, calling it "the freak show." Her essay by that name is discursive and cantankerous, but it is a testament to Sexton's anxieties about her own popularity. In it, she describes poetry as sacred and intimate, "the handwriting on the tablet of the soul...the most private, deepest, most precious part of us." Why, she wonders, are poets "asked to make a show of it?" (35). Most of the audience, she asserts, comes to see the "freak" and knows little about her verse. Questioning that characterization of her listeners, Luedtke argues that Sexton developed it late in her career, as her illness became more pronounced and she became increasingly disil-lusioned with her work (167). One fan, Diane Vruels Friebert, who had attended the reading Sexton describes in "The Freak Show," wrote a furi-ous response to Sexton's essay. She defends the earnestness of her fellow audience members and argues that they did not come to "see a crazy lady falling off a podium," nor did they "come as executioners. We came to hear your living voice" (qtd in Luedtke 186). Listening to Sexton, for this writer, was a means to connect, and in a deeply apologetic response, Sexton pleads, "I want you. I need you. There are few of you...For those I would climb a rope ladder or even crawl on stage on hands and knees and as I said in my column, 'read my God-damned heart out'" (*Letters* 398). Sexton wants and needs them because they authenticate her "living voice"—the voice that, as she would have it, comes from the heart.

I would argue that as versions of the beautiful throat, what Sexton's performances bring most clearly into focus are these questions about the nature of the self as relational—to the audience and to past selves. In a psy-choanalytic study of Sexton's poetry, Diane Hume George identifies five different "I's" or personae and maintains that for Sexton, as for Whitman and other poets who sing the self, the "poem can only grope in the direc-tion of the secret life" (96). Sexton's performance of "Music Swims Back To Me"—recorded in 1959 and 1974—dramatizes her first recognition of the self as an other. In this respect, the poem in performance recalls Millay's "Renascence"—the poet re-embodies an earlier version of the self. Speaking to an unnamed "Mister," she hears music that calls back to mind her first night in the "institution on a hill." Surreal imagery, cir-cular thinking, and a voice of naïve surprise re-actualize an experience of disorientation. For example, when reading "and everyone here was crazy," Sexton raises her pitch, lightens the mood, and laughs, her voice cracking on that last word; the effect is especially pronounced in the Caedmon reading. At her best, as here, Sexton communicates the feeling of an experience being relived. Katha Pollitt observes that "Sexton's poems about her hospitalizations . . . are sadder, humbler, less literary than Lowell's—closer, one feels, to the inmate's sense of infantilization in the face of psychiatric authority and the madness itself" (qtd in Wagner-Martin 68). Pollitt, like many others, implies that the "less literary" is more authentic, and on the whole, she characterizes Sexton's work as too "histrionic" (68). But the "sense of infantilization" in "Music" comes across most clearly in Sexton's measured theatricality, as when she calls out "Wait Mister" in a voice that echoes the prototypical kid from the Golden Age of Hollywood film.

There is an irony here that, as I have argued, balances the sentimentality so closely identified with Millay's version of the beautiful throat. There is no vibrato in this voice, and sternness is a ballast for expressions of melancholy and sweetness, as we heard in "Her Kind." But these vocal registers are still essential to Sexton, and among the available Sexton recordings, those of her reading "The Truth the Dead Know" best illustrate how she successfully negotiates between irony and sentiment, both in her poetics and in her performance. The poem was first published in the *Hudson Review* in 1961, but Sexton had been recorded reading it on at least two occasions before publication: at a reading at Harvard on December 8, 1959, and at Fassett Recording Studio in Boston in May 1960.[15] Of these two, the most intriguing is the first, for Sexton reads an unpublished manuscript that is substantially different from the published variant. According to Sexton's biographer Diane Middlebrook, Sexton had begun corresponding and exchanging poems with James Wright in February 1960, and Wright had "a direct influence on several of the poems," including "The Truth the Dead Know," which along with "A Curse Against Elegies" may have begun as a poem called "Refusal" (128–30). At the Harvard event, after she reads the poem's title, Sexton explains that "it was written after my father's funeral, which was just three months after my mother's." The first stanza is the same as the published variant. The rest differs remarkably. Sexton reads the poem in a tired, dark voice, with very little shift in dynamic range until the final line, in which the dead are said to "mutter, 'Live now, live now'" (Sexton "Truth"). On the whole, it is an unremarkable performance, just as the manuscript itself is a lesser version of the poem.[16]

Between the time of this reading and the poem's publication, Sexton alters the opening of stanza two. Having originally called herself a "blushing hermit" before the sun, she dismisses the hackneyed trope to place emphasis on a more powerful image of the sun "guttering." She builds tension into the second stanza by changing the final line—a largely positive proclamation of young love in the early version becomes "and we touch," followed by "In another country people die" (43). The irony here is perhaps too easy, but it is characteristic of Sexton's work, and it initiates the juxtaposition of romance and suffering that arises again in the third stanza. In the Harvard reading, "Touch" at the end of the second line had originally been both a means of unity and a sign of singularity: we are "twice marked and twice alone." Compared to this koan, Sexton's revisions simplify the message, and the second and third lines of stanza three become the thematic center of the poem: physical connection reminds us that we're never fully alone. This is evident in how she reads the lines in the May 1960 recording. She pauses, as though for a full stanza break, before reading "and when we touch," and then again before "No one's alone." That becomes a declaration of faith—the "when" or moment of touch being the moment of recovery from mourning. Of the changes Sexton makes, those in the final stanza are the most perceptive and are characteristic of her better verse. She deletes a macabre carpe diem of the manuscript, in which the corpses speak through "tiny smiles" arranged, presumably, by an embalmer. Instead, she closes the poem with a cold existentialism that communicates the message "live now" by sheer contrast with the warmth of her momentary escape with her "darling."

Like the print version, Sexton's last audio version—again, for Caedmon in 1974—is superior to the readings from 1959 to 1960. It is most suitable to the poem, which Bogan might have warned borders on melodrama, tipping into it at the end of the first stanza with "I am tired of being brave," but pulling back with the darkness of the last. That is to say, Sexton does not seem inhibited by a fear of the histrionic. Confident in her performance, she manages the poem's emotional sincerity and its irony equally. As an audio work, the poem's most sentimental moment— its claim about "touch"—has particular resonance. Sexton and her lover "enter touch entirely": it is a claim that the "we" is preferable to the "I." What Sexton attributes to touch in the poem is carried forward by speech and listening in her reading. Speaking and being heard actualize the self inside another.

★　★　★

The aesthetic of the beautiful throat and the examples of Millay and Sexton indicate that in studies of twentieth-century expressive poetry, the audio archive has vital role to play. Moreover, the aural traces of these poets—both on record and in the response of listeners—bring acutely into focus how authenticity and sincerity are negotiated in performance. Listening to Millay, we are confronted by the shifting grounds of reception, by the fact that what was heard and appreciated then differs from now. I have argued, however, that while we need to take Millay's "deliberate grand manner" seriously, as her listeners did, we're also right to recognize her self-consciousness. In her performances, Sexton often perfected that balance of sincerity and irony, and her vocal effects were received as authentic expression by her listeners. Near the end of her life, Sexton sought to guard against full identification with the "Anne" of page, stage, or record, but as I listen to her recordings now, she proves most effective when she sets out to connect with us, to pull us into the world she inhabits, one in which the self is conflicted but sincere in its desires. In this respect, she is the forerunner of poets such as Sharon Olds and Annie Finch, whose work and readings resemble hers.[17]

For Sexton and Millay's listeners alike, the voice of the poet carries the self. Like Millay's, Sexton's readings were transformative experiences, even for skeptical listeners, and our study of her work should therefore include close listening to her recordings in the context of her critical heritage. I end with an example of just such a listener, Muriel Rukeyser, who, like Sandra Gilbert and Adrienne Rich, deeply appreciated Sexton's groundbreaking content but worried that unchecked confession compromises artifice. In a 1973 review in *Parnassus,* Rukeyser recalls hearing Sexton read at the Guggenheim Museum in New York. At the end of a poem (Rukeyser cannot recall the title), Sexton declared "But it is not true" (qtd in McClatchy, *Artist* 155). To Rukeyser, this indicated a self-awareness she had not recognized in Sexton before hearing her. "She had cut through the entire nonsense about confessional writing," Rukeyser claims, "and returned me to the poem" (155). That is to say, Sexton's earnest reading, followed by her ironic disclaimer, had called attention to the poem as artifice, which is not to say artificial. She had made "the long walk out the other side of the struggle, madness, into the other struggle, to use madness" (160). Audiences will, Rukeyser admits, gladly consume pure confession, but they won't be "nourished" by it (160). Like many of Millay and Sexton's listeners, then and now, Rukeyser is nourished by the poetry of personal experience artfully rendered in the poet's voice. Listening connects her to poet and poem, and involves her in the revitalization of both.

CHAPTER 4

IMPERSONATIONS: POETS, PREACHERS, TEACHERS, AND THE REMAKING OF *GOD'S TROMBONES*

The old-time Negro preacher is rapidly passing. I have here tried sincerely to fix something of him.

—James Weldon Johnson, Preface to *God's Trombones*

The aesthetic of the beautiful throat brings to the surface a value that, I have argued, is fundamental to the audio archive: that the voice of the poet is the primary voice in which a poem should be performed, heard, and preserved. But while recorded modernism privileges the poet's reading of her work, forms such as the dramatic monologue, vernacular writing, multi-vocal poems, and documentary pastiche often position the poet outside of the poem she speaks, or within the poem as the voice of another. I want to propose that as recorded speech, audio poems in the latter category—which I will call voice impersonations—demand particular attention.

The impersonation in performance differs from poetry spoken "in first person," for the poet seeks to make present not necessarily a version of himself but the self of another. While any performance in character or "in persona" might be considered a mode of impersonation, I distinguish voice impersonation as the poet's attempt to re-actualize another by closely imitating the form and content of her characteristic discourse. Whether the subject is a London barmaid or Southern preacher, voice impersonation, I suggest, is procedurally similar to translation, insofar as the translator speaks for another or rewrites her text, attempting to capture essential semantic content as it is conveyed by the full range of another's linguistic expression. Assuming that a text's meanings lie beneath language, Walter Benjamin argued that the successful translation seeks to be transparent. To allow the original to manifest fully in the new language, it hews close to the "original's mode of signification," even to the point of a "literal rendering of the syntax" (81). Voice impersonation makes a similar attempt at transparency through close imitation, and we might equate the self or character of the impersonated with Benjamin's "meaning." On these terms, the ideal voice impersonation would be an echo, the inevitable distortion kept to a minimum by the quality of the poet's performance.

Of course, neither translation nor impersonation can be fully transparent. Post-structuralism poses a challenge to Benjamin's position, in that meaning is an effect of the play of language, not an essence toward which it gestures. Moreover, the translator cannot simply mime the original, for his own language and culture are always already implicated in the mimesis. According to Lawrence Venuti, the translator's response must be to make himself fully visible by drawing attention to his moves as translator and to the choices he makes in recasting the original (498–99). I would argue that the tension here—between on the one hand believing in the integrity of the original and desiring to be transparent, and on the other recognizing the limits of imitation and laying bare one's methods— surfaces in the work of the poet as voice impersonator. Interest in the sounds of another, often in her regional speech and particular linguistic and rhetorical patterns, motivates close approximation, but imperson- ation inevitably involves the reinscription of another's voice. In listen- ing to an impersonation from the archive, we are compelled to consider the impersonator's intent, the qualities of the impersonation, and their effects. Among modernist recordings, voice impersonation takes many forms, from Eliot's Cockney maid in *The Waste Land* (1922) to the imita- tion of local voices in Williams' *Paterson* (1948–56) and Rukeyser's "Book of the Dead" from *U.S. 1* (1938). But as in the previous chapters, I will focus here on a particular example that draws to it a host of recordings and audible traces: James Weldon Johnson's *God's Trombones: Seven Negro Sermons in Verse* (1927). Just as listening to Millay and Sexton provided a model for studying archival recordings of poetry "in first person," espe- cially those in the tradition of the beautiful throat, I intend this chapter to be a model for using audio and a text's aural reception to address modern- ist poetry performed in the voice of another.

As performance pieces, James Weldon Johnson's impersonations of the "old-time negro preacher" never failed to please audiences, as Johnson once attested to his editor, Marshall Best. Across their rich reception his- tory, these poems were as often encountered aurally as visually, notwith- standing the fact that the first edition of *God's Trombones* was a finely wrought work of modernist book art. In pages ahead, I will describe many of the significant ways that the poetry was heard, from Johnson's readings of "The Creation" in the studio in the mid-1920s to commercial recordings of dramatic renderings from the early 1970s. Drawing on theoretical models of oral composition and on Johnson's writings on dialect and folk culture, I will examine the relationship between the voice and style of preachers recorded in the early twentieth century and Johnson's fictitious black preacher—both the voice Johnson impersonated in print and in 1938 Musicraft recordings of the *God's Trombones* poems. The differential effects between live and studio recordings will again come into play as I consider the spontaneously composed audio sermon and Johnson's crafted impersonations. Like the field recordings of preachers from the first half of the twentieth century, Johnson's efforts were in part archival, and I will show that Johnson's effort to "fix something" of the black preacher—to save him from oblivion, but also to "fix" his rough, often parodied art—was redoubled by mass culture, where sounding *God's Trombones* became a pastime of both popular musicians and speech and rhetoric instructors in the U.S. public school (*God's Trombones* 841). As in Johnson's own work, preservation entailed revisions that would make the art of black preaching palatable for a largely white audience, and the audio legacy of *God's Trombones* illustrates how impersonations take on their own life, distinct from either the poet or his original subject.

Imitating Composition-in-Performance, Impersonating Vernacular

"The Creation" is a noisy poem. God bats his eyes, claps his hands, and shouts nature into existence. Ironically, he creates less by speaking than in the familiar priestly version from the opening of Genesis, for Johnson's purpose is to attune our ears not to God's words but to the drama and poetry of the preacher's voice. According to Johnson's accounts in his preface to *God's Trombones* and in his autobiography *Along This Way* (1931), "The Creation"—the first of the *God's Trombones* poems— originated in his own ecstatic reaction to hearing an evangelist. Johnson was on a lecture tour on behalf of the NAACP in 1918, raising awareness of the findings in the organization's *Thirty Years of Lynching in the United States*. Many of these lectures were given in small churches, and it was in such a church in Kansas City that Johnson was "perhaps against [his] will, deeply moved" by a sermon (*God's Trombones* 838). After a dull beginning, which Johnson attributes to nervousness in the presence of "distinguished guests," the preacher shuts his Bible and begins "intoning the old folk-sermon that begins with the creation of the world and ends with the Judgment Day":

> He was at once a changed man, free, at ease and masterful. The change in the congregation was instantaneous. An electric current ran through the crowd. It was in a moment alive and quivering; and all the while the preacher held it in the palm of his hand. He was wonderful in the way he employed his conscious and unconscious art. He strode the pulpit up and down in what was actually a very rhythmic dance, and he brought into play the full gamut of his voice, a voice—what shall I say?—not of an organ or a trumpet, but rather of a trombone, the instrument possessing above all others the power to express the wide and varied range of emotions encompassed by the human voice—and with greater amplitude. He intoned, he moaned, he pleaded,—he blared, he crashed, he thundered. I sat fascinated; and more, I was, perhaps against my will, deeply moved; the emotional effect upon me was irresistible. (837–38)

Johnson describes the sermon as a performance, which, as Richard Bauman has argued, "involves on the part of the performer an assumption of accountability to an audience for the way in which communication is carried out, above and beyond its referential content" (11). The dynamic between audience and performer is familiar to us from the previous chapter, and like Millay and Sexton's audience, Johnson finds himself "deeply moved" by the vocal effects of the performer. Johnson and the congregation respond to the "act of expression itself," to use Bauman's phrasing, as well as to what is being expressed. While the preacher's staging is fundamental, it is not just his persona but, as Bauman explains, the sermon that emerges from an interplay of planned and unplanned elements mediated by the congregation. It is significant that Johnson describes the preacher's art as both "conscious and unconscious." His performance is based on formulae—a dramatic closing of the Bible, a stepping out from behind the pulpit, an invoking of a sermon with elements that everyone knows—and its success depends on the preacher's mastery of these. The "instantaneous" change in the congregation is in part a sign of recognition: now they are going to get what they came for. Within this conscious structure, however, the preacher gains emotional freedom, expressed most effectively in the dynamic range and varied modes of his voice. His sermon is "intoned"—Johnson uses the word twice, and many years later Carl Van Vechten would use it when referring to how Johnson himself read "The Creation." But before turning to Johnson as a performer of his sermons in verse, I want to consider more fully his response as a congregant in light of recent theories of the sermon as "composition-in-performance."[1]

When Johnson impersonates the preacher, he likewise imitates the poetics of the folk sermon. The sermon is his preacher's characteristic discourse, and translating it into verse requires an understanding of its discursive structures. What Johnson calls "Negro preaching" has been the subject of several anthropological and linguistic studies that seek to describe the folk preacher's compositional process and the structure of his sermon, the two being inextricably intertwined. For many of these studies, Albert Lord's analysis of oral composition, particularly his concepts "formula" and "theme," has proven useful. In *The Singer of Tales* (1988), a study of the Serbo-Croatian epic singer, Lord argues that oral poetry is built of formula, or repeated phrases, and themes, or clusters of formulae that express a particular idea or problem. Over time, formulae and themes recur and modulate, as oral poets receive and remake them. Becoming a poet initially involves close listening and imitation and eventually includes interaction with a critical audience. Bruce Rosenberg applies Lord's theories to the American folk preacher. The "chanted sermon"—Bruce Rosenberg's name for the kind of sermon that Johnson experienced—is "spontaneously composed, orally presented, and metrically ordered" (10). The sense of spontaneity—that sermon and response alike rise up from the fervent spirit of the moment—belies the skilled preacher's invocation of traditional formulae and themes, his echoing and even parodying of popular sermons, and his careful cultivation of personal cues and phrases that buy time and remind him of what might come next in the tale he's spinning. This is not to say that there is nothing new under the sun, or that the preacher has succumbed to the anxiety of influence; but students of performed sermons, like those of traditional oral poetries, have noticed the particular importance of intertextual reference and generic frameworks in the onstage composition of these works. This onstage composition is what Gregory Nagy calls "composition-in-performance" and has proven to be common to oral literatures across time and place. Referring to the epic poet in the Homeric tradition, Nagy argues that

> each occurrence of a theme (on the level of content) or of a formula (on the level of form) in a given composition-in-performance refers not only to its immediate context but also to all other analogous contexts remembered by the performer or by any member of the audience. (50)

The sermon, no less than the poem, is situated in a literary and performance history, one that the congregation knows and the preacher invokes.[2]

The folk sermon is transactional, partially dependent on the live event, and Johnson was keenly aware of how this limited his impersonations.

As Johnson implies in the preface, he and the Kansas City congregation expected to encounter specific traditions and tropes, what Gerald Davis has called "ideal forms and ideal standards," and responded to their artful representation (26). Acknowledging the role of the audience in the composition-in-performance of the sermon, Johnson regrets that he is unable to recreate in his own work "the fervor of the congregation, the amens and hallelujahs, the undertone of singing which was often a soft accompaniment to parts of the sermon," though as we shall see performances of *God's Trombones* often incorporated some or all of these (*Trombones* 840). Davis considers the audience an integral part of the composition process in the "African-American narrative performance":

> During a performance, when both "performer" and "audience" are actively locked into a dynamic exchange, the audience compels the performer to acknowledge the most appropriate characteristics of the genre system—the ideal in terms of that particular performance environment—before permitting the performer sufficient latitude for the individuation of his genius and style. (26)

Certainly Johnson's awakening was part of such a dynamic exchange, and responses to Johnson's own performances of *God's Trombones*—responses that I will discuss in detail later in the chapter—indicate that a version of this exchange took place when he read from his work.

While spectacle, tradition, and audience play a role in the performed sermon, the preacher's voice is the instrument "above all others" in importance, and the experience of the sermon is fundamentally aural. In an essay on the writing down of ancient oral texts, Roger Chartier describes a dilemma that Johnson faced in his project to "fix" the African American sermon. The "transformation of ritual event into poetic monument," Chartier writes, "had considerable consequences": "The most fundamental of these was the introduction of a gap between the circumstances of actual enunciation...and the fictional scene of enunciation in the poem itself, which reflected a vanished situation..." (59). Where the live ritual actualizes sermon and preacher, the "poetic monument" will depend on a reading—at best, an oral reading—to re-actualize them. Johnson was anxious about the "vanished situation" of his sermons-in-verse—the scene of the church under the spell of the evangelist—but sought ways to compensate. Acknowledging that his poems would be better "intoned than read," Johnson provided cues for oral performance in his preface to *God's Trombones*, in his careful imitations of sermon style in the structure of the poems, and in his actual performances of the poetry. I will turn next to recordings of African American preachers from the early twentieth century and to Johnson's own recording of his poems, in order to consider what Johnson may have heard, how he impersonated it, and how and why he sought to elevate it. For Johnson's goal was not merely to celebrate an African American cultural form, but to raise it to the status of art—a goal that betrays his assumptions about the very art form he sought to honor and that influenced the nature of his (and subsequent) performances.

Bearing in mind that Johnson wrote the poems from *God's Trombones* in two bursts of activity during the 1920s,[3] and read them frequently throughout the next decade, I will focus on African American preachers from the era whose recordings are still commercially available.[4] The first are studio sessions by a popular preacher from Mount Calvary Church in Atlanta, Ga., Reverend James M. Gates. Gates recorded with Columbia in the 1920s and 1930s, and his recordings sold in the tens of thousands. Although elements of Gates' performances seem staged for recording— for example, in lieu of a church, he is often provided with an amen corner consisting of Sisters Jordan and Norman and Deacon Leon Davis—it is nonetheless clear that his sermons arise in the moment, preached to a virtual congregation he imagines beyond the studio walls. His sermon "The End of the World and Time Will Be No More," recorded October 3, 1927, is typical and built on common formulae and themes that Johnson uses in "The Judgment Day." Gates begins in a conversational voice, subdued and matter-of-fact. The transcription and line breaks are mine:

> Uh, children, as I look at this great number this morning
> It brings this great subject to my mind
> The end of the world
> When time will be no more

With this last phrase, Gates begins to intone, his voice trembling slightly. The sisters offer "amens."

> As I look at this great congregation this morning
> It tells me that a time will come
> When there will not be a living being on this globe
> The end of the world,
> When time shall be no more

Little content is added here, but much is happening that points us to the poetics of the sermon. Gerald Davis writes that "circularity" is an essential organizing principle of the African American sermon, allowing the preacher to build his themes gradually as he pulls together Biblical allusion and sermon formulae (28). As Gates preaches, the circularity also proves essential to pace, the building of intensity and of volume. In the following lines, Gates increases tempo by launching off of his slant-rhymed couplet into a series of short lines; in each, his voice swoops upward to the final word:

> There will be a time
> When the sun will refuse to shine,
> And the moon will run down in blood,
> And some shall fall
> As a peach tree casts an untimely fruit
> When she is shaken by a mighty wind

Gates' text is Revelation 6:13, no doubt spoken from memory and cleverly altered to suit his imagined Southern congregation—figs become peaches, and "some" in his audience, rather than the stars, are destined to fall.[5] By now Gates is intoning loudly, his voice cracking and angry. He chants at this high pitch, at times almost singing, for several lines:

> There was one theologian said the sun
> Will be three hours high,
> One for the Father,
> And one for the Son,
> And one for the Holy Ghost three in one.
> I don't know
> I don't know
> I don't know about this hour
> But I'm prepared to meet my God.
> Ahh, there will come a time
> When the old rocks will melt,
> Ahh and the mountains will reel and rock like a drunken man,
> And the earth will have a spasmodic fit.
> There'll come a time
> When the dead in Christ shall rise,
> Get up, out of the sleeping grave,
> Come moving into judgment
> Ohohh-uh, there'll come a time
> The end of the world
> When time shall be no more.
> Can you hear me over in my [sound distorted]

At this point, Gates bursts into the chorus of "When the Saints Go Marching In," following cues from his two congregants, the "sisters," who have been singing throughout this ecstatic portion of the sermon. Together with Deacon Davis they sing two verses of the hymn, punctuated by Gates' proclamation that no matter whether you're "high or low, rich or poor, white or black / you'll be there when they crown him Lord of All."

Transcription diminishes the art and effect of Gates' sermons, but the look of the text is suggestive. It is a poem, and I would argue that Johnson recognized this in his Kansas experience. While he impersonates another—a preacher whose belief he no longer shares—difference is, to some extent, mitigated not only by Johnson's sense of relationship to the preacher as an African American, but also by their shared artistry. In my transcription, I have attempted through lineation and punctuation to represent Gates' pacing, if not precisely his rhythm. But many integral sounds—his vocal qualities, hums, grunts, and vibrato; the equally diverse responses of his "congregants"; the spinet, slightly off-key—are silenced. Beyond the sounds of the event, there is the steady hiss of the record, a sound that now signifies "historic." As we saw in chapter two, recordings bring to the event ambient noises that, in the moment of listening, become part of the experience. The experience of the recording per se notwithstanding, Johnson worried about such aural matters in the print representation of a sermon. "There is, of course, no way," he laments in the preface to *God's Trombones*, "of recreating the atmosphere…nor the gestures of the preacher—his physical magnetism, his gestures and gesticulations, his changes of tempo, his pauses for effect, and, more than all, his tones of voice" (840). "More than all"—Johnson believed that when preacher and congregation were "swept away" by the sounds of the inspired voice, the sermon became "not prose but poetry" (837). To say that Gates' art aspires to the condition of music would hardly be an exaggeration, for his lines in performance often become precisely that.

Johnson's ear for the poetics of the sermons he had heard is evident in his own end-of-time sermon, "The Judgment Day." The poem includes many of the structural elements and sampling from Biblical apocalyptic texts that we've found in Gates:

> In that great day,
> People, in that great day,
> God's a-going to rain down fire.
> God's a-going to sit in the middle of the air
> To judge the quick and the dead. (865)

The repetition of "God's a-going," in this section and throughout the opening, has both thematic and compositional purposes, much like

Gates' variations on "there will be a time." On judgment day, human free will ends, and God takes charge, dividing the "sheep from the goats" (866). The refrain drives home the message that all agency, in the end, belongs to a judge who will "stop up his ears" to the pleas of the wicked (867). Insofar as "Judgment Day" is an imitation of a "composition in performance," however, the refrain has an additional, structural purpose. It organizes composition, structures its unfolding. We are to imagine the preacher building up to these lines, marking the pace of his sermon with an emphatic repetition of the sermon's essential message about the agency of God. Much of what Johnson's preacher declares that God will do comes from Revelation, as did Gates' text, though Johnson weaves in allusions to the valley of dry bones from Ezekiel. The moon bleeds in both sermons, and the earth melts. Indeed "Judgment Day" is arguably the purest imitation among the *God's Trombones* sermons. Unlike "Let My People Go" or "Noah Built The Ark," its message is exclusively religious, and because we know that as an agnostic Johnson had no evangelical designs on his audience, the purpose of this sermon seems to be mimesis: to mime the sermon of an old-time Negro preacher.

While with the aid of Gates, we can imagine the "voice tones" of Johnson's judgment-day preacher, those tones do not translate into print (840). There is, however, another significant component of the preacher's sound that Johnson chose not to represent, even though print has the potential to do so: the preacher's vernacular or dialect. After having been an admirer and writer of dialect verse, Johnson came to consider it a flawed practice for African Americans who wanted to raise the status of black literature; "a-going" and an occasional "ev'ry" are the only examples of vernacular representation in *God's Trombones*. At the turn of the century, Johnson's artistic career had been launched with songs such as "Run, Brudder Possum, Run," "Nobody's Lookin' but the Owl and the Moon," and "Congo Love Song," all composed with his brother Rosamond and Robert Cole for Broadway and off-Broadway musicals. He had emulated Paul Laurence Dunbar, and most of his early poems are in dialect, including some that he would publish in *Fifty Years & Other Poems*, despite his change of heart about representing black speech in nonstandard English.

That change of heart began, he claims in *Along This Way*, in the summer of 1900 when he read *Leaves of Grass*. Johnson seems to have read Whitman as the quintessentially American poet, the democratic voice, a convention that was already well-established by the time he would have turned to "Song of Myself." While reading Whitman, "I got a sudden realization of the artificiality of conventionalized Negro dialect poetry," he writes,

> of its exaggerated geniality, childish optimism, forced comicality, and mawkish sentiment; of its limitation as an instrument of expression to but two emotions, pathos and humor...I could see that the poet writing in the conventionalized dialect, no matter how sincere he might be, was dominated by his audience; that his audience was a section of the white American reading public; that when he wrote he was expressing what often bore little relation, sometimes no relation at all, to actual Negro life; that he was really expressing only certain conceptions about Negro life that his audience was willing to accept and ready to enjoy; that, in fact, he wrote mainly for the delectation of an audience that was an outside group. (*Along* 306)

We may speculate that Johnson here attributes to a youthful epiphany a complex argument against dialect writing that actually took him decades to develop fully. As Caroline Gebhard has argued, Johnson's story of how he came to disown dialect writing is difficult to separate from his rivalry with Dunbar. Certainly, the sentiments recorded in *Along This Way* can be found in his letters, in his introduction to the *Book of American Negro Poetry* (1922) and in the preface to *God's Trombones* (1927). But the fact that Johnson revisits this argument so frequently across his career suggests the strength of his opposition, who demanded that he uphold his side of the "racial contract" in representing "actual Negro life."[6] "Actual," under the terms of this contract, meant according to acceptable codes, such as those made popular by Dunbar. As George Hutchinson has pointed out, "using marks of race, as in most dialect poetry, just for the sake of marking race and dividing audiences—or dividing speakers and audiences—went against [Johnson's] grain" (337). Hutchinson maintains that Johnson sought "interracial communion in the experience of art," but in dialect poetry, black writers principally served the dish their white readers delighted in (337).

That dialect poetry was not so clearly a sell out to white tastes has been the topic of several revisionist critical efforts.[7] I would argue that by avoiding dialect, Johnson shrewdly recognized a danger inherent in impersonations of black speech patterns. Regardless of his benign intent, to compose a sermon in verse in vernacular was to risk associating it with pernicious stereotypes of blackness. But Johnson was also clearly concerned that something was lost in African American writing, such as his own sermons in verse, when black vernacular was not represented—indeed, when the folk voice was flattened out into standard English. What might have happened, Johnson speculates, if "Negro dialect...had come to [Dunbar] fresh and plastic," unencumbered by stereotype and malleable (*Along* 306)? For Johnson, the temptation to experiment is great but must be resisted until, as he writes in "The Dilemma of the Negro Author" (1928), there comes "a breaking up and remodeling of most of white America's traditional stereotypes, forced by the advancement of the Negro in the various phases of our national life..." (751). In the present "phase" of art, African American interests would be most quickly advanced by poets who successfully assimilated black concerns and forms to recognized models of high art—what Marcellus Blount calls Johnson's "strategies of authentication" (590). Johnson would say as much to Dunbar, who would defend his own decisions as pragmatic, but whose chief ambition, Johnson surmises, was to write an epic "in straight English that would relate to the Negro" (*Along* 308).

Whether or not Johnson was right about Dunbar, his comments on dialect poetry not only indicate his awareness that the reception of black writing was racialized; they also betray his own doubts that the sermon was an art fully equivalent to the poetry he most admired. Fahamisha Patricia Brown writes that

> For James Weldon Johnson, African American folk and popular art form the basis for the creation of serious art, but are not themselves serious art. Using the critical standards of his day—of established cultural arbiters—he cannot affirm African American cultural production on its own terms, even as he acknowledges its merits. (10)

For Johnson, the sermon could not in its own right compete with the art of a Whitman. While he defended ragtime and the Negro spiritual as the "gift of the Negro" to U.S. and European high culture, he argued that the "production of genuine Aframerican folk art must, sooner or later, cease" and be replaced by the work of "Negro artists" who moved above and beyond it (*Negro Spirituals* 741). Johnson felt that this would be easier for painters and musicians than poets, whose principal medium was fraught by the popularity of dialect and whose charge it would be to deal in "racial themes." But, Johnson argues, "the sooner they [young African American poets] are able to write American poetry spontaneously, the better" (*Negro Poetry* 713). American poetry is presumably a literature that rises above racial concerns and does not include the actual sermons of the old-time Negro preacher, no matter how effective his voice or poetical his lines. Johnson seems to have held these things in tension: the African American artist must express his "racial spirit" and shed light on his culture's contributions, and he must rise above both.

In this regard, Johnson's impersonation of the preacher is an effort at improvement—at a "fix." It is arguable that even as Johnson hears the preacher's poetry, he underestimates the preacher's and the dialect poet's "mastery of form," as Houston Baker puts it—their self-conscious donning of racialized tropes and traditional forms as signifying masks (41). In such terms, Brown makes a strong case for Dunbar's "Ante-Bellum Sermon," the use of vernacular there being instrumental in Dunbar's development of a double-consciousness. Certainly, as we've seen in James Gates' sermon, performed naïvete—"I don't know, I don't know, I don't know"—signifies its opposite: an absolute certainty that the end of time respects no racial or economic differences, even if the preacher cannot say when that end will finally arrive. Furthermore, that naïvete belies the preacher's fluent limning of Revelations. But in the following pages, I will argue that in his performances of his most widely admired sermons in verse, "The Creation" and "Go Down, Death," Johnson carefully reintegrated the sounds of the preacher, including vernacular speech— "carefully," in that his oral imitations of the preacher are restrained. Emotion is tempered; poetic and elocutionary elegance trump raw expressiveness. I will argue that his performances set a precedent that was carried forward across the reception history of *God's Trombones*, in which readers and interpreters remade the work, much as Johnson had remade the African American sermon, in order to "fix something of" the old-time Negro preacher. That fix resulted in impersonations of the preacher and imitations of his sermons largely distinct from the folk preaching that had inspired Johnson.

Sounding and Responding to *God's Trombones*

Johnson's performances of *God's Trombones*—both the recordings and the aural traces of his readings—are critical to the study of his project, in that they lift his impersonation of the preacher off the page and literalize it. In performance, Johnson embodies his "old time Negro preacher." By all accounts, Johnson read his sermons in verse regularly for friends and family and for audiences who attended the hundreds of lectures he gave in churches, schools, and conference halls. Carl Van Vechten, who was among Johnson's closest friends, recalled hearing him intone "The Creation" many times, "one evening after dinner at HIS apartment before the enthusiasm of Clarence Darrow and Newman Levy; several times at my apartment; certainly on one occasion when Paul Robeson sang 'Let My People Go' and 'Little David, Play on your Harp'...."[8] Johnson provides similar accounts in *Along This Way,* adding that Robeson read "The Creation" and "Listen, Lord," and that the first audience for "Go Down, Death" were his and Grace's Thanksgiving dinner guests (*Along* 554–58). In his correspondence are dozens of requests for him to lecture and read his poetry at high school graduation ceremonies and literary contests, such as the one at the Germantown Friends' School on March 5, 1937, where Johnson gave an "address on the contribution of the Negro to the literary culture of America" and read from his sermons in verse.[9] Not unlike Edna St. Vincent Millay, who was his neighbor at Five Acres, Johnson was a poet with a mass audience by the late 1920s, an audience that wanted to hear him perform his work.[10]

What did Johnson's audience hear, or put differently, how did they listen to Johnson's readings? In the poet's correspondence there are a few intriguing clues. On April 12, 1936, Johnson read "The Creation" in the second half of a Fisk University Singers concert, broadcast in England over NBC radio. Writing to his Viking editor Marshall Best, Johnson indicates that he received around forty letters, half of which asked whether *God's Trombones* could be purchased in England. A "Miss" M. Price-Morgan of Swansea, for example, asked "if it is possible for me to have a copy of that beautiful & so real a composition called 'Creation,' so that I can read & enjoy the beautiful lines once more, in my solitude" (Price-Morgan). Her earnestness echoing the letters of Millay's listeners, Ms. Price-Morgan is so moved by the "beautiful lines" that she wants to relive the experience; one imagines her reading "The Creation" aloud in her "solitude." This is analogous to what Louis Untermeyer claims about his reading of Johnson's "resonant renderings of Negro sermons": "in my private capacity as a mere reader, I expect to return to the volume again and again." Price-Morgan and Untermeyer describe a kind of religious experience, brought on by a form of devotion—the repeated reading of Johnson's sermons in verse in solitude. Writing about the connection between religious experience and aurality, Leigh Eric Schmidt describes prayer as at once an experience of speaking and listening. As in all "Religious ways of knowing that emphasize the aliveness of sounds," prayer and scripture reading immerse the faithful "in inescapable relationships of exchange" with another (the evangelist, gospel writer, God) that are carried out orally and aurally (35). For Price-Morgan, Untermeyer, and many of Johnson's enthusiastic correspondents, private rereading of Johnson's sermons in verse seems to have had this effect.

In at least one case, a listener describes her experience in the language of conversion. Johnson had read from a manuscript of *St. Peter Relates An Incident* (1935) at New York University School of Education in December 1931. In a letter thanking him for the reading, Professor Hughes Mearns includes a note that he had received from an audience member Louise Mendenhall. Her note is worth quoting at length:

> After hearing him speak and read his poems the very last vestige of race prejudice oozed away and I found that I'd be not only willing but really proud to have our daughters marry his sons (if he has sons). This is I believe supposed to be the ultimate test! What Mr. Johnson so aptly said about the inner core of prejudice being reached by art more easily than any other way actually happened. What differences exist between races seem interesting, attractive—not at all repellant. (Mendenhall)

What is the "art" that reached Ms. Mendenhall? Her language suggests it was Johnson's performance, his speaking and his reading. It is significant that she doesn't mention the texts themselves. Recall listeners to Millay and Sexton's "beautiful throat," and Johnson's claim in the preface to *God's Trombones* that the congregation responds to the ebb and flow of the preacher's voice as much as to his words. The message is carried by the poet's sincere performance and performed sincerity.

Perhaps in recognition of this, Johnson acted quickly when given an opportunity to record his work. He recorded the first four sermons in verse between February 10 and 17, 1938, for Musicraft Corporation, a small label in New York City that had recently recorded Sandburg and would come to be known primarily for its jazz recordings in the 1940s. Johnson wrote to Best on February 17 that he had run "right off the street to make them [the audition records] and wasn't in anything like the proper mood" (Letters to Best). He made similar remarks to Fanny Strassman at Viking, who was responsible for setting up the recording. However, he subsequently proved keen on having his records heard and on making more; when issuing the recordings proved difficult for Musicraft, Johnson and Strassman approached NBC to talk about making a new set. The NBC audition never happened, and the Musicraft records were not issued until August 1938, two months after Johnson's untimely death.[11]

Disagreeing with Johnson's self-critique, Strassman loved his readings and considered his performance of "Go Down, Death" "particularly fine...I was moved by it all over again" (Strassman). H. L. Mencken, who had seen an advance copy of *God's Trombones*, called this poem, "one of the most remarkable and moving poems of its type ever written in America."[12] "Moving" could be the sign under which Johnson performs his piece. In the Musicraft recording, he begins by entering into character, announcing before he begins, "Go, Down Death, in which the old-time preacher sang the last words over one of the faithful members of his little flock." Johnson affects a quiet, consoling voice in the opening stanza, allowing his voice to trail off after the refrains of "weep no more" and when he calls the name "Jesus." This lilting, trailing voice returns throughout the performance when the preacher addresses the mourners or speaks specifically of Sister Caroline.

We hear a similar technique in the Easter Day sermon of Johnson's contemporary Sin-Killer Griffin recorded by John A. Lomax in Texas, 1934. Griffin places himself on Golgotha during the crucifixion of Jesus and imagines the sun when "it recognized its Maker" collapsing in grief. Like Johnson's, his voice trails, as if he is weeping, a technique he uses again when the centurion cries out in epiphany, "Sholy, sholy, this must be the Son of God" (9–10). Johnson's technique changes when his preacher imagines God summoning Death. Volume and tempo increase as God sits back on his throne and commands his angel:

> Call me Death!
> And that tall, bright angel cried in a voice
> That broke like a clap of thunder:
> Call Death!—Call Death!
> And the echo sounded down the streets of heaven
> Till it reached away back to that shadowy place,
> Where Death waits with his pale, white horses. (849)

Johnson shouts the summons, and his quick, dramatic delivery continues until we are again in the presence of Sister Caroline. Johnson shifts to a calm, confident voice, rendering placid the potentially macabre scenes in which the dying lady sees Death and he takes her up "like a baby...in his icy arms" (850). I imagine a similar performance of the poem at Johnson's funeral, when the poem was read chorally to powerful effect.[13]

In describing Johnson's performance, I mean to suggest that "Go Down, Death" and the sermons in verse demand oral interpretation and aural reception, for it was the sound of the poems that made their reputation. More to the point, Johnson's performances return sounds to his impersonation that elude print or that he had chosen to silence. Not least among these is his performance of vernacular. As Johnson reads them, the following lines, "Day before yesterday morning, / God was looking down from his great, high heaven" (849) might be more accurately represented thus, "Day before yestuhdee morning, / Gawd was looking down from his great, high heaven." A few lines later, "thunder" becomes "thunduh" and "heaven" becomes "heav'n." Conversely, Johnson carefully articulates "-ing" endings throughout this poem—it is difficult to see this as other than deliberate, given how frequently dialect poetry does the opposite. There is, in short, an important disjuncture between Johnson's script and his oral reading, a disjuncture precisely at the point of enunciation. It is clear that Johnson does not merely slip into the vernacular; rather, he performs it sparingly *and* deliberately. The sound lends his preacher's voice authenticity, and that, I would argue, accounts for Johnson's careful use of it. For Johnson is restrained, lest his impersonation invite the kind of racialized response that, in his opinion, dialect writing insured. To be taken seriously, Johnson filters, or perhaps *fixes,* the old-time preacher's dialect—the dialect that is fully, unapologetically present in Griffin's and Gates' performances—even as he closely follows other aspects of the preacher's compositional structures and vocal techniques.

The same argument can be made about Johnson's performance of "The Creation," though the salient characteristic of that performance is what Van Vechten called his intoning. In his preface to *God's Trombones,* Johnson provides notes toward an oral reading of his poetry:

The tempos of the preacher I have endeavored to indicate by the line arrangement of the poems, and a certain sort of pause that is marked by a quick intaking and an audible expulsion of the breath I have indicated by dashes. There is a decided syncopation of speech—the crowding in of many syllables or the lengthening out of which must be left to the reader's ear. The rhythmical stress of this syncopation is partly obtained by a marked silent fraction of a beat; frequently this silent fraction is filled in by a hand clap. (840)

Brown referred to these as the "elaborate stage directions" that the poet preferred to dialect, and to some extent, Johnson follows them in his reading of "Creation" (21). The first two dashes we encounter in the poem are, in his reading, long pauses, but in the following lines we also hear the "audible expulsion of breath" that Johnson claims the dashes indicated:

So God stepped over to the edge of the world
And he spat out the seven seas—
He batted his eyes, and the lightnings flashed—
He clapped his hands, and the thunders rolled— (*Trombones* 843)

The long valleys in a waveform of these lines represent Johnson's breath. It is audible, a sweep of air that connects "seas" and "He" (the first long valley in the waveform), or the sudden "expulsion" of "spat" "batted," "clapped," and "thundered" (the largest peaks in the image; see figure 4.1, which shows a waveform of James Weldon Johnson reading "The Creation").

Figure 4.1

When Johnson comes to lines crowded with syllables, lines such as "The lakes cuddled down in the hollows of the ground, / And the rivers ran down to the sea," he reads with a syncopated rhythm. As in "Go Down, Death," Johnson again uses crescendo to build up to God's commands, as in the lines leading up to "Bring forth! Bring forth!" (849). The total effect of this breath-work, the syncopation, and volume dynamics is an impersonation that closely approximates Gates and Griffin, but with the finished quality that one might expect of a carefully rehearsed recitation. With their delicate balance of ethnographic authenticity and polished realization, Johnson's impersonations inspired his listeners to remake the sermons in verse for teaching elocution and for choral performance. How the poems were remade and what became of Johnson's hope of fixing the old-time Negro preacher are matters I want now to treat in some detail.

Re-sounding *God's Trombones*

For many listeners, the impersonation becomes their primary contact with the voice or kind of voice being impersonated. Johnson's preacher had a long afterlife in the U.S. classroom and on the popular stage, suggesting on the one hand that his archival intent was successful—his preacher was a fixture of U.S. culture. On the other hand, as we have seen, his impersonations were intentional revisions, improvements as he saw them. That revisionist impulse continued as Johnson's own work was remade for public school and stage.

Having always believed that his sermons-in-verse needed to be heard, Johnson responded enthusiastically when he learned of "a somewhat unique use" being made of them by secondary and college speech programs. In a letter to Marshall Best from May 1932, Johnson writes about a "speaking choir" from Talladega College that "gave the Creation with thrilling effect" and of a "dozen or so letters" requesting permission to use *God's Trombones* for performance:

> We at once realized that these poems are singularly good material for this use that is being made of them. There are not many American poems as well fitted to be used for this purpose. Now, I am wondering if the Viking [Press] couldn't do something to call wider attention to the adaptability of *God's Trombones* for use in the speech departments of schools and colleges, and as speaking poems. I do not need to say that if this can be done,

it will go far toward insuring a long and steady circulation for this book. (Letters to Best)

The utilitarian language of this letter is important. Johnson is pleased to find that his poems are useful, and he imagines that this "unique use" will increase and perpetuate sales of his book. Interestingly, he does not mention the principal use he attributed to the poems in the preface to *God's Trombones*—that is, sustaining the art and image of the old-time Negro preacher. Rather, he pointedly describes his sermons-in-verse as *American* poems, the "somewhat unique use" having the potential to give Johnson what he hoped for young black poets: a chance to be read as American, rather than American Negro. As part of speech and elocution training, the poems will be instrumental in a quintessentially American project of self-improvement. Perhaps in the course of such training, students will arrive at an appreciation of the preacher, as is suggested in a letter from Lillian Washington of Bluefield State Teachers College:

> Now I use *God's Trombones* for verse-choir work in my speech class— because of the richness of their emotional and spiritual qualities and for the sake of their profound sincerity. Our students so much need all those things; and I am glad to see them acquire, also an appreciation for the old time Negro preacher, at whom too often they are disposed to laugh. (Washington)

Given that many of the letters Johnson mentions were requests for permission to use his verse for recitation, Johnson's supportive response should be considered instrumental in the direction his *God's Trombones* poems took in popular culture toward the end of his life and after his death. In short, his "negro preacher" became a speech coach, and the sermons became scripts for dramatic reading practice.

What Johnson had encountered on his lecture tours and heard about in letters were practices and pedagogies that came under the rubric "oral interpretation." Quick to distinguish their work from nineteenth-century elocutionism, the artificiality and excesses of which were often the subject of parody, advocates of oral interpretation could be found in popular and academic circles from the late 1920s until the early 1970s, the gap between town and academy being bridged by a shared belief in the connection among socialization, poetic interpretation, and refined oral reading. The public, oral performance of literature underwent a revival in 1920s England with the work of John Masefield and Marjorie Gullan, and a similar revival soon followed in the United States.[14] Oral interpreters claimed that their techniques were organic and that performances depended upon a deep understanding of the author's intent in the text being read. Although the oral interpreter might share some techniques with actors, he should be primarily "identified with the audience...He is one of them, sharing with them communicatively his reading experience" (Dolman 29). Unlike the readings from students of the "outmoded...mechanical school of elocution," a successful oral interpretation amounted to a "total synthesis" of literary work and the well-trained "instruments of communication," the voice and body (Lee 17). The performed poem was, therefore, an interpreted poem. Performance, that is to say, embodied interpretation.

Unsurprisingly, oral interpretation ran directly counter to the New Critical emphasis on writing and the self-contained integrity of the poem as text, and oral interpretation advocates maintained that studied recitations rivaled close reading as a demonstration of one's understanding of a poem. While mid-century formalism institutionalized skepticism toward performance, oral interpretation tried, with limited success, to reclaim recitation from its detractors. In this mode, a recitation sounds like several of the recordings we've encountered in this study—Sexton's "The Fury of Sunrises" and Frost's "Stopping By Woods on a Snowy Evening," for example, or any of Johnson's sermons in verse. Lowell's "Skunk Hour" might qualify with more energy, Thomas' "Do Not Go Gentle Into That Good Night" with less ego. For oral interpretation advocates, the poetic text should be treated as a script for performance. Of secondary concern, but significant nonetheless, was the quality of the speaker's elocution.

In both teaching and performance, one of the most popular formats for oral interpretation from the 1920s forward was the verse-speaking choir. As Joan Shelley Rubin has demonstrated, the social goals of these choirs in the United States were consistent with the goals of elocutionary instruction advocated by the popular McGuffey readers of the nineteenth century.[15] In *The Reading Chorus*, a choral recitation manual from the late 1930s that contains "The Creation," Helen Gertrude Hicks identifies three ways in which the work of a reading chorus helps achieve desirable social ends. First, and perhaps fundamentally, speech is normalized because participants learn "how to breathe correctly, how to phrase, how to produce a clear, pleasing tone, how to enunciate well. Ear-training makes them more alert to correct sound and language patterns" (3). Vocal training here is at once a form of discipline—students' habits of speech and listening are corrected—and a way of tuning up the "instruments of communication" for optimal choral performance. This training/tuning has further benefits. Participants learn "group co-operation" by reading with others and "social understanding" or empathy by reading work about unfamiliar subjects (5). Although later in the century, writing on oral interpretation becomes increasingly interested in the connection between oral reading and literary analysis, there is a remarkable consistency in its assumptions about the social benefits of recitation. Even when choral recitation per se is not at issue, popular textbooks such as Charlotte Lee's *Oral Interpretation* (1965), Lew Sarett's *Basic Principles of Speech*, which saw several editions after its initial publication in 1946, and Karl Robinson's *Speech in Action* (1965) contain Johnson's poems and suggest that speech refined through practiced recitation of literature improves the person and elevates her socially. It is important to recognize that in all these texts, performing literature is not just presented as a fine art, though that presentation is critical. Rather, learning to speak well through the oral performance of literature is considered basic to a liberal education.

Given the social purposes of oral interpretation, what made Johnson's "The Creation" so attractive? I have argued that Johnson was particularly concerned about the voice of his sermons in verse: that it be authentic, but that it be refined, that it capture something of the old-time Negro preacher but not risk sounding like his minstrel-show impersonation. What Johnson did for his preacher, that is, Hicks and others would do for their students. Johnson wrote a poetic variant of the African American folk preacher that assimilated much more readily to the bourgeois goals of speech training than, say, Dunbar's preacher in the "Ante-Bellum Sermon." At the same time, "The Creation"—unlike Dunbar's poem or Johnson's "Let My People Go," which was frequently left out of performances of *God's Trombones*—doesn't bring up the uncomfortable subject of race relations. In Sarett's *Basic Principles*, "The Creation" is in the "Vocal Expression" section of "Mastering the Skills of Speech," a chapter that begins with detailed instruction in "Improving Your Voice and Pronunciation" and "Communicating Your Meaning Through Language." Like many such texts, Sarett's provides illustrations of the anatomy of voice production—cross-sections of the throat and mouth, for example—and descriptions of ways to produce elegant and forceful speech. "The Creation" is among a variety of poems—including "The Hope of Their Religion" from Vachel Lindsay's "The Congo"—that follow instructions on vocal "melody," as well as on integrating action into effective oral recitation of literature.

Though Johnson's old-time Negro preacher and Lindsay's "good old negro in the slums of the town" are both modernist impersonations that would lend themselves to the performance techniques Sarett stressed, it is a cruel irony that they're paired (Lindsay 278). Lindsay's stage directions—he instructs his readers to perform with "a literal imitation of camp-meeting racket, and trance"—and his "Never again will he hoo-doo you," which he performed with relish repeatedly in the early decades of the century, present exactly the image of the preacher that Johnson wanted to erase (278–79).[16] Writing about the social construction of whiteness in modernist poetry, Rachel Blau DuPlessis begins with the nonword "hoo," meant to invoke Africanness in works by Vachel Lindsay, Wallace Stevens, and T. S. Eliot. Noting the word's origin in "hoodoo" and "voodoo," and the "sardonic mocking tone" in which the poets use it, DuPlessis argues that deploying the word is part of a poetical strategy to demean African and African-diasporic culture and expunge whiteness of "social guilt" (670). Of Lindsay's "The Congo," DuPlessis notes, "the very rhythm and rhetorics of poetry have been harnessed to uphold the formation of whiteness" (675). While the poem purports to be a "Study of the Negro Race," Lindsay's exuberant performance exoticizes African drumming, chant, and dance. As his performance notes indicate, he impersonates several voices, all from the point of view of an unnamed observer. For instance, in part one, "Their Basic Savagery," Lindsay begins as a white observer who describes the drunken revelry and drumming of "Fat black bucks in a wine-barrel room" (275). In an affected, nasal chant, Lindsay reads with increasing speed as the observer is caught up in the drumming, climaxing in a change of voice. This is his conscience, in the voice of a preacher, who sternly asserts the observer's responsibility to pay attention to the revel: "Then I had religion, Then I had a vision/ I could not turn from their revel in derision" (275). Other voices come into the first section: Lindsay's parodic take on Congolese speech, his version of a disinterested academic, and his imitation of "witch doctors" casting a spell (276). This pastiche of voices is controlled by the white poet as actor, whose performance affirms the power of whiteness as a subject position.

While Lindsay's performance is offensive, it convincingly stages his racist text. That is to say, it is an effective "oral interpretation," and given its popularity, Sarett likely knew it. In the poem's final section, "The Hope of Their Religion," Lindsay reduces the "race" to two, competing voices, presented as civilized versus savage. Civilization is expressed by the "good old negro in the slums," Lindsay's version of the African American preacher. Ostensibly, as Sarett's pairing suggests, Lindsay and Johnson share an ethnographic interest in the preacher's voice. Johnson's respect for high-cultural forms tempered his admiration of the "old time Negro preacher," and yet *God's Trombones* evidences his belief in the artistic potential of the folk sermon. In contrast, even as Lindsay casts the preacher as a sign of hope for the "negro's" salvation from savagery, he clearly doubts that the "hoo-doo" can ever be fully suppressed. A variation on the witch doctors of section one, Lindsay's preacher howls and beats his Bible. Lindsay's "negro nation" sings a hymn of triumph over "Mumbo-Jumbo," but Lindsay ends his poem with the "Congo tune" and directs the reader to speak in "a penetrating, terrified whisper" (279–80). As in the previous sections, the observer's agitated, rhythmic chant provides the ground for the overlay of other voices, and as such it delivers the message that blackness is inherently suspect. Fear and fascination clearly provide the energy of Lindsay's 1931 performance, which ultimately treats black voice as a deviant form of white.

While Johnson's impersonations more closely approximated his source and evidence a respect and affection for the preacher that Lindsay's lack, it is important to note that neither his nor Lindsay's performance offends against the tastes of a largely white congregation in the first half of the twentieth century. What I propose here is that the work Johnson began on the old-time Negro sermon—work that he saw as a mode of refinement that elevated a beautiful folk form to the level of art—had racialized consequences. I do not mean to suggest that Johnson should be faulted for this, insofar as his intent was to bring the art of the preacher to a wider audience. Moreover, as we have seen throughout this study, the poet's voice is subject to the vicissitudes of reception. An impersonation, just like a persona, is taken up by readers and listeners and recast. In his writings and recordings, Johnson managed to "fix" his source for a bourgeois audience while honoring many of the fundamental qualities of the sermon's structure and the preacher's delivery. But Johnson's model altered further as it became a fixture in popular culture through speech and literature textbooks.

The most dramatic change came in the structure of the widely anthologized sermon-in-verse, "The Creation." As a result of the popularity of choral reading, the poem is often presented in parts—boys chorus, girls chorus, male solo, and mixed chorus—with simple vocal markings, such as "swift and clear" or "quietly." The voice of the old-time Negro preacher is quieted, if not entirely silenced, as in these prefatory remarks in Hicks' textbook:

> The author tells us that the old-time Negro preacher so loved the sound of the language of the Bible, that he would never speak in dialect when he was preaching. The more grand and beautiful the picture in Biblical literature, the more he loved it. So the Creation is one of the favorite subjects of the Negro preachers. Certainly they couldn't find any greater idea, could they? (146)

Dialect offends against the beauty of the Bible: that, it would seem, is Hicks' reading of Johnson. In commenting, however misguidedly, on

Johnson's old-time Negro preacher and the question of dialect, Hicks is unusual; only one other text in my sample, Charlotte Lee's popular *Oral Interpretation*, mentions dialect, and in that case, only to point out that "the poet has *not* used dialect. Let him have his way" (69; emphasis in the original). For the most part, textbooks across the century say little about "The Creation" as a representation of an African American cultural form; rather, with the poem commonly offered up for oral reading, the texts consistently focus on its dramatic biblical content. Literature textbooks such as *Adventures for Today*, a grade nine anthology from the mid-1950s, and *Adventures for You,* a grade seven text from the late 1960s, commonly frame the poem as an example of religious expression and ask such questions as what the poet thinks about God and how God created the world. In a grade eleven text from 1970, *Ideas and Patterns in Literature,* "The Creation" is used to illustrate the importance of the Bible as "a source of our literature." In none of the textbooks is the matter of the old-time Negro preacher broached. For the purposes of literature and language arts instruction, "The Creation" became a poem about a Judeo-Christian myth, artfully rendered for oral performance.[17]

However, the story of Johnson's "The Creation" told by these anthologies and speech texts is complicated by evidence in recordings of *God's Trombones* in performance. On the one hand, recordings of "The Creation" in isolation from the other *God's Trombones* poems have tended to mute the preacher's voice, much as the textbooks had. In a 1968 United Artists recording called *Poetry of the Black Man,* Sidney Poitier reads "The Creation" dramatically, backed by a chorus and orchestral effects, but without a hint of the intoned style we heard in Gates or Johnson; Poitier's voice is breathy and serious, and he seems to be speaking in an empty hall, perhaps to suggest God speaking into the void. It resembles nothing so much as Dylan Thomas' Caedmon recordings. Conversely, Arna Bontemps' reading of "The Creation" on a 1955 Folkways recording called *Anthology of Negro Poets in the U.S.A.* is restrained, far more so than Johnson's, and focuses our attention on the words of the poem, rather than on its rhythms and sounds. In short, the performance is consistent with mid-century practices we heard on the LOC recordings of chapter one. Despite their considerable differences, the Poitier and Bontemps readings effectively erase the preacher.[18]

On the other hand, recordings of choral renderings of *God's Trombones* resurrect a version of the old-time Negro preacher, even as they edit out the sermons with the most to say about racial inequality. In 1959, United Artists issued a recording of *God's Trombones,* with the actor Harold Scott in the role of preacher. The album was marketed as a commemorative edition in honor of Johnson. Scott's readings closely resemble Johnson's, though he is backed by an African American chorus that sings spirituals between the poems and often hums melodies as he reads. Tympani supply thunder in "The Creation"; the chorus shouts "Crucify him!" in "The Crucifixion." The performance is not, however, an attempt to "recreate the atmosphere" of the church that Johnson lamented his book would necessarily lack (*Trombones* 840). Rather, the recording has high-brow aspirations, as is evidenced not only in its tastefully restrained and carefully orchestrated drama, but also in the album's packaging.[19] Carl Van Vechten writes the liner notes. Lorraine Hainsberry provides an angry assessment of the "failure to use the Negro in the theatre," perhaps balancing the fact that "Let My People Go," a thinly veiled commentary on racial oppression, has been left out of the performance. Harold Scott's Harvard credentials are trotted out in an extended excerpt from *The Harvard Crimson*. Finally, there is the jacket of the album, adorned by an off-centered, black-and-white photo of Scott on a wintry hillside, leafless tree bent by the cold, Scott dressed in all black, his hand on the brim of an itinerant preacher's hat. He is staring at the sky, his eyebrows raised, as if he is asking, "Why?" In sum, the Scott recording provides the visual and aural experience of *God's Trombones* that Johnson wanted: an authentically high brow, if not high art, rendering of the African American preacher and sermon, comparable to his and Aaron Douglas' own artful book, but with the tantalizing addition of sound.[20]

A very different, middle-brow rendering of *God's Trombones* was performed in 1963 by Fred Waring's Singing Pennsylvanians, with Frank Davis as preacher. Broadcast on television and recorded by Decca, the fully orchestrated Waring version verges on camp. With its church bells and medleys of Negro spirituals, the performance calls to mind Claude McKay's angry objection to spirituals tricked up "for virtuoso wonders" in the "garish marble hall."[21] Be that as it may, Davis imitates the fiery evangelist, not with the uninhibited gusto of Gates or Griffin, but with more flair than Johnson.[22] Primarily an occasion for the Pennsylvanians to try their skill at singing spirituals, the Waring performance includes only three of the sermons-in-verse, "Listen Lord," "Creation," and "Judgment Day," with the first poem divided to serve as prelude and postlude to the "service."[23] Waring's notes to the album explain that he had wanted to record spirituals for many years, but had felt unable "to do full justice" to them before finding the right soloists. The implication is that the white Pennsylvanians chorus needed black voices and found them before striking out on *God's Trombones*. For all these differences from the Scott version, however, both are presented as tributes to African American preaching and singing and both assume that the framework for such a tribute is best taken from Johnson's example. Recall Johnson's prediction in his letter to Best: attention to this "somewhat unique use" being made of his poems might insure the longevity of his project.

Given its wide distribution through school anthologies and its frequent performance by verse choirs and musical groups, *God's Trombones* effectively became middle-class America's experience of the old-time Negro preacher and sermon—that is, in the cases where the preacher's voice and the poetry's status as sermons in verse had not been erased. I have argued that Johnson carefully remade an African American folk form in ways that honored it while (in his estimation) elevating it, but that his impersonations became themselves subject to revisionary impersonation. The old-time Negro preacher who is fixed in the collective unconscious of (e.g.) students of the Harcourt-Brace versions of "The Creation," or of people who sat by their radios and televisions for the Waring *God's Trombones* concert, is a pale shadow of the Kansas evangelist whose performance inspired the composition of *God's Trombones.*

★　★　★

Johnson's example extends to many different kinds of recordings "in another's voice" that we find in the audio archive. In conclusion, I want to look briefly at one of these recordings that is especially close to the issues raised by sounding *God's Trombones*: the *Anthology of Negro Poets* issued in 1954 by Folkways and edited by Arna Bontemps.[24] The album gathers a variety of poems in first person and in another's voice, all in the interest of defining the "Negro Poet" much as Johnson sought to "fix something" of the preacher. The Folkways anthology is an exemplary period piece, presenting the "Negro Poet" as a naïve, natural genius whose lyrics embody universal concerns. In his notes on the reverse of the original album, Arna Bontemps claims that the six writers on the album—Langston Hughes, Sterling Brown, Claude McKay, Countee Cullen, Margaret Walker, and Gwendolyn Brooks—have rarely had "the inclination or detachment or even the time to make the niceties of prosody their central concern. By and large, they have written spontaneously out of the well-springs of their own hearts" (*Anthology*). Invoking the rhetoric of Wordsworth's 1800 preface to *Lyrical Ballads*, Bontemps attempts to forestall critique of the poetry, which has sprung "spontaneously" from its makers. His dismissive reference to "detachment" sets the "negro poet" at odds with Eliot's poetics of impersonality; these poets are, in his estimation, unapologetically attached to their roles as "spokesman [*sic*] for the human spirit" (*Anthology*). Like Johnson, Bontemps lays claim to the universality of the "Negro Poet's" voice, even as it issues from experience that is particular to African Americans.

Bontemps' presentation is reinforced by the album's cover art.[25] In the heavy brushstrokes and thick lines generally associated with American "naïve" style, two Africans are depicted in flowing robes and headdress. One sits on a stone and reads; the other releases a dove. Between them grows a cotton plant. Symbolically, the painting blends Africa and the American South, biblical and contemporary times. The voice of "Negro Poet," as the album wants us to understand her, speaks simply and power-fully, across time and from the heart.

As is often the case, however, this collective, metaphoric "voice" is not always evident in the specific, human voices on the album, or in the kinds of texts they perform. Bontemps acknowledges the differences among the poets' "writings and…personalities," and two contrasting examples—one "in first person," the other an impersonation—will suffice to begin to illustrate how the album's soundings complicate the Romantic, univo-cal characterization of the "Negro Poet" presented in the album's materi-als. Among the poets, Claude McKay speaks directly to Bontemps' claims in remarks that precede his recitation of "If I Must Die." His remarks recall those of his mentor, James Weldon Johnson, prophesying an end to race-distinctions among artists:

> "If We Must Die" is the poem that makes me a poet among colored Americans. Yet frankly I have never regarded myself as a Negro poet. I have always felt that my gift of song was something bigger than the nar-row, confining limits of any one people and its problems. Even though many of my themes were racial, I wrote my poems to make a universal appeal…(*Anthology*)

Published in 1922, McKay's sonnet is an inspirational call-to-arms, a St. Crispin's Day speech to rally African Americans to meet violence with vio-lence, justifiable as the last, honorable resort. McKay reads with heat and passion in the mode of the beautiful throat, closely akin to Millay. But if the content of "If We Must Die" makes McKay "a poet among colored Americans," the form of his poem—a strictly observed Shakespearean sonnet—aligns him with an English tradition. McKay imagines that this makes his work more "universal"—a suspect category that, as race theorists have argued, is synonymous with "white."[26] While McKay's deft use of the sonnet hardly substantiates Bontemps' representation of the "Negro Poet" as unconcerned with the "niceties of prosody," McKay shares Bontemps' desire for the elusively "universal." In their estimation, as in Johnson's, "Negro" is a category to be embraced in the interest of ultimately transcending it.

In contrast with McKay's sonnet are vernacular pieces by Margaret Walker, whose *For My People* won the Yale Younger Poets award in 1942. Walker's spirited reading of her ballad "Kissie Lee" suggests a reclamation of the possibilities of dialect writing that Johnson had doubted was possible in the earlier contexts of the 1910s. In "Kissie Lee," an admiring speaker tells the story of the "toughest gal I ever did see" (38). Initially "young and good," Kissie was a victim of bullying until she "learned to stab and run"—a lesson taught by her "Grammaw" who is "tiahed of yoah whinin'" (38). Thematically, the ballad echoes McKay as an endorsement of violent self-defense, for the speaker's infectious enthusiasm encourages us to admire Kissie's aggression. Walker impersonates the ballad speaker with bravado. Always in voice, she takes advantage of a wide dynamic and tonal range—a high-pitched announcement in the opening lines, a matter-of-fact claim that Kissie "got herself a little gun" at the poem's center, a deep rumbling in the grandmother's stern advice (38–39). Walker's vernacular performance conveys the speaker's sheer pleasure in telling Kissie's tale, and we are as attracted to the speaker as to her subject. In Walker's example, the voice of the "Negro poet" is local and naïve, and while it contrasts with McKay's, in the context of the album it seems to fill the "common voice" role in an essentially Romantic project. Despite the small number of poets on *An Anthology of Negro Poets,* the generational span gives rise to a remarkable catalog of reading styles: Cullen and McKay in the beautiful throat, Brown and Walker in impersonations, Hughes and Brooks performing variations of both. Notably absent is the understated mid-century mode that was beginning to take hold in the late 1940s and early 1950s. As the album presents it, the voice of the "Negro Poet" is always engaged. It may be theatrical, emotional, or eloquent, but it is not impersonal.

Much more research and analysis is needed to do justice to Walker's vernacular impersonations and the voices on this album. As with Johnson, Walker's reading should be placed alongside recordings of the voices she impersonates, and it should be contextualized not only in the Bontemps' anthology, but also in the later fortunes and purposes of dialect writing. Likewise, my claims here about the purpose and effect of Bontemps' project are conjectural, meant primarily to gesture toward the ways that my sounding of *God's Trombones* could factor into work with related projects in the archive. Johnson's sermons in verse are nested in an ever-expanding circle of soundings and re-soundings.[27] This holds true for any poem on record, in that the poet's reading, while at the center of critical attention, resonates with its remakings in other voices. For the modernist imperson-ation and its analogues, these remakings are balanced by voice recordings of the impersonated. Close listening to this variety of recordings—with poet's audio and textual performances as points of departure—is integral to the study of modernist poetry in another's voice.

AFTERWORD

OUT OF THE AUDIO ARCHIVE

Writing about an archive organizes it, and organization is a system of priorities. "The question of the archive remains the same," Jacques Derrida claims in *Archive Fever*. "What comes first? Even better: Who comes first? And second?" (30). Derrida questions what is lost when the archivist determines what or who comes first, when he classifies, historicizes, and evaluates the meanings of the materials he's gathered. At the end of this study, I am keenly aware of both the strengths and limitations of my approach to the archive—the system of organization I've modeled, the poets and recordings I've chosen as examples. Organizing principles, such as those I've developed in the structure of this study, facilitate research and analysis; the general categories "in the studio" and "on stage" usefully sort the scenes of recording, and "in first person" and "in another's voice" describe in broad terms the two prevalent subject positions of modernist poets who recorded their work. While I do mean to suggest that these categories play a meaningful, practical role in gathering the dispersed recordings of the archive, the boundaries are porous, and the labels not always satisfying. I focused on Sexton and Millay as examples "in first person," but what differences would surface were we to compare their studio and live recordings, or if we were to listen to Sexton as an oral storyteller in her few recorded performances of poetry from *Transformations*? Lowell's recordings from the 1960s might, for that matter, be studied as expressive work, if not that of the "beautiful throat." Thomas' recordings of Auden, Yeats, and Hardy's poetry could serve as a point of departure for studying how poets and actors have performed others' work; these are not precisely voice impersonations, but they are a variety of performance in another's voice. Systems of classification—the kind that archival study necessitates—are suggestive in part by virtue of their limitations.

By that same token, my decision to focus in detail on a few poets whose recordings are representative within these categories has meant that there are many important voices we have not heard over the course of this book: Olson or Ginsberg, for instance, the New York School or the Black Arts movement. For all of these and other poets who recorded in the decades from the 1930s to 1970, audio and the aural were central. A companion volume would bring them in to sound off against and, at times, harmonize with the voices included here: Ashbery as a reader whose performance style echoes Bishop's, Ginsberg or Di Prima as preachers, or the relationship between Amiri Baraka or Wanda Coleman and the beautiful throat aesthetic. Given the sheer quantity and diversity of recordings in the archive, there is much to be gained by listening to a different set of recordings and poets within the framework suggested by this book. For example, what first-person aural aesthetics competed with or departed from the beautiful throat? How might an extensive study simply of commemorative recordings, such as the Oppen centennial recently archived on PennSound, the numerous memorial service recordings housed in the Woodberry Poetry collection, and the audio/video recordings of tributes held by the Poets House, further or complicate the conclusions I've drawn about the occasional poetry recording? Along those same lines, do poets' readings of documentary poetry offer a different perspective on "in another's voice" than Johnson's impersonations? In short, notwithstanding the limits of my study, I want to believe that close listening of the kind I've modeled in the foregoing chapters can carry forward our understanding of particular poets' works even as it illuminates characteristics of poetry on record and how it functioned in the development of modernism. One thing I hope to have accomplished here is to have provided a useful approach for future endeavors in the archive.

Artifacts in the archive exist largely on tape and disc, and audio in those formats has been the primary material of this study. But even during the period of my research, recordings that I traveled to hear became available online; audio that I studied first on tape or record has been digitized, and I have converted some myself. In these closing pages, therefore, it is worth briefly considering what is at stake in digitizing the archive. Re-archiving poetry on record—digitizing dated formats and making the audio more widely accessible online—at once preserves and alters it. In his deconstruction of "archive fever"—the internal tension between our desire to preserve and the fact that inscription delimits and, in effect, destroys—Derrida reflects upon typing his lectures on his "little portable Macintosh," which has led him to question when, precisely, something becomes archived (*Archive* 25). Is it at the moment of writing, he asks, or when he hits "save"? And doesn't saving the writing make it available for printing, yet another impression of the original (26)? Applying the analogy to memory and Freud's impulse to articulate, transcribe, and interpret memories, Derrida suggests that each impression reinscribes and alters the putatively static, archived object (30–31). Digital status redoubles the tension between a document's "irreplaceable singularity" in the archive and its malleability under scrutiny and reiteration (90).

The "trouble" Derrida identifies in the archival impulse points us again to McGann's concept of the "textual condition," which has been influential in the development of online archives. As language, the text resists boundaries, and its possible meanings are ever renewing. At the same time, the materiality of the text binds it to specific historical moments, just as its reception historicizes its meanings. In *Radiant Textualities*, McGann argues that moving print to online forms should involve the same level of detailed bibliographical work demanded by critical editing of a print text, lest the historical traces of a text's meanings be obscured. The same holds true for the digitization of archival recordings. At their best, digital audio archives will of course take advantage of the improved capabilities of the new format, but they will also attempt to represent the meaningful codes of the tape or disc. Specifically, as I have suggested in this study, those meaningful codes include information about the time, place, and scene of the recording, album materials and liner notes, the sequence of readings and commentary, and at times audience response and other ancillary sounds. Particularly in its digitization of live recordings, PennSound has been a model, with information on site as well as imbedded in downloadable files.[1] Smithsonian Folkways has made similar efforts to represent fully its commercially produced recordings, with digital photos of albums and liners.

Having devoted hours to the painstaking process of transcribing from reel-to-reel tape, I am not nostalgic for record or tape players. But I do want to note an important difference between listening online and listening in a library's archive, strictly speaking. Downloading an archival recording brings the sound into the present—one's presence, in fact, at the computer and in the moment. Poetry on record has always promoted an illusion of presence, as we have seen, but the ease and immediacy of the digital transaction contrasts with going to the archive as separate place and retrieving the recording as material object. In their introduction to a collection of essays on archival research, historians Gesa Kirsch and Liz Rohan suggest that going into the archive helps us "better understand [our] own historically situated experience" (2). When the Internet brings the archive to us, difference is less apparent because distances have been reduced and materials changed. This is not an argument in favor of limited access or difficulty, but it is another important reason to develop digital archives that carefully contextualize materials.

If listening to the archival recording reaches back, it also brings the voice forward into the present scene of the listening. I have argued that each listening is a remaking, and it is this effect that caused Derrida to question the "place proper" of the archived object (30). The flickering cursor on his screen anticipates the inscription of a letter, but hasn't the archiving begun before the writing, and doesn't it continue after it? The ions on a magnetic tape collected the poet's voice in the 1950s, but digitizing the voice re-collects it, both in the sense of gathering it again and remembering it. Recollection is also a revaluation. Derrida notes that the root of "archive" denotes both commencement and commandment (1–2). To digitize a poet's tape or disc recording is to set in motion a revaluation, for the act itself declares that the voice and recording have value. From economic imperatives to elective affinities, what drives our choices of poetry to re-archive is complex. But in my analyses, I have attempted to make a case for ephemera such as the occasional recording and, more generally, for the wealth of recording by modernists whose work has lived primarily on the page in our scholarly research. The modernist text and our subvocalizations of it in silent reading should be put in dialogue with its audio variants.

As I have argued, whether in the studio or on stage, the poet was recorded to preserve the voice and the performance. Archives are assertions against loss, and the "scriptal spiral" was audible writing to hold the poet's reading in place for the future. When Lowell gazes at the record, when Johnson gets behind the microphone at Musicraft studios, when listeners since the advent of tape have pressed "record" during a reading or a poets' forum, the expectation has been that the poetry on record will be heard again and again. However, forms of audio inscription have yet to achieve the simple durability of print, and the transfer of voices from disc to tape, from tape to digital formats is in part an effort to prevent inaccessibility. My college owns one functioning reel-to-reel player—a durable, impressively heavy ReVox—and close to one hundred 3 ¾ ips recordings of poetry readings from the 1960s and 1970s. The ReVox seems likely to outlast my laptop, but neither will play a record, and all of that tape is fragile. There should be a sense of urgency behind the digitization of poetry audio in order to bring the voices back to our attention, but concomitantly, archivists must work against the deterioration of original materials and their playback devices.

Moving the audio archive to digital, online formats takes us back to an essential question: what do we hope to hear from the poet's recording of her work? Whether the poet's voice comes to us or we go to it, whether that voice has been translated to disc, tape, or digital code, the poet's recording makes us conscious of the sounds internal to the text and those sounds and voices surrounding it. Throughout this study, my method of close listening has involved formal analysis that compares a poem's sounds and a poet's soundings. "A line such as this," a college professor of mine once declared, "repays close scrutiny." He then drew the following, which represents some phrases cast forward from the initial sounds, on the board:

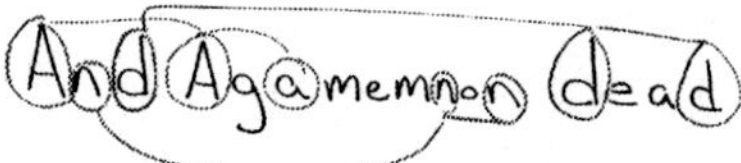

Some phrases, poetical and musical alike, cast forward from their initial sounds, and the work moves toward order as we listen. Yeats may have blotted this line; he completely reworked the initial stanza of "Leda and the Swan" after publication.[2] I want to believe, however, that "Agamemnon dead" came from "And" as surely as a chestnut tree from its bole.

Whether or not that is so, I have argued that when we close listen, we hear not only the sounds of the poem and the poet's voicing of them, but also the echoes of previous scenes of reading and listening. The recorded poem inscribes an interaction between a voice and listeners, most obviously in the "on the stage" recording, but equally in the performance style of the studio reading. Moreover, whether we download a sound file or attend a performance, our listening now, as I claimed in chapter three, differs from, and yet is influenced by, our listening then. I first heard Johnson's "The Creation," for example, in the early 1970s, during a recitation at my elementary school in rural North Carolina. The poem was a mainstay of my school's annual contest, where it was performed from memory alongside a collection of Psalms, poems, cautionary tales, and historical speeches. The quality shared by these texts was not so much literary as moral—they were considered good for the soul of the speaker and the listener alike. Reciting "The Creation," my cousin Lisa won the contest in the year that I best recall. She was soft-spoken but clear, accurate, and sincere, this final quality giving her an edge over her stammering elocutionist competitors. I have now listened to numerous soundings and re-soundings of Johnson's poem, but Lisa's doleful "I'm lonely still" resonates deepest.

As the audio archive moves online, what we hear may alter, and should at least influence, the stories we tell about modernist poetry. Opportunities to involve our students in archival research of real consequence present themselves, and I will reflect on some of these opportunities in appendix A, a description of a course on poetic sound and voice. But I want to end by recounting a shared experience of close listening that took place as I wrote this book. My son Samuel and I had just heard John Ashbery read at a celebration of his eightieth birthday. Samuel is eight, bright and earnest, and generally enjoys "grown-up" events. Nevertheless, the teacher in me was concerned that without a few directions for listening, he might get frustrated. So I told him to listen for words or sentences that he liked, and we would talk about them later. Ashbery read a wide range of poems, including the two-voiced "Litany," joined by Ann Lauterbach. Afterward, as soon as we were away from the crowd, Sammy volunteered, "I didn't understand much but I liked the line, 'The man with the red hat / and the polar bear, is he here too?' because you just don't expect to hear that in a poem."

The line comes from "Glazunoviana," a short poem from an early Ashbery book *Some Trees* (1956), and like many Ashbery poems, it defies easy summarization. For Sammy, instructed to listen for sentences he liked, red hat and polar bear were memorable because they defied his expectations. True, Sammy had been frustrated, minimally, by what he didn't understand, but not knowing exactly what to make of Ashbery's poetry let him listen to it. On an ordinary day, to hear something unexpected requires willfulness and patience, but listening to poetry is, in my experience, extraordinary in its challenges to the familiar and its tests of patience, especially for those of us who get our poetry primarily from the page, in silence. What stayed with me from Ashbery's reading were the unsettling fact that the bear "drops dead in sight of the window" and that what makes the evening flicker will also blot it out: "In the flickering evening the martins grow denser. / Rivers of wings surround us and vast tribulation" (*Mooring* 13). For several days, I worried at the worried syntax of the last line, always in Ashbery's plain, undramatic voice. I had known of the poem before the reading, only because I was familiar with *Some Trees*, but I had never really heard the understated drama of its ending, or recognized how ominously it answers the burlesque of the opening stanza. Listening to Ashbery read it changed the quality of my attention. And given that the celebration was recorded, there will be opportunity to listen more closely.

APPENDIX A

LEARNING TO LISTEN: POETRY RECORDINGS IN THE CLASSROOM

This study has been dedicated to the premise that listening to poetry, especially in the poet's voice, should be integral to scholarship in modern poetics and reception. Audio recordings and other traces of the aural/oral life of a poem belong among the "texts" that scholars research, analyze, edit, and disseminate. By that same token, they belong in the classroom as more than ancillary materials or adjuncts to the anthology. In this appendix, I provide the syllabus for a course on poetic sound and voice in which audio plays a central role. In effect, this course is a seminar on the questions raised when we approach poetry as a speech act, when we listen to it as crafted sound, and when we participate in it as a situated performance. Roughly, the course mirrors the design of *Recorded Poetry and Poetic Reception,* insofar as it begins with varieties of poetry "in first person" and "in another's voice," then modulates to considerations of studio and stage performances as they are captured on record and in a poet's reception. While "Poetic Voices" is a specialized seminar, the course's guiding principles and sample lessons are readily transferable to the general modernist survey. All of the recordings I include are available commercially or from libraries, except when the lesson involves students in archival research. As a context for the syllabus, I want to describe in detail an essential pedagogical principle of the course and two of the course assignments that involve research in the audio archive.

Leading with the Poet's Voice

In the college literature course, students typically first encounter assigned reading at home, in advance of an upcoming class meeting. Class time is then devoted to discussing students' responses to the literature, elaborating on those based on information brought to the table by the instructor, and correcting misperceptions. Without discounting the virtue of expecting students to arrive at provisional readings of texts on their own, I want to suggest that this way of doing business favors the stronger, better-prepared students, who can readily find points of entry into the text at hand and, by extension, the class discussion. Moreover, it tends to turn the class meeting into a series of reports and response, in which a student reports her interpretation, confusion, or reaction, and the instructor responds, usually in a way intended to improve or correct. The situation deteriorates further when the texts under consideration are some of the particularly challenging poems of "high" modernism. Baffled students come to class seeking clarity from the professor, and if there is discussion at all, it involves only a few.

The instructional challenge here is to encourage students to consider modernist poetry open to inquiry, puzzled response, and hypothesis precisely because of its density. Leading with a poet's voice in advance of reading—when possible, listening more than a single time—can be a fruitful response. In the three different cases I am about to describe, students listen and respond to a poet reading his work before they leave to read the work on their own, or at home using an online archive and prompts I have prepared. Before we listen, I establish the fact that a poet's reading is not authoritative—like their own, it's a mode of interpretation—though it does carry a certain authority. We should hear it as the author's attempt at getting across the sound and sense of his work. Listening without a "script," we will necessarily miss specific words or phrases, but we may well hear something that we wouldn't see.[1]

For students new to Gertrude Stein, for example, listening to the text can mean the difference between engagement with Stein's linguistic play and frustration at the portraits' density and abstraction. Students often speak of needing to read Stein aloud, and in an essay on Stein's portraits, Ulla Haselstein's observations about Stein's writing and performance suggest why. Haselstein argues that the portraits depend upon a reader's active involvement to complete them:

> In order to be able not only to make sense of the text but to get through the text at all, the reader must embody and enact it by reading it out aloud and translating it into a dramatic performance. Only if the reader lets herself be drawn into a transferential relation with the text and repeats the portrait situation, will the long and meandering repetitive sentences make sense as intimations of a self characterized by obsessive thought patterns, resonating with self-doubt and exultation following the changing tides of public recognition. (732–33)

Haselstein points out the power of recitation in re-actualizing Matisse's character as Stein presented it in her poetic portrait of the artist. To introduce the poem, however, asking students to listen—in the active manner described by Nancy, Stewart, and others whom this study has cited—can be more successful than expecting them to read Stein's unorthodox sentences aloud without practice. Stein recorded several portraits in 1935, and I begin with her performance of "Matisse." First, having been prompted simply to attend to Stein's manner of reading, students should listen without text or notebook. Stein's reading is rhythmic and brisk; her voice communicates confidence—her confidence in the portrait, as opposed to Matisse's in himself, for Matisse's ostensible anxiety is a motif in the poem. This tends to come forward when students listen to the reading a second time, now with the prompt to write down two phrases that they hear. Everyone reads these phrases aloud, around the classroom and without commentary. Commonly called "text rendering," the exercise generally has two, thought-provoking results. First, listeners tend to gravitate toward language punctuated by Stein's reading, phrases that include "again and again" and variations on "certain." The exercise itself, thereby, draws attention to Stein's patterns of repetition and to the poem's interrogation of certainty. Second, the class' reading of the phrases, without interruption, effectively creates a found poem that can be compared to "Matisse" in order to shed light on Stein's craft. Having heard Stein's and their "poem," students write briefly to the statement "Our poem and Stein's sound alike. Believe and doubt." The believing and doubting exercise, crafted by Peter Elbow for writing workshop, requires students to test a thesis or point of view. Applied here, it highlights the sense beneath densely arranged unpunctuated syntax such as, "One was quite certain that for a long time in his being one being living he had been trying to be certain that he was wrong in doing what he was doing," as well as Stein's use of volume and rhythm to communicate that sense.

To push deeper into the implications of Stein's formal experiments and toward the goal of understanding how modernism deconstructed the art of representation, we turn next to Picasso and Stein, comparing paintings, text, and audio. Leading up to Stein's portraits of Picasso, the class views Ingres' 1832 portrait of Louis Francois-Bertin and Picasso's 1906 portrait of Stein, which takes Ingres' as a point of departure. Asked, "What is your impression of Bertin, and what gives you this impression?" students will note that closely observed, naturalistic details—such as Bertin's claw-like hands and his intense, impatient gaze—are a window on character. In contrast, Picasso's portrait does not try to pass as "real." Picasso has begun to break apart and examine the forms within the form— the angles, for example, of Stein's face—in a style that anticipates *Les demoiselles d'Avignon* and future cubist works. The portrait of Stein calls attention to the procedures of its making and the components of its artifice in much the same way as Stein's linguistic portraits of Picasso.

This is particularly apparent in "If I Told Him: A Completed Portrait of Picasso," written in 1923 in a form similar to Picasso's art of the same period. In his study of Stein and Picasso's relationship, Vincent Giroud argues that the 1923 portrait is more abstract and difficult than the one in 1912, an evolution in Stein's portraiture that is mirrored by the shift from Picasso's Stein portrait to the figures of *Les demoiselles*. Giroud writes:

> Combining a rebuslike quality and associations of words and ideas that proceed as much from sound as from sense, it illustrates what the Stein critic Ulla Dydo calls "the primacy of naked words" (along the same lines, Kahnweiler had argued that Stein went even further than Marinetti in using "mots en liberte"). (39–40)

That the language of a portrait would not proceed from an intended sense may seem counterintuitive to students, as it did to Stein's contemporaries.[2] As Giroud implies, one sound generates another in the text, such that Stein seems to have chosen words partly on the basis of the words that came before in a line or verse paragraph. This process of sound-association does, however, come to sense—at times, to a sense of Picasso. For example, the chiasmus of the opening verse paragraphs is simultaneously visual and aural. We see the mirror effect of "If I told him would he like it. Would he like it if I told him," but listening to Stein we also hear it in the way the rhythm reverses at the full stop after "it" (*Writings* 506). The sense here *is* the text's making, and it is that consuming preoccupation with making that Stein associates with Picasso. Sounds also communicate Stein's critique of Picasso's domineering competitiveness. He is a Napoleon, concerned with who came first. Voicing the verse paragraph that begins "He he he he and he," Stein seems to be imitating a child's snickering (507). "He is and as he is"—an echo of I am that I am—is thus a proclamation made in laughter. When students listen to Stein, they become aware of her humor as well as of her aural poetics.

As with Stein's portraits, I lead with the poet's voice in teaching Ezra Pound's "The Seafarer."[3] Pound's reading of "The Seafarer" is an intriguing impersonation of an imagined Anglo-Saxon. Audio and print versions of the poem can be introduced together, framed with a question: what might be the purpose of Pound's deliberately archaic mode of translating the poem, in writing and in sound? For his 1939 Harvard Vocarium session, Pound incants the poem in a haunting, guttural voice, backed by a drumbeat that occasionally underscores the end of a hemistich. Throughout, Pound affects simmering anger and reads with foreboding. Volume increases with the seafarer's anger or dread, as when he declares, "Not any protector / May make merry man faring needy" (510). Pound rolls—practically trills—the r's in his lines and accentuates alliteration. Importantly, he does not modulate his voice or tempo in ways that would compensate for the often-confusing grammatical inversions. His performance is therefore consistent with his decision not to modernize the Anglo-Saxon original. Writing about translations of "The Seafarer," John Corbett argues that Pound's use of antiquated vocabulary and syntax is a variety of literal translation, not in the conventional sense of exact parity with the original, but "in a deliberate construction of strangeness" that calls attention to difference and to the translator as maker (161). In this respect, Pound's impersonation differs from Johnson's, who would make the preacher familiar to us. However, if text and performance locate the seafarer's voice in the distant past, other elements of the poem place it in the twentieth century. Corbett notes that Pound omitted the final lines of the poem, which complete a Christian allegory he wished to undermine. Pound's impersonation thus implies that the Seafarer's voice is contemporary. His performance furthers the point: we end in darkness, without a hope of redemption.[4]

Pound's performances often provide insight into his perspective on the personae of his works, as in his wry, melodramatic reading of "Cantico Del Sole," and in the classroom the recordings shed light on notoriously opaque verse. They serve a similar purpose in lessons on Eliot's *The Waste Land* (1922), but the focus shifts to responding to the poem's multiple voices.[5] Students listen, without the text, and make note of the different voices Eliot performs. Rather than playing the entire poem during this initial foray, I focus on Eliot's reading of part two, "A Game of Chess." In the 1933 recording of this part, he shifts tone and volume appreciably to indicate the several voices. The shifts are consistent, and after listening twice, students offer up names for and descriptions of what they've heard. For example, the pompous speaker of the ornate opening stanza is interrupted first by the nightingale's muted "Jug Jug," then more fully by Eliot's agitated, feminized, "My nerves are bad to-night. Yes, bad. Stay with me" (2.102, 111). The most provocative, and disturbing, voice that Eliot "does" in "A Game of Chess" is the gossiping maid's, sporadically interrupted by Eliot's loud and impatient "HURRY UP PLEASE ITS TIME" (2.141). Ennui, frustration, impatience, pathos: much of the tone of the section is communicated by how Eliot performs it.

Be that as it may, Eliot's performance, while diverse, is limited by his capacity to embody the multiple perspectives of his work. The opening stanzas of "The Burial of the Dead" and "The Fire Sermon," as well as the lines of the fisherman and blind Tiresias, are all delivered in the same voice. Eliot's reading, in this respect, narrows the vocal range of the text. For even if Eliot were able to embody the multiple personae of *The Waste Land*, the poem is filled with words and phrases that seem to speak themselves. Referring to *The Waste Land* and Pound's *Hugh Selwyn Mauberley*, Denis Donoghue writes:

> One's first reading of these poems leaves an impression of their poetic quality as residing in their diction: the animation of the verse arises from the incalculable force of certain individual words and phrases which stay in the mind without necessarily attracting to their orbit the words before or after. The memorable quality of those phrases seems to require a clear space on all sides, and it has little need of before and after. (219).

Donoghue's observation and the limit of Eliot's performance raise the question of what voice, if any, centers *The Waste Land*. In the audio, some of the most compelling voices are the most troubling; for example, Eliot reads the neurotic wife and vulgar maid with disturbing gusto that borders on the misogynistic. But the sounds that linger—jug jug, Shantih shantih shantih—do not so much generate a center of gravity as signify the irreducibility of voice. In a classroom that leads with Eliot's recording, a critique of his performance can be a means not only of opening up a complex poem, but also of confronting the differences between reading and listening to modernist poetry.

Students in the Archive

As I argued in the introduction, the audio archive of poets reading their work is widely dispersed, inconsistently cataloged, and underutilized by scholars and students. However, for this reason, and given the fact that digitization and library interconnectivity are making the recordings increasingly accessible, research in this unconventional archive can play a key role in students' learning about twentieth-century poetry specifically and scholarly inquiry generally. Two assignments from Poetic Voices foster such research.

In an assignment called "Into the Archive," students research, annotate, and report on a poetry recording made locally at our college. Like nearly every college and university, ours has audio-taped readings by visiting poets for decades. Until 2007, most of the pre-1970 recordings remained un-cataloged, on cassettes and aging 3 ¾ ips reel-to-reel tape. They include a wide range of voices from the 1960s in particular, such writers as Leroi Jones (later, Amiri Baraka), Robert Bly, Diane Di Prima, Anne Waldman, and Allen Ginsberg. While preserving and fully cataloging such materials is beyond the scope of a small undergraduate or graduate cohort, listening, tracking down titles, and sleuthing dates and locations is not. With assistance from the college librarian, groups of students in the course choose a tape and, as a result of their research, produce notes that can be used by catalogers and bibliographers. For the purpose of assessment in the course, the notes include titles and publication data for the poetry, as much information as the students are able to obtain about place and occasion of the recording, and brief analyses that highlight the poet's remarks, audience feedback, and variants in the audio poem. In the syllabus given here, I have included examples of notes submitted by students from their research in recordings by Diane Di Prima and Robert Lowell. Because the assignment is contingent on the holdings of our college, it often takes the students away from the specific poets on our syllabus and, occasionally, outside the timeframe. The former is not a problem, for it tends to fill in the inevitable gaps in a survey. I handle the latter by asking students to relate the work they're researching to that of the course. Given the history of poetry readings at our college, this often leads to a dialogue between modernism and the kinds of poetry that formed in response or reaction to it.

A second assignment also diversifies the syllabus and carries students out to the larger archive of sound recording. In "Found Sound," students choose a poet whose work is represented online in a reliable digital audio archives. As with any work online, we review the criteria for "reliability," and I use our course website as a portal to the best examples. Students are asked first simply to explore and listen, one goal of the assignment being to introduce them to the breadth of modern poetry audio. When they've chosen a reading that interests them, they are charged with researching the poet's life and tracking down a published version of her poetry in book form or as a journal contribution. They are to write a commentary in which they compare the text and the audio and speculate on the two different states of the poem. Students may choose performance pieces, in which print plays at best a minor role. Their commentary then becomes an exercise in rendering the aural into print, and they consider the issues involved in transcribing and writing about performed sound.

In a course meeting near midterm, students present their findings to small groups. A variation on the Found Sound presentation, in which the poet's reading is played, includes the student's recitation of and commentary on a poem. By "recitation," I do not mean to imply exercises in memorization and elocution of the kind described in Joan Shelley Rubin's social history of poetry in the United

States, *Songs of Ourselves* (2007). Students simply read the poem to the group in a manner that demonstrates their grasp of its sounds and meanings. Writing about recitation and the novel, Jerome McGann argues that "negotiating language in an articulate way" is often a difficulty for students—one that can be overcome in part by short but regular and practiced readings in class ("Reading" 147). As we saw with the discourse of oral interpretation in chapter four, interpretive recitation is not the same as stammering elocution, and in this assignment students' performances are preceded or followed by response and analysis—not unlike the kind practiced by many poets at public readings.

★　★　★

As a review of the syllabus will quickly demonstrate, the lessons and assignments I've described could readily be extended to include other recordings, other sounds. Muriel Rukeyser's wit and passion, for instance, often resound in performance— her own, and those of later poets and composers who've paid tribute to her work. Given that Rukeyser drew up plans for a radio drama of the events recounted in "The Book of the Dead," a carefully researched, reader's theatre production of that poem could be a powerful assignment.[6] In choosing poets, I err on the side of those for whom recordings are available, but as in this study, "audio" can include other aural traces, such as the letters and commentaries of a poet's audience, or recent attempts to voice the poetry of writers such as Burns and Barnes. The key is that audio in general, and poetry on record in particular, be integral course materials—just as they are integral to the poet's output and reception.

★　★　★

Syllabus for LI 526 Poetic Voices

Rationale and Goals

Sound is essential to the effects and meanings of poetry in its infinite varieties. We listen to a poem's sounds—whether the poem is being read, or we are reading it silently—and it is common to refer to a poem's voice, suggesting that something humanizes the text, that something or someone speaks. But when we read a poem—especially a lyric poem—who speaks? For that matter, who is listening?

This brings me to the essential questions that will frame our study of poetic sound and voice:

What do we mean by "voice" in the poem?
How is it the same as/different from the poet's voice? How are voice and sound related?
Where does it come from?
Who speaks, and who listens to, the poem? How does a printed poem communicate sound and voice? What elements of style mark a poem as unique to a particular writer?

How do we pay attention to it?
Is there a difference between close reading and close listening to a poem? What is the value of hearing a poet read her own work? What place do recordings of such readings have in our study of poetry? What should we pay attention to besides the text of the poem?

To address these questions, we will read and listen to a variety of poems in English—mostly lyrical poems that call attention to matters of voice, speech, and sound. We will give special emphasis to twentieth-century poetry, for which there are extant recordings of poets reading their work. Public readings and performance played a critical role in the dissemination of modern poetry. Audio recording—a technology born just before the turn of the twentieth century— captured the "voice" of the poet on stage, on radio, and in the studio, making it possible for us to consider a poet's voicing alongside the texts. By that same token, the rapid, recent growth of online archives of poetry recordings have made voiced poems—by the poets, by fans, by performers—widely available. These archives will be important for the class and, I hope, useful for your subsequent study and teaching.

For you as future middle and high school teachers, this course is intended to model a way of organizing an in-depth study of poetry around a problem or issue that is essential to the form. There are other time-honored and equally valid ways of organizing a course: for example, by period, by "school" or group of poets, by genre. It is my hope that approaching poetry through sound and voice will not only deepen your understanding of how poetry speaks, but also provide ideas and resources for your own future curriculum planning.

Course Materials

M. H. Abrams, et al., eds. *Norton Anthology of English Literature, Volume E: The Victorian Age.* Eighth edition.

Edna St. Vincent Millay. *Selected Poems.* Ed. J. D. McClatchy. Library of America, 2003.

T. S. Eliot. *The Waste Land and Other Writings.* Ed. Mary Carr. Modern Library Classics, 2002.

James Weldon Johnson. *God's Trombones: Seven Negro Sermons in Verse.* Ed. Henry Louis Gates. Penguin Classics.

Anne Sexton. *Selected Poems.* Ed. Diane Wood Middlebrook. Mariner, 2000.

Gertrude Stein. *Writings 1903–1932.* Library of America, 1998.

All other texts are on Reserve Web or online, per the schedule given later. All recordings can be accessed via the course Moodle site.

Graded Course Assignments and Assessments

Found Sound (30 percent)
For this assignment, you will broaden our horizons by adding to the reading/ listening list. Each of you will choose a poet whose reading of her/his work

is represented in an online archive. There are many, but for the purposes of this assignment, please limit yourself to PennSound (http://writing.upenn.edu/pennsound/), the Academy of American Poets (http://www.poets.org), Ubuweb (http://www.ubuweb.com), or the Poetry Foundation (http://www.poetryfoundation.org/). You will then post a commentary on our Moodle site that includes the following components:

- Text of the poem and a link to the audio.
- Commentary (five pages): Your commentary should include information about when/where the poem was first published and, if available, when the recording was made. The bulk of the commentary, however, should address some aspect of the question: what is the relationship between text and performance in this reading?

Note that this assignment must be posted in advance of the class meeting. In class, your postings/audio will be the primary "texts" for class discussion, supplemented by the Charles Bernstein essay on Reserve Web and materials I'll bring to class.

Into the Archive (30 percent)

This college has an impressive history as a place for poets. Its archive of recordings is currently being digitized and cataloged, and this provides us with a meaningful research opportunity. In two groups, you will listen to a selection of these recordings. Each group will consider a different poet; we will determine the poets based on input from the college librarian, so that our research supports the real archival work of the college. Because your group will have eight–ten members, you should divide and conquer in accomplishing the following tasks:

Preparing Notes

Your first goal will be to discover what poems are being read and to annotate the recording. It's probably best to imagine your work as the preparation of liner notes. The notes should include information about the poet, a list of the poems (or sections of poetry) from the recording that indicates where we can find published texts, information about the time and location of the recording, and a description of the poet's readings and commentary. The notes should also include a works cited page. Your group's notes (maximum of ten pages, DS, twelve-point font, in .doc or .rtf format) are due electronically on the day of your presentation.

Presenting Research

After carrying out the research and preparing the notes, your group will be responsible for presenting its findings. This will take place during weeks eight and nine of class. The presentation should be limited to thirty minutes and should seek to engage the class in thinking about your text or audio; that is to say, imagine this presentation as a brief episode of teaching. It may include PowerPoint or a podcast, or it may simply be you, the audio, and us. There will then be time for Q&A. Any materials besides your group's notes associated with your presentation are due electronically by class time.

Here is some advice about sharing the labor: while you should divide the tasks of preparing notes and presenting the research, everyone should listen to and discuss the recording. Preparing the notes will likely require more hands than preparing the presentation, and it makes sense to have most of your group involved in this piece of the research. For a half hour presentation, two–three members should suffice. Finally, all of your written work will need to be collated and edited, a task that may fall to one or two members of the group. In short, manage your distribution of tasks so that everyone devotes (approximately) equal time to the project.

As a model, I include here two examples of notes from past projects:

On "Middle Age," by Robert Lowell, from a reading at Bard College in November 1973 When Lowell introduces his next poem, "Middle Age," he is again intent on giving background to the audience. He is self-deprecating and amusing. He says: "Middle age—a period I'm beginning to look back on with nostalgia. But I didn't then. And it's about New York. I'm very versatile. I can handle both Maine and New York." He also speaks very personally about this poem, which deals with the memory of his father, his painful relationship with his father, and his relationship with his memory of his father as he himself ages. He says the poem is

> about [sensitively] my father who died rather young—62—and he'd been dead um, oh, about fifteen years when I wrote this. And you'll find that dead people change in a way after they die that um, I mean of course they change then, but um, as time goes by, they're not the same as they were at the beginning cause you're different, I think. The person who remembers is different. One thing that's very striking is when you become the same age as someone like your father that is, he died at 62. I remember him as something like 40, a sort of composite age of different ages, and suddenly you find you've reached that age and it's—I don't know—it does something. Um. [Long pause] The other is that, I suppose, it's a commonplace really, it's harder to forgive people you've injured than people who've injured you—that oughta be written into the Lord's Prayer, I suppose [chuckles].

Lowell's commentary before the reading of "Middle Age" feels intimate and generous. His ideas about forgiveness are hardly commonplace and yet, he speaks to the audience as if they surely understand the likes of his complex emotions. His effort to resolve his feelings about his father, and the sense of his father as great—leaving "dinosaur death-steps" where he must walk—is reflected in his earnest delivery of the poem. There is a particularly powerful sense of intimacy

Lowell creates when he recites, "At forty-five, / what next? what next?" This is of course a question the speaker of the poem addresses to himself, but the audience is privy to this private introspection.

On "Revolutionary Letter #49" by Diane Di Prima, from a reading at Bard College in October 1973 This poem shows Di Prima taking ideas and concepts from a variety of traditions—political, musical, philosophical, poetic—and reworking them into a radical and transcendent piece of living poetry; it is an invocation to free a variety of figures, all of whom she identifies as "political prisoners." In her introduction to the poem, Di Prima mentions that it was inspired by protest rallies common in those days: the repetitive chants and the call and response with the audience: people shouting free so-and-so—an endless stream of people who needed to be freed. But the poet then transcends the form, a list of demands, and expands on the ideas beyond the political into the historical, ecological, personal, and metaphysical. She also infuses the poem with a syncopated rhythm common in Beat poetry, inspired by bebop in a rhythmic tradition that can be traced back to Africa.

She attacks not just the artificial relationships and constructs of law, class, race, gender, and government but everything and anything that constrains or restricts or separates, anything that isn't natural. All of the individuals Di Prima mentions in the opening chant were contemporary and historical figures who fought against the status quo, from revolutionaries such as Angela Davis, Native Americans leaders, labor leaders such as Big Bill Hayward, to religious, philosophical, scientific visionaries such as Jesus, Socrates, and Galileo. By populating her poem with lists of people and categories of people, by bringing them into the architecture of her art, Di Prima is also firmly rooting her poetry in the American tradition of that great American poet and iconoclast Walt Whitman.

The project will be graded as follows:

- Notes accurately cover all of the information specified earlier: 30 percent
- Notes are well-written and carefully edited: 20 percent
- Presentation has been thoughtfully planned: 30 percent
- Presentation is engaging and informative: 20 percent

In short, the notes and presentation each count for roughly 50 percent, though it should be clear that each of these components is dependent on the other.

Your group should feel free to consult me at any time during this research, perhaps especially at the beginning, when you have listened to the recording and begun to make a plan.

Essay (40 percent)
The final assessment for the course is a fifteen-page essay. The essay should focus on poetry from the syllabus, though research into such supplemental sources as the poet's letters or secondary criticism of the poet's work is expected. Clearly,

your research will not be exhaustive, and I will not set a minimum number of sources. *The most important feature of this paper will be your careful close reading of or close listening to poetry in order to establish a claim about it.*

The essay must consider at least two different poets from the syllabus. You must meet with me about your paper topic before the end of Reading Week; to this meeting, you should bring written notes toward your essay, including a draft of your thesis statement. This preliminary writing will not lock you in; rather, it will give us a point of departure as we plan your work. You may of course meet with me more than once, and you should feel free to ask me to read drafts of your paper before week ten. The essay will be assessed according to the following criteria:

1. Convincingly argued thesis, supported by perceptive close reading and relevant research (40 percent).
2. Thoughtful composition—carefully structured and stylistically engaging (40 percent).
3. Timely completion of work with attention to details of citation and mechanics (20 percent).

This essay is due electronically (.doc or .rtf) by class time in week ten.

An important note on citation format: All written work for the course should conform to MLA documentation style as outlined in chapter five of the *MLA Handbook* (seventh edition).

"How To" Hints for Reading

In the interest of accruing the full benefits of both quantity and quality, you should consider the following approach to each week's reading list:

1. I will always introduce a new poem or set of poems before sending you off to read them. This introduction will often include listening, writing, and thinking. Use your notes from this introduction as a scaffold for your subsequent reading. Audio that is used in class will always be available to you, for a second listening, through Reserve Web.
2. Read all of the poems as a group once through. Do this in one sitting, preferably at a time of day when you're moderately to fully awake, or at least within arm's reach of the coffee pot. Being alert is key. Listen again to poems for which there is a recording. Mark poems, lines or words that stand out for you. Use simple annotations: a question mark for something that puzzles you or to which you want to return, an exclamation point for something that shocked or otherwise surprised you, and a check for something that seems to make sense to you.
3. Go back to *selected* poems and linger with them. How you select is up to you. You might, for example, choose only the poems that you marked with question marks; you might choose a mixture. In any case, you should reread the chosen poems two–three times each. This time,

make your notes more extensive. I suggest that you try the following system, called a "double-entry journal." Draw a vertical line down the middle of a page in your notebook. In the left column, write the poem's title and, underneath it, line numbers that you want to comment upon, question, and so on; in the right column, write your thoughts about those lines.

4. Finally, before you declare yourself finished, spend five minutes writing your general impressions of the work you've read.

Even if you choose not to keep notes in a journal, I cannot overemphasize the importance of step four. A few minutes of writing after you read usually goes a long way toward improving retention and advancing understanding.

★　★　★

Class Schedule

Week One: Overheard Utterance

Shelley, "To A Skylark"; Hardy, "The Darkling Thrush"; Yeats, "Sailing to Byzantium"; Frost, "The Oven Bird"; Stevens, "Not Ideas About the Thing but the Thing Itself" and "The Idea of Order at Key West"; Lesley Wheeler, "Sounding Poetic Voice" (all from Reserve Web). John Stuart Mill, "What is Poetry?" (from the Norton *Victorian*).

Week Two: Who Speaks? (Dramatic Monologues)

Elizabeth Barrett Browning, "Runaway Slave at Pilgrim's Point"; Alfred Lord Tennyson, "Ulysses"; Robert Browning, "Andrea Del Sarto" and "Childe Roland to the Dark Tower Came"; D. G. Rossetti, "Jenny"; Mary Elizabeth Coleridge, "The Other Side of a Mirror" (all from the Norton *Victorian*). T. S. Eliot, "The Love Song of J. Alfred Prufrock" and "Gerontion"; E. Warwick Slinn, "The Dramatic Monologue" (from Reserve Web).

Week Three: "He Do the Police in Different Voices"

T. S. Eliot, *The Waste Land*; Ezra Pound, "The Seafarer"; Wimsatt and Beardsley, "The Intentional Fallacy" (from Reserve Web).

Week Four: Two Women's Voices

Edna Millay, "First Fig," "Second Fig," "Only until this cigarette is ended," "I shall forget you presently, my dear," *Sonnets from an Ungrafted Tree*, "Elegy," "Recuerdo," and Sonnets 11 and 52 from *Fatal Interview*; Gertrude Stein, "Idem the Same: A Valentine for Sherwood Anderson," "Picasso," "If I Told Him: A Completed Portrait of Picasso," "Matisse," and "Patriarchal Poetry"; Marion Thain, "What Kind of Critical Category is Women's Poetry?" [*Victorian Poetry* 41.1 (Winter 2003), from *Project Muse*].

Week Five: Recordings as Literary Artifacts

To class, please bring four copies of your poem/notes from close listening to found sound; read Charles Bernstein, Introduction to *Close Listening* (from Reserve Web).

Note: Found Sound *must* be posted on Moodle by Monday at 5:00 of this week.

Week Six: Versions of Vernacular

Robert Burns and William Barnes, Selections (from Reserve Web). Paul Laurence Dunbar, "An Ante-Bellum Sermon" and "When Malindy Sings" (poems and audio at http://www.dunbarsite.org/gallery.asp). James Weldon Johnson, *God's Trombones*; Marcellus Blount, "The Preacherly Text: African American Poetry and Vernacular Performance" [*PMLA* 107.3 (May 1992), available through *JSTOR*].

Week Seven: Documenting Sound

Muriel Rukeyser, *The Book of the Dead*; William Carlos Williams, selections from *Paterson* (all from Reserve Web).

Week Eight: Mid-Century Modernism on Record

Dylan Thomas, "The Force that Through the Green Fuse," "Do Not Go Gentle Into that Goodnight," "Fern Hill," "Poem in October," "Hunchback in the Park"; Robert Lowell, "Quaker Graveyard in Nantucket," "Home After Three Months Away," "Skunk Hour"; Louise Bogan, "The Alchemist", "Medusa," and "Women"; William Carlos Williams, "The Young Housewife," "Pastoral," "Paterson: The Falls," and "The Dance" (all from Reserve Web).

Due: Lowell Presentation

Week Nine: Howls

Allen Ginsberg, "Howl," "Supermarket in California," and "America"; Anne Sexton, "You, Doctor Martin," "Music Swims Back to Me," "Her Kind," "The Truth the Dead Know," "The Operation," and "Little Girl, My Stringbean, My Lovely Woman"; Lucy Collins, "Confessionalism" (from Reserve Web).

Due: Di Prima Presentation

Week Ten: Sound Experiments

Gerard Manley Hopkins, "God's Grandeur," "As Kingfishers Catch Fire," "The Windhover," "Pied Beauty" "Carrion Comfort," and "That Nature is a Heraclitean Fire"; Lewis Carroll, "Jabberwocky"; Edward Lear, "The Jumblies" (all from the Norton *Victorian*). Steve McCaffery, "Sound Poetry: A Survey" and selections by Jaap Blonk (at http://www.ubu.com/papers/mccaffery.html).

Due: Long essay, due electronically by class time, in .doc or .rtf format.

APPENDIX B

SELECTED LIST OF MODERNIST AUDIO ARCHIVES

Breadth and depth of the collection, its accessibility, and its cataloging in ways that facilitate research have been the criteria in my selection of the archives for this list. I have also limited the list to library archives in the United States and online sources. For the researcher of modern poetry, these audio archives are indispensable.

Archive of Recorded Poetry and Literature, Recorded Sound Reference Center, Library of Congress

This collection includes all of the recordings made in the library's recording laboratory, as well as live recordings of readings and other poetry events at the Library. The Brander Matthews collection from Columbia University as well as NBC's recordings from the early part of the century are part of the Recorded Sound Reference Center.

Woodberry Poetry Room Collection, Lamont Library, Harvard University

The Woodberry collection includes all Harvard Vocarium recordings, recordings of poetry events at Harvard from the 1930s to the present, and a wealth of commercially produced poetry recordings. A few recordings from the Woodberry collection are now available online at http://hcl.harvard.edu/libraries/houghton/collections/poetry_room.html.

The Rodgers and Hammerstein Archive of Recorded Sound, New York Public Library for the Performing Arts

The NYPL collection is especially valuable as a resource for commercial recordings, from the widely available to the highly specialized. It includes a wide range of recordings of poets reading their work, as well as other musical and spoken word renderings of modernist poetry.

The Poetry Audio Archive of the Academy of American Poets

Beginning with John Berryman's recordings of *The Dream Songs* in 1963, the Academy of American Poets' collection includes numerous recordings of readings, forums, and other poetry events. Many recordings of individual poets/poems are available on the Academy's website at http://www.poets.org/page.php/prmID/361. Entire readings are available for purchase, and video is now part of the collection.

The Naropa University Audio Archives

Founded by Anne Waldman and Allen Ginsberg, the Naropa archives include thousands of hours of recordings, primarily of avant-garde poetries from the 1970s forward. The archives holdings are currently being digitized and made available online at http://www.archive.org/details/naropa.

Axe-Houghton Multimedia Archive, The Poets House (New York)

This is a collection of live recordings from Poets House events, but also of many rare commercial recordings of twentieth-century poetry.

PennSound

The principal online archive of contemporary poetry audio, PennSound (http://writing.upenn.edu/pennsound) is a major source not only of poetry readings but also of occasional recordings, lectures, and other poetry events held at the Kelly Writer's House.

Poetry Foundation Audio Archives

The Poetry Foundation houses the *Essential American Poets* project, a collection of archival and recent readings selected by Donald Hall. In addition, the Foundation's website is a portal to other poetry audio on the web.

Ubuweb

For sound and performance poetry, Ubuweb (http://www.ubu.com/) is the most comprehensive collection on the Internet.

NOTES

Introduction: Listening to Recorded Poetry

1. Jed Rasula traces this mainstream to a source in what he calls the "poetry establishment" of the 1950s, led by Robert Lowell, who was himself "hand-picked" by the New Critics. Rasula's provocative narrative of the poetry establishment (so-called) and the avant-garde since mid-century has correlates in the works of Charles Bernstein and Joan Retallack. See Rasula, *The American Poetry Wax Museum*; Bernstein, *A Poetics*; and Retallack and Spahr, ed., *Poetry and Pedagogy*.

2. Al Filreis begins each podcast with this claim about close reading. I will consider the relationship between close reading and close listening later in this introduction.

3. Here, I mean to invoke Richard Schechner's perfomance-theory concept of the "actual," in which the drama is created as it is performed. I discuss Schechner's work in chapter three. On text versus audio in Antin's talk poetry, see Raphael Allison, "David Antin's Pragmatist Technophobia," in *JML* 24.8 (Summer 2005): 110–34. On Blonk's performances, consult "hold your breath and gag," PoemTalk no. 6 (May 4, 2008) http://poemtalkatkwh.blogspot.com/2008/05/hold-your-breath-and-gag-poemtalk-6.html.

4. For an overview of the debate regarding archives and digitization, see the essays in Kathryn Sutherland, ed. *Electronic Text: Investigations in Method and Theory* (New York: Oxford UP, 1997). For work that questions the archival impulse in literary and cultural studies, see Helen Freshwater, "The Allure of the Archive," *Poetics Today,* 24.4 (Winter 2004): 729–58.

5. The past twenty years has witnessed the growth of a video archive of poetry readings and interviews. But visual media brings an additional layer of issues that fall outside the scope of this study. Hence, "audio" archive.

6. The literature on the relationship between sound and print in reading acquisition, and on the continued importance of sound in silent reading, is vast. For a survey of the field, see Michael Kamil, Peter Mosenthal, P. David Pearson, and Rebecca Barr, eds. *Handbook of Reading Research,* vol. 3 (Mahwah: Erlbaum, 2000).

7. Stevens' reading is available online at the Academy of American Poets
   website. The recording is from *Wallace Stevens Reads* (Caedmon TC 1068).

8. Stein recorded several pieces at Columbia on January 30, 1935, including
   "Matisse," "If I Told Him: A Completed Portrait of Picasso," an excerpt
   from The Making of Americans," selections from "Madame Recamier:
   An Opera," and "A Valentine for Sherwood Anderson." These were part
   of the Columbia University Press Contemporary Poetry Series and were
   released on 78 rpm records. They were reissued in 1951 on LP by Harcourt
   Brace and again in 1956 on Caedmon. Stein's recordings are now available
   on the Ubuweb and PennSound sites.

1 Making Poetry Records, Remaking Poetic Voices: Caedmon and the Library of Congress

1. These ephemeral audio/video recordings are rapidly expanding the
   archive of late-twentieth/early-twenty-first-century poetry recordings,
   as a search on YouTube makes readily apparent.

2. For a fascinating account of the Browning and Tennyson recordings, see
   Picker.

3. Not all of the poets on Caedmon's list were actually recorded with
   Caedmon. The Stein recordings, for example, were made for Columbia
   University Press on January 30, 1935, during Stein's U.S. lecture tour.
   Several projects similar to that of the Library of Congress coincided with
   or followed it, chief among them the work of Harvard Vocarium. The
   Library of Congress project, however, came to be the largest of its kind,
   and was closely affiliated with the powerful influence of the New Critics,
   not to mention the U.S. government.

4. During the question and answer session of a panel on modern poetry
   and sound at MSA 2006, Michael Davidson referred to this as the
   "Caedmonization" of modern poetry.

5. I borrow this phrase from Davidson's study, which took it from Wallace
   Stevens' "The Idea of Order at Key West."

6. On the technology of phonograph sound reproduction, see Eargle. I am
   also grateful to Professor Louis Ramaley of Dalhousie University for his
   lucid explanations of the physics of sound.

7. Note that the series is dated 1949, though Lowell's contributions were
   made during his tenure in 1947–48.

8. I compiled this list by collating Library of Congress bibliographic records
   and the 1951 commercial catalog, supplemented by information from
   Lowell's letters. A few of the poets recorded during Lowell's tenure had
   no records issued in the original series. By that same token, a small number
   of the recordings issued in 1949 predated Lowell or were acquired from
   the Harvard Vocarium. The recordings of Eliot reading *The Waste Land*
   fit into this category.

9. Lowell never writes about his role in grouping the poets, and neither is there any record of this from other participants in the process. However, it's reasonable to assume that Lowell suggested groupings for the 78 rpm records, and it's clear that some effort was made to maintain these later, although in both cases, space constraints on the discs must have factored into final groupings and the order of poems.

10. In her edition of Bogan's letters, Ruth Limmer characterizes the poet's reading as " 'dry,' slowly paced—as opposed to the very swift tempo of her conversation—and each vowel sound and consonant is given full measure in a pure contralto that never lost its New England shading" (Bogan, *Letters* 370n). See *What the Woman Lived: Selected Letters of Louise Bogan*.

11. I am indebted to Sarah Parry's article on Caedmon, cited later, in which she notices that Dylan Thomas seems never to breathe on many of the Caedmon recordings.

12. "Paratext" refers to elements such as epigraphs, notes, typeface, and so on outside the strictly lexical elements that influence meaning. For a theory of "paratext," see Gerard Genette, *The Architext: An Introduction*, trans. by Jane E. Lewin (Berkeley: U California P, 1992).

13. In a special issue of New Verse, dedicated to Auden, Thomas writes "I think he [Auden] is a wide and deep poet, and that his first narrow angles, of pedantry and careful obscurity, are worn almost all away" (25). It's ironic that Thomas would accuse another poet of obscurity, though "careful" suggests that Auden is obscure by design. Thomas also refers to Auden's poetry as "a hygiene." Thomas did not record Auden's early, political verse, which seems to be the primary target of these negative comments.

14. This recording is now available on the Woodberry Poetry Room's homepage, listed in the bibliography. Note that Lowell reads an early variant of the poem, "Passages from the Quaker Graveyard," published in *Partisan Review*, 13.1 (1946), 76–78.

15. Later, in his essay, "On 'Skunk Hour,' " Lowell further elaborated on this and other references in the poem. See *Collected Prose*, as well as Frank Bidart's footnotes in *Collected Poems*.

16. I discuss this in detail in the next chapter.

2 Poets and Critics Live at the Forum: The Occasional Recording and Elizabeth Bishop

1. The term "occasional" also invokes another subset of live recordings of political events and state occasions where poetry plays a supporting role— for example, protests such as recorded Vietnam teach-ins of the 1960s. Even as I write this, poet Elizabeth Alexander prepares to read her work at the presidential inauguration of Barack Obama. The December 19,

2008, podcast of *Poetry Off the Shelf* included Alexander's interview with Linda Pasten, who recalled Robert Frost's reading at Kennedy's inauguration. Aged and bothered by the brilliant sunlight, Frost could not read the poem he had composed, and after a few tense moments of silence on the frigid January stage, he instead recited from memory "The Gift Outright." Alexander notes that the poem's unabashed patriotism was true to Frost's character late in life, and the poem's meaning in context becomes part of the discussion during the podcast. I would argue that the podcast itself becomes an instance of reception for both Alexander and Frost, placing the two in dialogue and offering a host of paratextual and sociohistorical data-points that should be considered—from the music that introduces the podcast to the exuberant atmosphere of Obama's anticipated inauguration.

2. Recent insights into the psychology of embarrassment and self-consciousness are usefully synthesized in the essays collected in W. Ray Crozier, ed. *Shyness and Embarrassment: Perspectives from Social Psychology* (Cambridge: Cambridge UP, 1990). An illuminating study of embarrassment and poetics is Christopher Ricks' *Keats and Embarrassment* (Oxford: Clarendon, 1974).

3. Five of these from a recording in New York, October 17, 1947, are included on the *Voice of the Poet* cassette, cited in the bibliography: "Cirque d'Hiver," "The Fish," "Varick Street," "Roosters," and "Sleeping on the Ceiling."

4. In her letter to Lowell, August 28, 1958 (*One Art* 361).

5. See especially her comments on *The Dolphin*, in her letter to Lowell, March 21, 1972 (*One Art* 561ff.)

6. In my analysis of the "North Haven" drafts, I have encountered many of the issues discussed by Millier and Harrison in their analyses of the drafts of "One Art." See Millier, "Elusive Mastery" and Harrison, *Poetics of Intimacy,* cited in the bibliography.

7. For a detailed look at Bishop's debt to Auden, see Costello's "A Whole Climate of Opinion," cited in the bibliography.

8. Alternately, they suggest an entirely different approach to the occasional recording than the one I take here. One might listen to the ambient sounds as part of the entire texture of the event, equal in importance to the poetry or anecdotes. The recorded memorial would become, under such conditions, similar to the chance operation "compositions" of John Cage or George Maciunas.

9. Interestingly, this Lutheran hymn was actually translated by a New Englander and Harvard man Frederic Henry Hedge (1810–90), who pastored various churches in the northeast, taught at Harvard, and edited *The Christian Examiner.*

10. On the topic of Bishop and Protestantism, see Cheryl Walker's *God and Elizabeth Bishop.*

11. Sacks develops this theoretical application of Freud in "Interpreting the Genre: Elegy and the Work of Mourning," in *The English Elegy.*

12. See, for example, Travisano's reading of "First Death in Nova Scotia," in *Midcentury Quartet*, 248–53. Travisano cautions against reading the poem as factual and points out the significant changes that Bishop made in the "facts" for the sake of the art.

13. In just this way, "Twelfth Morning or What You Will," which Anne Hussey reads after Giroux speaks, falls flat. Following the sentimentality of Giroux's story, the poem seems particularly recondite—an effect, I would argue, of context.

14. Hans Jauss, Joseph Grigely, Jerome McGann, and other textual theorists refer to the publication or going public of text as a "literary event," drawing attention to the temporal and social dimensions of literary texts and their meanings. See Grigely's *Textualterity*, McGann's *Textual Condition*, Jauss' *Towards an Aesthetic of Reception*, and most recently the essays in *Reimagining Textuality*, all cited in the bibliography.

3   Authenticity and Audience: Millay, Sexton, and Vocal Connections

1. For a fascinating history of this symbol, see Picker's *Victorian Soundscapes*.

2. For a detailed account of Millay's stage persona, see Wheeler, *Voicing American Poetry*.

3. Millay was clearly aware of her Byronism. Her visit to Albania in 1921 is recorded in a photo that invokes the famous Phillips portrait of Byron in Albanian dress. Deborah Forbes has compared Byron and Byronism to Millay's poetic heir, Anne Sexton. See her chapter on Sexton and Byron in *Sincerity's Shadow*.

4. The importance of radio to the development of literary modernism has been a subject of recent critical studies. Aside from *Wireless Imagination*, cited in the introduction, see Susan Merrill Squier, ed., *Communities of the Air: Radio Century, Radio Culture* (Durham: Duke UP, 2003) and Todd Avery, *Radio Modernism: Literature, Ethics, and the BBC, 1922–1938* (Burlington: Ashgate, 2006).

5. Cuthbert was also instrumental in broadcasting Millay's dramatic poem, "The Murder of Lidice." The radio script of the poem is part of a collection of NBC scripts from the era of World War II, *Adventure in Radio*, Margaret Cuthbert, ed. (New York: Howell, Soskin, 1945).

6. Douglas' book, cited in the Works Cited section, provides useful insights into early, popular perceptions of radio. For commentary on the uses/ abuses of poetry on contemporary radio, see Martin Spinelli, "Not Hearing Poetry on Public Radio," in Squier, ed., *Communities of the Air*.

7. There are two extant recordings of Millay reading her work. The first was made on January 8, 1933, at Columbia University and is a recording of Millay's radio broadcast from that evening, the third broadcast in the series that began on Christmas of the year 1932. The second was a

studio recording for RCA Victor, made in 1941. This is the only studio recording of Millay reading her own work, and Millay asked Dorothy Leffler, an assistant editor who was in essence playing nurse to her during a bout of depression, to choose the poems. The radio recording was originally made on instantaneous disc and is now archived at the Library of Congress in the Brander Matthews Dramatic Museum Collection. The Millay readings of "City Trees," "Elaine," and sonnets 11, 38, and 52 from *Fatal Interview* on the "Five Women Poets" compilation in the series *Voices of the Poet* (Random House, 2001) are duplicates of the Matthews recordings. The RCA recordings were later reissued on Caedmon (TC-1123), and while out of print, are held by numerous libraries. Millay's reading of "Recuerdo" on the Random House cassette is from the RCA studio recording. There are few surprises; the poems on the album are the perennial favorites among Millay's listeners. Moreover, despite the passing of nearly a decade, and the very different circumstances of these readings—live radio versus commercial studio—Millay's readings of poems shared by the two recordings are often virtually identical.

8. In addition to Jauss and McGann, cited in the argument, see Vernon Lionel Shetley's *After the Death of Poetry: Poet and Audience in Contemporary America* (Durham: Duke UP, 1993). Shetley applies reception theory to readings of American poets from the second half of the twentieth century.

9. See the essays in Neil Fraistat, ed. *Poems in their Place: The Intertextuality and Order of Poetic Collections* (Chapel Hill: U North Carolina P, 1986).

10. Michael Chasar treats the popular reception of "Lidice" in his dissertation, "Everyday Reading: United States Poetry and Popular Culture, 1880–1945" (University of Iowa, 2007).

11. The most comprehensive, commercially available recording of Sexton still in print is *The Voice of the Poet: Anne Sexton*, ed. J.D. McClatchy (Random House, 2000). Recordings on this disc span Sexton's career but draw heavily on a live reading in Boston from September 14, 1959, and a studio reading from May 1960. Sexton recorded for Caedmon on June 1, 1974; see *Anne Sexton Reads Her Poetry* (Caedmon TC 1441). This recording is out of print. Sexton is also featured on *Poetry Speaks* in a recording I discuss later, and a small selection of her readings are available on the Poetry Foundation and Academy of American Poets websites.

12. Writing about a cluster of British women poets, Laura Severin proposes that such a conflict was shared by Edith Sitwell, Stevie Smith, and others, who reached their readership through performance. See *Poetry Off the Page: Twentieth-Century British Women Poets in Performance* (Burlington: Ashgate, 2004).

13. This anxiety about giving readings is one of the few characteristics that Sexton shared with Elizabeth Bishop. Bishop was among the poets who identified Sexton with Millay and excess. In a letter to Lowell from July 17, 1960, Bishop wrote that Sexton has "a bit too much romanticism

and what I think of as the 'our beautiful old silver' school of female writing…" (*One Art* 386–87).

14. Schechner alludes to Levi-Strauss' important work *Le cru et le cuit,* published in 1964 and later translated as *The Raw and the Cooked.* Earlier, in his acceptance speech for the National Book Award in 1960 for *Life Studies*, Lowell used the "raw" and "cooked" metaphor. His acknowledgment, however qualified, that in subject matter, his recent work could be considered more raw than cooked became an essential reference point for criticism of confessional poetry.

15. The Harvard reading is among those held in the Woodberry poetry room; it also seems to be the recording on the compilation *Poetry Speaks*, though the acknowledgments do not indicate as much. The Fassett Studio recording is available on the Voice of the Poet series.

16. *Poetry Speaks* does not provide a transcript of the early version; rather, we get the later, published version of the poem. Her reading matches the language in an undated typescript of the poem, held in the Anne Sexton Papers, Harry Ransom Center, given in the Works Cited.

17. I have in mind, in particular, Finch's *Calendars* (Tupelo, 2003), her readings from that book on the *From the Fishouse* website (www.fishousepoems.org) and a performance I attended at the 2008 Lifting Belly High women's poetry conference in Pittsburgh, PA. An excellent example of Sharon Olds' readings can be found on a live recording, along with Yusef Komunyakaa, from 1993 issued by the Academy of American Poets and available from their website, www.poets.org.

4 Impersonations: Poets, Preachers, Teachers, and the Remaking of *God's Trombones*

1. Gregory Nagy's term, discussed later.

2. In addition to the critical works mentioned in these paragraphs, Albert J. Raboteau provides a concise and engaging account of African American preaching. See his *A Fire in the Bones*.

3. As he describes it in *Along This Way*, Johnson "surreptitiously jotted down some ideas" for "The Creation" during the 1918 sermon. That poem was published in *The Freeman* in 1920. Six years passed before he resumed work on his project. Between Thanksgiving and Christmas of 1926, he wrote "Go Down, Death" and "Listen, Lord." The book of seven poems, illustrated by Aaron Douglas, was published by Viking in the spring of 1927. Anne Carroll has written an important analysis of *God's Trombones* as book art, particularly of the relationship among text, illustrations, and Johnson's "authority." See Carroll, "Art, Literature, and the Harlem Renaissance."

4. Recordings of African American preaching from later decades are plentiful and easier to come by. For an example of the kinds of preaching upon which he bases his analysis, Rosenberg recommends any of the

recordings of the Reverend C. L. Franklin, many of which have been reissued on compact disc by MCA.

5. "And the stars of heaven fell unto the earth, even as a fig tree casteth her untimely figs, when she is shaken of a mighty wind" Revelations 6:13 (King James Version).

6. I borrow the term "racial contract" here from Jennifer L. Schulz, who argues that the American social contract is predicated on "racial hierarchies of citizenship" and that Johnson becomes gradually more aware of this and of his complicity in it. See "Re-staging the Racial Contract."

7. In addition to Gebhard, see Marcellus Blount, mentioned in Works Cited. Blount focuses principally on Paul Laurence Dunbar. He defends Dunbar's use of dialect by reading "An Ante-Bellum Sermon" as a self-conscious performance that manages to "master and manipulate the expectations of various audiences" (590). Importantly, Hutchinson strongly disagrees. See Hutchinson, 113. While he devotes little attention to Johnson, Michael North writes persuasively about the centrality of dialect and racial representation to the development of high modernism. See *The Dialect of Modernism*.

8. In Van Vechten's liner notes for the Harold Scott recording of *God's Trombones*, mentioned in the Works Cited.

9. This information is gathered from a poster contained in the James Weldon Johnson Correspondence at the Beinecke Rare Books and Manuscripts Library, Yale University, Box 22, Folder 511. Many such playbills, posters, and press releases can be found scattered among Johnson's voluminous correspondence.

10. Johnson and Millay are related in many, often curious ways. See letters between Boissevain, Millay, and Johnson in Box 14, Folder 323, of the James Weldon Johnson Correspondence, Beinecke Rare Books and Manuscripts Library, Yale University.

11. The recordings were issued as Musicraft 1083–1084 and are now available on Naxos *Voices of Black America*, given in the Works Cited. This is Johnson's only commercial recording, though at least one noncommercial recording was made: at Columbia University, December 24, 1935, with Johnson reading "The Creation" and "We Too America." This is now available on Rhino World Beat *Our Souls Have Grown Deep Like the Rivers*, R2 78012. Throughout my analysis of Johnson's recordings, I refer to the Musicraft performances, although there are no appreciable differences between his Columbia and Musicraft readings of "The Creation."

12. Mencken's praise was used on the original dust jacket for the 1927 first edition of the book.

13. See Van Vechten's letter to Grace Nail Johnson, July 2, 1938, collected in the *Letters of Carl Van Vechten*.

14. Academic writing on oral interpretation often centered upon a debate with the New Critics over oral reading, as opposed to analytical writing, as a critical exercise. See, for example, Don Geiger, "New Perspectives in

Oral Interpretation," *College English* 14 (Feb. 1953): 281–86, and George F. Reynolds, "Oral Interpretation as Graduate Work in English," *College English* 11 (Jan. 1950): 204–10. A detailed account of Masefield and Gullan's work can be found in Mark Morrisson, "Performing the Pure Voice: Elocution, Verse Recitation, and Modernist Poetry in Prewar London," *Modernism/Modernity* 3: 3 (1996): 25–50, and Ronald E. Shields, "Like a Choir of Nightingales: The Oxford Recitations, 1923–1930," *Literature in Performance: A Journal of Literary and Performing Arts* 3 (Nov. 1982): 15–26.

15. Rubin discusses these matters in "They Flash Upon the Inward Eye."

16. Lindsay recorded "The Congo" and several of his works at Barnard College, Columbia University, in 1931. These recordings form part of the Brander Matthews Collection housed at the Library of Congress. Many appear on the Caedmon LP *Vachel Lindsay Reading* (TC 1041). "The Congo," "The Flower Fed Buffaloes," "The Mysterious Cat," "General William Booth Enters Heaven," "The Moon's the North Wind's Cooky," and "The Chinese Nightingale" can be found in the PennSound online archive.

17. It is also worth noting that while some of the literature anthologies, by the mid-1960s, offer poetry by Langston Hughes and (occasionally) Claude McKay and Gwendolyn Brooks, they never make explicit connections between these poets and Johnson.

18. Like so many recorded anthologies, the Poitier and Bontemps records are worth deeper investigation in their own right. It could be argued, for example, that differences in reading style have to do with differences in intended audience. The Poitier is a popular recording on a major label; the Bontemps is intended primarily for academic libraries. Note also that the Bontemps anthology should not be confused with a similarly titled Folkways disc he edited, in which poets read their own work. I discuss this anthology in the conclusion of the chapter.

19. For the distinction between high- and middle-brow, I follow Bourdieu's *Distinction* and Rubin's *The Making of Middle Brow Culture*.

20. I am aware that other factors might have led to the deletion of "Let My People Go"—its length and limited recording space being significant. But "Noah Built the Ark" is nearly as long and lacks the direct connection to the long struggle for civil rights that the Israel in Egypt story has.

21. In his sonnet "Negro Spiritual," first published in *The Liberator*, May 1922. Included in *American Poetry: The Twentieth-Century. Vol. 1: Henry Adams to Dorothy Parker* (New York: Library of America, 2000), 832.

22. This rendering is similar to Bryce Bond's on a Folkway recording from 1965, FL 9788.

23. It is interesting to note that Waring uses the same echo effect for Davis' reading of "The Creation" that Poitier would later use.

24. A reproduction of the anthology can be purchased from Smithsonian Folkways. Liner notes and album cover can now be viewed online at the Folkways website, www.folkways.si.edu. Note that Bontemps and Langston Hughes had previously collaborated on a recording, *Anthology*

of Negro Poets in the USA, 200 Years, first released by Doubleday and later reissued by Folkways. Bontemps reads on that recording.

25. According to Jeff Place and Margaret Asch of Smithsonian Folkways, the cover art for this album was originally signed "Carlis." Whether this Carlis was John Carlis, an African American artist from mid-century, is uncertain. According to Ms. Asch, "there is so little (easily) known about Carlis and the original work is so vivid and stunning as the covers cannot be…he clearly was an important collaborator in the Folkways project early on. Moe [Asch, founder of Folkways] turned to him to create images for what I believe would have been some of Moe's favoured projects (Talking Union, Story of Jazz/Langston Hughes)" (Email correspondence, January 23, 2009).

26. The literature on whiteness is now vast. For a survey of the field, see Ashley Doane and Eduardo Bonilla, eds, *White Out: The Continuing Significance of Race* (New York: Routledge, 2003).

27. Note, as a further example, that some of the recordings on Bontemps' album are combined with Johnson's and other in a recent audio anthology, *Our Souls Have Grown Deep Like the Rivers: Black Poets Read Their Work.* This anthology, issued by Rhino World Beat in 2000, compiles archival and commercial recordings from the 1930s to the late 1990s.

Afterword: Out of the Audio Archive

1. The site's "manifesto" outlines a set of basic principles that, for the most part, audio files on PennSound adhere to. See http://writing.upenn.edu/pennsound/manifesto.php.

2. See the Yeats variorum: *The Variorum Edition of the Poems of W. B. Yeats,* Peter Allt and Russell Alspach, eds (New York: Macmillan, 1973).

Appendix A: Learning to Listen: Poetry Recordings in the Classroom

1. While it's been my experience that listening to modernist poetry often improves students' experience and comprehension, I regularly teach students whose instructional needs make attention to sound texts too difficult or impossible. As the syllabus indicates, I handle this by inviting students to speak to me early in the semester about their learning needs. In class, as in this book, I take "audio" to include not only sound recording but also writings that address the aural experience of poetry. When necessary, print can be substituted for sound.

2. See, for example, the reviews collected in *The Critical Response to Gertrude Stein,* Kirk Curnutt, ed. (Westport, CT: Greenwood Press, 2000).

3. A collection of Pound recordings is available on the PennSound website. For this lesson, I use Pound's 1939 reading for Harvard Vocarium.

The history of Pound's recordings is summed up in an essay by Richard Sieburth, also on the PennSound site.

4. Critics have also noted that the poem's publication in *The New Age* in 1913 highlights its appeal to guild socialists and suggests Pound's interest in leftist causes before World War I. See Lee Garver, "Seafarer Socialism: Pound, *The New Age,* and Anglo-Medieval Radicalism," *JML* 29.4 (Summer 2006), 1–21. The seafarer's contempt for privilege is evident in Pound's delivery of such lines as "Burgher knows not— / He the prosperous man—what some perform / Where wandering them widest draweth" (510).

5. Swigg, mentioned in Works Cited, offers a detailed comparison of Eliot's *Waste Land* recordings. The 1933 recording is available on the *Voice of the Poet T.S. Eliot.* J. D. McClatchy, ed. Compact disc (Random House, 2005).

6. In their edition of Rukeyser's poetry, Kaufman and Herzog refer to a manuscript note in which Rukeyser refers to a "documentary radio oratorio" of the events (Rukeyser, *Collected* 605). "Reader's theatre" is a common practice in language-arts classrooms. Students dramatize text with voice and, sometimes, sound effects, but no other props. They are limited to the language in the original text.

BIBLIOGRAPHY

Adorno, Theodor. "The Form of the Phonograph Record." *October* 55 (1990): 56–61.

Anthology of Negro Poets. Folkways, 1954. LP.

Ashbery, John. *The Mooring of Starting Out: The First Five Books of Poetry.* New York: Ecco, 1997.

———. *Some Trees.* New York: Ecco, 1956.

Auden, W. H. *Collected Poems.* Ed. Edward Mendelson. New York: Random House, 1976.

Badia, Janet. "'One of Those People Like Anne Sexton or Sylvia Plath': The Pathologized Woman Reader in Literary and Popular Culture." *Reading Women: Literary Figures and Cultural Icons from the Victorian Age to the Present.* Ed. Janet Badia and Jennifer Phegley. Toronto: U of Toronto P, 2005. 236–54.

Baker, Houston. *Modernism and the Harlem Renaissance.* Chicago: U of Chicago P, 1987.

Bauman, Richard. *Verbal Art as Performance.* Prospect Heights, IL: Wayland Press, 1977.

Benjamin, Walter. "The Task of the Translator." Trans. Harry Zohn. *The Translation Studies Reader.* Ed. Lawrence Venuti. New York: Routledge, 2004. 75–82.

Bernstein, Charles, ed. *Close Listening: Poetry and the Performed Word.* New York: Oxford UP, 1998.

———. "Creative Wreading: A Primer." *Poetry and Pedagogy: The Challenge of the Contemporary.* Ed. Joan Retallack and Juliana Spahr. New York: Palgrave, 2006. 275–81.

———. *A Poetics.* Cambridge: Harvard University Press, 1992.

Best, Marshall. Letter to James Weldon Johnson. February 8, 1938. TS. James Weldon Johnson Correspondence, Beinecke Lib., Yale University, New Haven.

Bishop, Elizabeth. *The Complete Poems, 1927–1979.* New York: FSG, 1979.

———. Interview by Susan Howe and Charles Ruas. Pacifica Radio. WBAI, New York. April 19, 1977. Radio. Now available as a digital audio file at http://writing.upenn.edu/pennsound/x/Howe-Pacifica.html. Accessed June 2009.

———. Memorial Service for Elizabeth Bishop. Rec. October 21, 1979. Audiotape. Woodberry Poetry Room, Harvard University, Cambridge.

Bishop, Elizabeth. "North Haven." N.d. TS. Elizabeth Bishop Papers, Vassar College Lib., Poughkeepsie.

———. *One Art: Letters*. Ed. Robert Giroux. New York: FSG, 1994.

———. Poetry Reading in Memory of Robert Lowell. Rec. March 1, 1978. Audiotape. Woodberry Poetry Room, Harvard University, Cambridge.

———. *The Voice of the Poet: Elizabeth Bishop*. Ed. J. D. McClatchy. New York: Random House, 2000.

Blount, Marcellus. "The Preacherly Text: African American Poetry and Vernacular Performance." *PMLA* 107.3 (1992): 582–93.

Bogan, Louise. "The Alchemist." *Twentieth Century Poetry in English: Louise Bogan, Paul Engle, Marianne Moore, Allen Tate*. Rec. Dec. 1947. Library of Congress, 1953. LP.

———. "Allen Tate's New Poems." Rev. of *Poems: 1928–1931* by Allen Tate. *New Republic* 30 Mar. 1932: 186–87.

———. *The Blue Estuaries: Poems, 1926–1968*. New York: Ecco, 1977.

———. Rev. of *Lord Weary's Castle,* by Robert Lowell. *The Critical Response to Robert Lowell*. Ed. Steven Gould Axelrod. Westport, CT: Greenwood, 1999. 28–30.

———. *What the Woman Lived: Selected Letters of Louise Bogan, 1920–1970*. Ed. Ruth Limmer. New York: Harcourt, Brace, Jovanovich, 1973.

Bontemps, Arna. Liner notes. *Anthology of Negro Poets in the U.S.A.* Folkways, 1955. LP.

Bourdieu, Pierre. *Distinction: A Social Critique of the Judgment of Taste*. Trans. Richard Nice. Cambridge: Harvard UP, 1984.

Bowdoin College. *Bowdoin College Centennial Celebration of the Class of 1825*. Conference program, May 4–16, 1825. Bowdoin College Lib., Brunswick.

Brown, Fahamisha Patricia. *Performing the Word: African-American Poetry as Vernacular Culture*. New Brunswick, NJ: Rutgers UP, 1999.

Bruns, Gerald L. *The Material of Poetry: Sketches for a Philosophical Poetics*. Athens, GA: U of Georgia P, 2005.

Caedmon Records. *Speaking of the Best for Over a Quarter Century: Caedmon 1952–1977*. New York: Caedmon, 1977.

Camelot, Jason. "Early Talking Books: Spoken Recordings and Recitation Anthologies, 1880–1920." *Book History* 6 (2003): 147–73.

Cameron, Sharon. *Choosing, Not Choosing: Dickinson's Fascicles*. Chicago: U of Chicago P, 1992.

Carroll, Anne. "Art, Literature, and the Harlem Renaissance: The Messages of *God's Trombones*." *College Literature* 29.3 (2002): 57–83.

Chartier, Roger. "The Text Between the Voice and the Book." *Voice, Text, Hypertext: Emerging Practices in Textual Studies*. Ed. Raimonda Modiano. Seattle: U of Washington P, 2004: 54–71.

Clark, Suzanne. "Uncanny Millay." *Millay at 100: A Critical Reappraisal*. Ed. Diane P. Freedman. Carbondale, IL: Southern Illinois University Press, 1995. 3–26.

Colburn, Steven, ed. *Anne Sexton: Telling the Tale*. Ann Arbor: U of Michigan P, 1988.

Corbett, John. "'The Seafarer': Visibility and the Translation of a West Saxon Elegy into English and Scots." *Translation & Literature* 10.2 (2001): 157–73.

Costello, Bonnie. "Elizabeth Bishop's Impersonal Personal." *American Literary History* 15.2 (2003): 334–66.

———. "A Whole Climate of Opinion: Auden's Influence on Bishop." *Literary Imagination* 5.1 (2003): 19–41.

Cuthbert, Margaret. Introductory Note to NBC Letters to Millay. N.d. TS. Edna St. Vincent Millay Papers, Vassar College Lib., Poughkeepsie.

Davidson, Michael. *Ghostlier Demarcations: Modern Poetry and the Material World.* Berkeley: U of California P, 1997.

———. "Technologies of Presence: Orality and the Tapevoice of Contemporary Poetics." *Sound States: Innovative Poetics and Acoustical Technologies.* Ed. Adalaide Morris. Chapel Hill: U of North Carolina P, 1997. 97–148.

Davis, Gerald L. *I Got the World in me, And I Can Sing It, You Know.* Philadelphia: U of Pennsylvania P, 1987.

de Man, Paul. *Blindness and Insight: Essays in the Rhetoric of Contemporary Criticism.* Second ed. Minneapolis: U of Minnesota P, 1981.

Dell, Floyd. *Homecoming: An Autobiography.* New York: Farrar and Rinehart, 1933.

Derrida, Jacques. *Archive Fever: A Freudian Impression.* Trans. Eric Prenowitz. Chicago: U of Chicago P, 1996.

———. "From Speech and Phenomena." *A Derrida Reader: Between the Blinds.* Ed. Peggy Kamuf. New York: Columbia UP, 1991. 6–30.

Dolman, Jr., John. *The Art of Reading Aloud.* New York: Harper, 1956.

Donoghue, Denis. "The Word Within A Word." *The Waste Land.* Ed. Michael North. New York: Norton, 2001. 216–29.

Douglas, Susan J. *Listening In: Radio and the American Imagination from Amos'n'Andy and Edward R. Murrow to Wolfman Jack and Howard Stern.* New York: Random House, 1999.

Drucker, Johanna. "Theory as Praxis: The Poetics of Electronic Textuality." *Modernism/Modernity* 9.4 (2002): 683–91.

DuPlessis, Rachel Blau. "'Hoo, Hoo, Hoo': Some Episodes in the Construction of Modern Whiteness." *American Literature* 67.4 (1995): 667–700.

Dylan Thomas Reading A Child's Christmas in Wales and Five Poems. Rec. February 1951. Caedmon, 1952. LP.

Eargle, John. *Sound Recording.* Second ed. New York: Van Nostrand Reinhold, 1980.

Elbow, Peter, and Pat Belanoff. *Sharing and Responding.* Second ed. New York: McGraw-Hill, 1995.

Eliot, T.S. "The Music of Poetry." *On Poetry and Poets.* New York: FSG, 1957. 17–33.

———. *The Waste Land.* Ed. Michael North. New York: Norton, 2001.

Epstein, Daniel Mark. *What Lips My Lips Have Kissed: The Loves and Love Poems of Edna St. Vincent Millay.* New York: Henry Holt, 2001.

Fan, Kit. "Imagined Places: Robinson Crusoe and Elizabeth Bishop." *Biography* 28.1 (2005): 43–53.

Ferry, Anne. *Tradition and the Individual Poem: An Inquiry Into Anthologies.* Stanford: Stanford UP, 2001.

Fish, Stanley. "Interpreting the Variorum." *Critical Inquiry* 2.3 (1976): 465–85.

Forbes, Deborah. *Sincerity's Shadow: Self-Consciousness in British Romantic and Mid-Twentieth Century American Poetry.* Cambridge: Harvard UP, 2004.

Foucault, Michel. *Discipline and Punish.* New York: Vintage, 1979.

———. *The History of Sexuality.* Trans. Robert Hurley. New York: Vintage, 1990.

———. "What is an author?" *The Foucault Reader.* Ed. Paul Rabinow. New York: Pantheon Books, 1984. 101–20.

Frost, Robert. *The Poetry of Robert Frost: The Collected Poems, Complete and Unabridged.* Ed. Edward Connery Latham. New York: Henry Holt, 1969.

Gates, James M. "The End of the World and Time Will Be No More." *Are You Bound for Heaven or Hell?: The Best of Reverend J.M. Gates.* Rec. 1927. Columbia Legacy, 2004. CD.

Gebhard, Caroline. "Inventing a 'Negro Literature': Race, Dialect, and Gender in the Early Work of Paul Laurence Dunbar, James Weldon Johnson, and Alice Dunbar-Nelson." *Post-Bellum, Pre-Harlem: African American Literature and Culture, 1877–1919.* Ed. Barbara McCaskill and Caroline Gebhard. New York: NYU Press, 2006. 162–80.

Geiger, Don. "New Perspectives in Oral Interpretation." *College English* 14: 5 (1953): 281–86.

George, Diane Hume. *Oedipus Anne: The Poetry of Anne Sexton.* Chicago: U of Illinois P, 1987.

Gill, Jo. *Anne Sexton's Confessional Poetics.* Gainesville: UP of Florida, 2007.

Gioia, Dana. "Elizabeth Bishop: From Coterie to Canon." *The New Criterion* 22.8 (2004): 19–26.

Giroud, Vincent. *Picasso and Gertrude Stein.* New Haven: Yale UP, 2006.

Gitelman, Lisa. "Souvenir Foils: On the Status of Print at the Origin of Recorded Sound." *New Media, 1740–1915.* Ed. Lisa Gitelman and Geoffrey B. Pingree. Cambridge: MIT Press, 2003. 157–73.

Griffin, Sin-Killer. "The Man of Calvary." *Negro Religious Songs and Services.* Rec. 1934. Rounder, 1999. CD.

Grigely, Joseph. *Textualterity: Art, Theory, and Textual Criticism.* Ann Arbor: U of Michigan P, 1995.

Hall, Donald. Interview by Curtis Fox. *Poetry Off the Shelf.* September 15, 2008. Now available as a digital audio file at www.poetryfoundation.org/podcast_ poetryofftheshelf.xml. Accessed October 1, 2008.

Harrison, Victoria. *Elizabeth Bishop's Poetics of Intimacy.* Cambridge: Cambridge UP, 1993.

Haselstein, Ulla. "Gertrude Stein's Portraits of Matisse and Picasso." *New Literary History* 34.4 (2003): 723–43.

Hayles, N. Kathryn. "Voices Out of Bodies, Bodies Out of Voices: Audiotape and the Production of Subjectivity." *Sound States: Innovative Poetics and Acoustical Technologies.* Ed. Adalaide Morris. Chapel Hill: U of North Carolina P, 1997. 74–96.

Hedley, Jane, "'I Made You to Find Me': Sexton, Lowell, and the Gender of Poethood," *Raritan* 19.3 (2000): 87–114.

Herbert, George. *The English Poems of George Herbert.* Ed. C.A. Patrides. London: Everyman, 1974.

Hicks, Helen Gertrude. *The Reading Chorus.* New York: Noble and Noble, 1939.

Hilberg, Evenlyn. Letter to Edna Millay. N.d. Edna St. Vincent Millay Papers, Vassar College Lib., Poughkeepsie.

Howard, Richard, ed. *Preferences: 51 American Poets Choose Poems From Their Own Work and From the Past.* New York: Viking Press, 1974.

Hutchens, John K. "Miss Millay's New Poem: 'The Murder of Lidice' Has Its First Radio Hearing, and Shapes A Crime Into a Symbol for All the World to Heed." *New York Times* October 25, 1942. *Proquest Historical Newspapers Database.* November 17, 2009.

Hutchinson, George. *The Harlem Renaissance in Black and White.* Cambridge: Belknap Press of Harvard University, 1995.

Jauss, Hans. *Toward An Aesthetic of Reception.* Trans. Timothy Bahti. Minneapolis: U of Minnesota P, 1982.

Johnson, James Weldon. *Along This Way. James Weldon Johnson: Writings.* Ed. William L. Andrews. New York: Library of America, 2004. 125–606.

———. *Book of American Negro Poetry.* New York: Harcourt, Brace, 1922.

———. "The Dilemma of the Negro Author." *James Weldon Johnson: Writings.* Ed. William L. Andrews. New York: Library of America, 2004. 744–52.

———. *Fifty Years & Other Poems.* Boston: The Cornhill Company, 1917.

———. "Four Readings from *God's Trombones.*" *Voices of Black America: Historical Recordings of Poetry, Humor, & Drama, 1908–1947.* Rec. 1938. Naxos, 2002. CD.

———. *God's Trombones.* New York: Viking, 1927.

———. *God's Trombones. James Weldon Johnson: Writings.* Ed. William L. Andrews. New York: Library of America, 2004. 834–67.

———. Letters to Marshall Best. May 9, 1932–May 17, 1938. TS. James Weldon Johnson Correspondence, Beinecke Lib., Yale University, New Haven.

———. Preface. *The Book of American Negro Poetry. James Weldon Johnson: Writings.* Ed. William L. Andrews. New York: Library of America, 2004. 688–719.

———. Preface. *The Second Book of Negro Spirituals. James Weldon Johnson: Writings.* Ed. William L. Andrews. New York: Library of America, 2004. 730–43.

———. *St. Peter Relates An Incident.* New York: Viking, 1935.

Kahn, Douglas, and Gregory Whitehead, eds. *Wireless Imagination: Sound, Radio, and the Avant-Garde.* Cambridge: MIT Press, 1992.

Kalstone, David. *Becoming a Poet: Elizabeth Bishop with Marianne Moore and Robert Lowell.* Ed. Robert Hemenway. New York: FSG, 1989.

Keppie, Elizabeth E. *Choral Verse Speaking: An Avenue to Speech Improvement and Appreciation of Poetry For Use in Senior High School and Colleges.* Boston: Expression Company, 1939.

Kirsch, Gesa E., and Liz Rohan, eds. *Beyond the Archives: Research as a Lived Process.* Carbondale: Southern Illinois UP, 2008.

Knapp, Edgar, H., ed. *Ideas and Patterns in Literature, III*. New York: Harcourt Brace, 1970.

Lee, Charlotte I. *Oral Interpretation*. Third ed. Boston: Houghton Mifflin, 1965.

Leighton, Lawrence B. "Miss Millay Charms Hearers With Readings From Poems." *Bowdoin Orient*, May 13, 1925: 2.

Levy, Eugene. *James Weldon Johnson: Black Leader, Black Voice*. Chicago: U of Chicago P, 1973.

Library of Congress Reference Department. *Catalog of Phonograph Records: Twentieth Century Poetry in English: Contemporary Recordings of the Poets Reading Their Own Poems*. Washington, DC: Library of Congress, 1951.

Lindsay, Vachel. "The Congo." *American Poetry: The Twentieth Century*. Vol. 1. Ed. Robert Hass, John Hollander, Carolyn Kizer, Nathaniel Mackey, and Marjorie Perloff. New York: Library of America, 2000. 275–79.

Lipking, Lawrence. *The Life of the Poet: Beginning and Ending Poetic Careers*. Chicago: U of Chicago P, 1981.

Logan, Julia Irene. Letter to Edna Millay. December 26, 1932. TS. Edna St. Vincent Millay Papers, Vassar College Lib., Poughkeepsie.

Loizeaux, Elizabeth Bergman, and Neil Fraistat, eds. *Reimagining Textuality: Textual Studies in the Late Age of Print*. Madison: U of Wisconsin P, 2002.

Lord, Albert B. *The Singer of Tales*. Second ed. Cambridge: Harvard UP, 1988.

Lowell, Robert. *Collected Letters*. Ed. Saskia Hamilton. New York: FSG, 2005.

———. *Collected Poems*. Ed. Frank Bidart and David Gewanter. New York: FSG, 2003.

———. *Collected Prose*. Ed. Robert Giroux. New York: FSG, 1987.

———. *Life Studies*. New York: Vintage, 1959.

———. "The Quaker Graveyard in Nantucket." Rec. March 20, 1946. Audiotape. Woodberry Poetry Room, Harvard University, Cambridge. Now available as a digital audio file at http://hcl.harvard.edu/libraries/houghton/collections/poetry_room.html. Accessed December 5, 2007.

———. *Robert Lowell: A Reading*. Rec. December 8, 1976. Caedmon, 1978. LP.

Luedtke, Janet E. "'Something Special for Someone': Anne Sexton's Fan Letters from Women." *Rossetti to Sexton: Six Women Poets at Texas*. Ed. David Oliphant and Robin Bradford. Austin: U of Texas at Austin P, 1992. 165–89.

Marks, Herbert. "Elizabeth Bishop's Art of Memory." *Literary Imagination* 7.2 (2005): 197–224.

Marshall, Carol, ed. *Designs for Reading: Poems*. Boston: Houghton Mifflin, 1969.

Marx, Patricia. "Interview with Anne Sexton." *Hudson Review* 18.4 (1965–66): 560–70.

Materer, Timothy. "Mirrored Lives: Elizabeth Bishop and James Merrill." *Twentieth-Century Literature* 51.2 (2005): 179–209.

McCabe, Susan. *Elizabeth Bishop: Her Poetics of Loss*. University Park: Penn State UP, 1994.

McCaffery, Steve. "From Phonic to Sonic: The Emergence of the Audio-Poem." *Sound States: Innovative Poetics and Acoustical Technologies*. Ed. Adalaide Morris. Chapel Hill: U of North Carolina Press, 1997. 149–68.

McClatchy, J.D., ed. *Anne Sexton: The Artist and Her Critics.* Bloomington: Indiana UP, 1978.

———, ed. *Five American Women. The Voice of the Poet.* Random House Audio, 2001. Audiocassette.

McGann, Jerome. *The Beauty of Inflections: Literary Investigations in Historical Method and Theory.* Oxford: Oxford UP, 1985.

———. *The Poetics of Sensibility: A Revolution in Literary Style.* Oxford: Clarendon, 1996.

———. *Radiant Textuality: Literature After the World Wide Web.* New York: Palgrave, 2001.

———. *The Textual Condition.* Princeton: Princeton UP, 1991.

McGann, Jerome, and Lisa Samuels. "Deformance and Interpretation." *NLH* 30.1 (1999): 25–56.

McGann, Jerome, et al. "'Reading Fiction/Teaching Fiction': A Pedagogical Experiment." *Pedagogy: Critical Approaches to Teaching Literature, Language Composition, and Culture* 1.1 (2001): 143–65.

McKay, Claude. "Negro Spiritual." *American Poetry: The Twentieth Century.* Vol. 1. New York: Library of America, 2000. 832.

Mendenhall, Louise. Letter to Hughes Mearns. N.d. Contained in Mearns letter to James Weldon Johnson. 19 December 1931. James Weldon Johnson Correspondence, Beinecke Lib., Yale University, New Haven.

Middlebrook, Diane Wood. *Anne Sexton: A Biography.* Boston: Houghton-Mifflin, 1991.

Middleton, Peter. *Distant Reading: Performance, Readership, and Consumption in Contemporary Poetry.* Tuscaloosa, AL: U of Alabama P, 2005.

Milford, Nancy. *Savage Beauty: The Life of Edna St. Vincent Millay.* New York: Random House, 2001.

Mill, John Stuart. "What Is Poetry?" *Norton Anthology of English Literature, Vol. E. The Victorian Age.* Eighth ed. Ed. Stephen Greenblatt, Carol T. Christ, and Catherine Robson. New York: W.W. Norton, 2005. 1044–50.

Millay, Edna St. Vincent. *The Buck in the Snow & Other Poems.* New York: Harper & Brothers, 1928.

———. *Edna St. Vincent Millay Reading Her Poetry.* Rec. 1941. Caedmon, 1961. LP.

———. *Fatal Interview: Sonnets.* New York: Harper & Brothers, 1931.

———. *The Harp-Weaver and Other Poems.* New York: Harper & Brothers, 1923.

———. *Huntsman, What Quarry?* New York: Harper & Brothers, 1939.

———. "Letter to Cass Canfield." January 8, 1946. *The Letters of Edna St. Vincent Millay.* Ed. Allan Ross Macdougall. New York: Harper & Brothers, 1952. 334.

———. *Make Bright the Arrows: 1940 Notebook.* New York: Harper & Brothers, 1940.

———. *Poems by Edna St. Vincent Millay.* RCA, 1941. LP.

———. *Selected Poems.* Ed. J. D. McClatchy. New York: Library of America, 2003.

———. *Wine From These Grapes.* New York: Harper & Brothers, 1934.

Millier, Brett Candlish. *Elizabeth Bishop: Life and the Memory of It.* Berkeley: U of California P, 1993.

———. "Elusive Mastery: The Drafts of Elizabeth Bishop's 'One Art.'" *New England Review* 13.2 (1990): 120–29.

———. "The Prodigal: Elizabeth Bishop and Alcohol." *Contemporary Literature* 39.1 (1998): 54–76.

Miller, Nancy. *Getting Personal: Feminist Occasions and Other Autobiographical Acts.* New York: Routledge, 1991.

Mitgang, Herbert. "Recorded Books Help Make The Ear Faster Than The Eye." *New York Times.* 27 Aug. 1987, Arts sec.: C19.

Monroe, Harriet. Letter to James Weldon Johnson. May 22, 1931. TS. James Weldon Johnson Correspondence. Beinecke Lib., Yale University, New Haven.

Monteiro, George, ed. *Conversations with Elizabeth Bishop.* Jackson: U of Mississippi P, 1996.

Morrisson, Mark. "Performing the Pure Voice: Elocution, Verse Recitation, and Modernist Poetry in Prewar London." *Modernism/Modernity* 3.3 (1996): 25–50.

Morton, David. L, Jr. *Off the Record: The Technology and Culture of Sound Recording in America.* New Brunswick: Rutgers UP, 2000.

———. *Sound Recording: The Life Story of a Technology.* Westport: Greenwood Technographies, 2004.

Moses, Kate. "Sylvia Plath's Voice, Annotated." *The Unraveling Archive: Essays on Sylvia Plath.* Ed. Anite Helle. Ann Arbor: U of Michigan P, 2007. 89–120.

Nagy, Gregory. *Poetry as Performance: Homer and Beyond.* Cambridge: Cambridge UP, 1996.

Nancy, Jean Luc. *Listening.* Trans. Charlotte Mandell. New York: Fordham UP, 2007.

North, Michael. *The Dialect of Modernism: Race, Language, and Twentieth-Century Literature.* Oxford: Oxford UP, 1994.

Olson, Stanley. *Elinor Wylie: A Life Apart.* New York: Dial, 1979.

Ostriker, Alicia. "Anne Sexton and the Seduction of the Audience." *Sexton: Selected Criticism.* Ed. Diana Hume George. Chicago: U of Illinois P, 1988. 3–18.

———. "That Story: Anne Sexton and Her Transformations." *Sexton: Selected Criticism.* Ed. Diana Hume George. Chicago: U of Illinois P, 1988. 251–73.

Parry, Sarah. "The Inaudibility of 'Good' Sound Editing: The Case of Caedmon Records." *Performance Research* 7.1 (2002): 24–33.

Picker, John M. *Victorian Soundscapes.* Oxford: Oxford UP, 2003.

Poitier, Sidney. *Sidney Poitier Reads Poetry of the Black Man.* United Artists, 1968. LP.

Pollard, Charles. *New World Modernisms: T.S. Eliot, Derek Walcott, and Kamau Brathwaite.* Charlottesville: U of Virginia P, 2004.

Pooley, Robert, ed. *Exploring Life Through Literature.* New York: Scott, Foresman, 1963.

Potell, Herbert, ed. *Adventures for Today.* New York: Harcourt Brace, 1955.

Pound, Ezra. "Hugh Selwyn Mauberley." *American Poetry: The Twentieth Century.* Vol. 1. New York: Library of America, 2000. 532–45.

———. "The Seafarer." *American Poetry: The Twentieth Century.* Vol. 1. New York: Library of America, 2000. 509–11.

Price-Morgan, M. Letter to James Weldon Johnson. June 15, 1936. TS. James Weldon Johnson Correspondence, Beinecke Lib., Yale University, New Haven.

Prins, Yopie. "Voice Inverse." *Victorian Poetry* 42.1 (2000): 42–59.

Pritchard, William. "The Anne Sexton Show." Rev. of *Anne Sexton: A Self-Portrait in Letters,* by Anne Sexton. *Hudson Review* 31.2 (1978): 387–92.

Pumphrey, Eva, ed. *Adventures for You.* Second ed. New York: Harcourt Brace, 1968.

Raboteau, Albert J. *A Fire in the Bones: Reflections on African-American Religious History.* Boston: Beacon Press, 1995.

Ramazani, Jahan. *Poetry of Mourning: The Modern Elegy from Hardy to Heaney.* Chicago: U of Chicago P, 1994.

Rasula, Jed. *The American Poetry Wax Museum: Reality Effects, 1940–1990.* Urbana: NCTE Press, 1996.

———. "Understanding the Sound of Not Understanding." *Close Listening: Poetry and the Performed Word.* Ed. Charles Bernstein. New York: 1998. 233–61.

Rees-Jones, Deryn. "Consorting with Angels: Anne Sexton and the Art of Confession." *Women: A Cultural Review* 10.3 (1999): 283–96.

Retallack, Joan, and Juliana Spahr, eds. *Poetry and Pedagogy: The Challenge of the Contemporary.* New York: Palgrave, 2006.

Reynolds, George F. "Oral Interpretation as Graduate Work in English." *College English* 11.4 (1950): 204–10.

Rich, Adrienne. "Anne Sexton: 1928–1974." *On Lies, Secrets, and Silence: Selected Prose, 1966–1978.* New York: Norton, 1979. 121–23.

Richards, I. A. *Practical Criticism: A Study of Literary Judgment.* New York: Harcourt, Brace and Company, 1949.

"Robert Frost, Miss Millay, Hatcher Hughes, Margaret Deland, Carl Sandburg, and James Stephens Speak Before Large Audiences." *Bowdoin Orient,* May 13, 1925: 1.

Robinson, Karl. *Speech in Action.* Chicago: Scott, Foresman, 1965.

Rosenbaum, Susan B. *Professing Sincerity: Modern Lyric Poetry, Commercial Culture, and the Crisis of Reading.* Charlottesville: U of Virginia P, 2007.

Rosenberg, Bruce A. *The Art of the American Folk Preacher.* New York: Oxford UP, 1970.

Rubin, Joan Shelley. *The Making of Middle Brow Culture.* Chapel Hill: U of North Caroline P, 1992.

———. "Modernism in Practice: Public Readings of the New Poetry." *A Modern Mosaic: Art and Modernism in the United States.* Ed. Thomas Fahy and Sarah P. Reuning. Chapel Hill: U of North Caroline P, 2000. 127–52.

———. *Songs of Ourselves: The Uses of Poetry in America.* Cambridge: Belknap Press of Harvard University, 2007.

Rubin, Joan Shelley. "'They Flash Upon That Inward Eye': Poetry Recitation and American Readers."
Proceedings of the American Antiquarian Society 106.2 (1996): 273–300.
Rukeyser, Muriel. *The Collected Poems of Muriel Rukeyser.* Ed. Janet E. Kaufman and Anne F. Herzog, with Jan Heller Levi. Pittsburgh: U of Pittsburgh P, 2007.
———. *U.S. 1.* New York: Covici, Friede, 1938.
Sacks, Peter. *The English Elegy.* Baltimore: Johns Hopkins, 1985.
Salvaggio, Ruth. *The Sounds of Feminist Theory.* Albany, NY: SUNY Press, 1999.
Sarett, Lew. *Basic Principles of Speech.* Boston: Houghton Mifflin, 1946.
Schechner, Richard. *Essays on Performance Theory, 1970–1976.* New York: Drama Book Specialists, 1977.
Schmidt, Leigh Eric. *Hearing Things: Religion, Illusion, and the American Enlightenment.* Cambridge: Harvard UP, 2000.
Schulz, Jennifer L. "Restaging the Racial Contract: James Weldon Johnson's Signatory Strategies." *American Literature* 74.1 (2002): 31–58.
Scott, Harold. *Poems from James Weldon Johnson's "God's Trombones."* United Artists, 1959. LP.
Sexton, Anne. *All My Pretty Ones.* Boston: Houghton Mifflin, 1962.
———. *Anne Sexton: A Self-Portrait in Letters.* Ed. Linda Gray Sexton and Lois Ames. Boston: Houghton-Mifflin, 1977.
———. *The Death Notebooks.* Boston: Houghton Mifflin, 1974.
———. "Her Kind" and "The Fury of Sunrises." *Anne Sexton Reads Her Poetry.* Rec. June 1, 1974. Caedmon, 1974. LP.
———. "Her Kind." *Anne Sexton: The Voice of the Poet.* Ed. J. D. McClatchy. Rec. September 14, 1959. Random House Audio, 2000. CD.
———. *No Evil Star: Selected Essays, Interviews, and Prose.* Ed. Steven Colburn. Ann Arbor: U of Michigan P, 1985.
———. *Selected Poems.* Ed. Diane Middlebrook. Boston: Houghton-Mifflin, 1988.
———. "The Truth the Dead Know." *Poetry Speaks: Hear Great Poets Read Their Work, From Tennyson to Plath.* Rec. December 1959. Sourcebooks MediaFusion, 2001. CD.
———. "The Truth the Dead Know." TS. Anne Sexton Papers, Harry Ransom Center, University of Texas at Austin.
———. *To Bedlam and Part Way Back.* Boston: Houghton Mifflin, 1960.
Shields, Ronald E. "Like a Choir of Nightingales: The Oxford Recitations, 1923–1930." *Literature in Performance: A Journal of Literary and Performing Arts* 3.1 (November 1982): 15–26.
Sisson, Lewis E. Letter to Edna Millay. January 5, 1933. TS. Edna St. Vincent Millay Papers. Vassar College Lib., Poughkeepsie.
Slaughter, Mary H. Letter to Edna Millay. January 16, 1933. TS. Edna St. Vincent Millay Papers, Vassar College Lib., Poughkeepsie.
Slawinski, Janusz. "Reading and Reader in the Literary Historical Process." Trans. Nina Taylor. *New Literary History* 19.3 (1988): 521–39.

Smith, Janet K. Letter to Edna Millay. January 9, 1933. TS. Edna St. Vincent Millay Papers, Vassar College Lib., Poughkeepsie.

Snow, Mr. and Mrs. Thad. Letter to Edna Millay. January 25, 1933. TS. Edna St. Vincent Millay Papers, Vassar College Lib., Poughkeepsie.

Stein, Gertrude. Interview by William Lundell. November 1934. Now available as a digital audio file at http://www.ubu.com/sound/stein.html. Accessed January 19, 2009.

———. *Writings, 1903–1932*. Ed. Catharine R. Stimpson and Harriet Chessman. New York: Library of America, 1998.

Stevens, Wallace. *The Collected Poems*. New York: Random House, 1990.

Stewart, Garrett. *Reading Voices: Literature and the Phonotext*. Berkeley: U of California P, 1990.

Stewart, Susan. *Poetry and the Fate of the Senses*. Chicago: U of Chicago P, 2002.

Strassman, Fanny. Letters to James Weldon Johnson. February10–March 7, 1938. TS. James Weldon Johnson Correspondence, Beinecke Lib., Yale University, New Haven.

Summers, Joseph H. "George Herbert and Elizabeth Bishop." *George Herbert in the Nineties: Reflections and Reassessments*. Ed. Jonathan F. S. Post and Sidney Gottlieb. Connecticut: George Herbert Journal Special Studies and Monographs, 1995. 48–58.

Swigg, Richard. "Sounding The Waste Land: T.S. Eliot's 1933 Recording." *PN Review* 28.1 (2001): 54–61.

Symes, Colin. *Setting the Record Straight: A Material History of Classical Recording*. Middletown: Wesleyan UP, 2004.

Tate, Allen. "Ode to the Confederate Dead." *American Poetry: The Twentieth-Century*. Vol. 2. Ed. Robert Hass et al. Washington, DC: Library of America, 2000. 269–72.

———. "Ode to the Confederate Dead." *Twentieth Century Poetry in English: Louise Bogan, Paul Engle, Marianne Moore, Allen Tate*. Rec. December 1947. Library of Congress, 1953. LP.

———. "Ode to the Confederate Dead." *Yale Series of Recorded Poets: Allen Tate*. Carillon Records, 1961. LP.

Thomas, Dylan. *The Collected Poems of Dylan Thomas, 1934–1952*. New York: New Directions, 1971.

Thompson, David. Rev. of *Twentieth Century Poetry in English: Contemporary Recordings of the Poets Reading Their Own Poems*. *American Quarterly* 2.1 (1950): 89–93.

Trams, A. Francis. Letter to Edna Millay. January 25, 1933. TS. Edna St. Vincent Millay Papers, Vassar College Lib., Poughkeepsie.

Travisano, Thomas. *Midcentury Quartet: Bishop, Lowell, Jarrell, Berryman, and the Making of a Postmodern Aesthetic*. Charlottesville: U of Virginia P, 1999.

Untermeyer, Louis. Letter to Viking Press. May 17, 1927. TS. James Weldon Johnson Correspondence, Beinecke Lib., Yale University, New Haven.

Van Vechten, Carl. *Letters of Carl Van Vechten*. Sel. and ed. Bruce Kellner. New Haven: Yale UP, 1987.

Van Vechten, Carl. Letter to James Weldon Johnson. May 9, 1927. TS. James Weldon Johnson Correspondence, Beinecke Lib., Yale University, New Haven.

Vendler, Helen. "Herbert and Modern Poetry: A Response." *George Herbert in the Nineties: Reflections and Reassessments.* Ed. Jonathan F. S. Post and Sidney Gottlieb. Connecticut: George Herbert Journal Special Studies and Monographs, 1995. 81–89.

———. "The Poems of Elizabeth Bishop." *Critical Inquiry* 13.4 (1987): 825–38.

Venuti, Lawrence. "Translation, Community, Utopia." *The Translation Studies Reader.* Ed. Lawrence Venuti. Second ed. New York: Routledge, 2004. 482–502.

Wagner-Martin, Linda, ed. *Critical Essays on Anne Sexton.* Boston: G.K. Hall, 1989.

Walker, Cheryl. *God and Elizabeth Bishop: Meditations on Religion and Poetry.* New York: Palgrave Macmillan, 2005.

Walker, Margaret. *For My People.* New Haven: Yale UP, 1942.

Waring, Fred, cond. *God's Trombones and Other Spirituals.* Decca, 1963. LP.

Washington, Lillian L. Letter to James Weldon Johnson. TS. November 12, 1934. James Weldon Johnson Correspondence, Beinecke Lib., Yale University, New Haven.

Wheeler, Lesley. *Voicing American Poetry: Sound and Performance from the 1920s to the Present.* New York: Cornell UP, 2008.

Williams, William Carlos. *Paterson.* New York: New Directions, 1946–58.

Wilson, Edmund. *The Fifties: From Notebooks and Diaries of the Period.* Ed. Leon Edel. New York: FSG, 1986.

———. *The Shores of Light: A Literary Chronicle of the Twenties and Thirties.* New York: FSG, 1952.

———. *The Twenties: From Notebooks and Diaries of the Period.* Ed. Leon Edel. New York: FSG, 1975.

Wylie, Elinor. *Black Armour: A Book of Poems.* New York: George H. Doran, 1923.

Yeats, William Butler. "On 'The Lake Isle of Innisfree.'" *Poetry Speaks: Hear Great Poets Read Their Work, From Tennyson to Plath.* Naperville: Sourcebooks MediaFusion, 2001. CD.

INDEX